PENGUIN B

JILL DAN

Born and educated in Ireland, Brian Cathcart was a Reuters correspondent before joining the *Independent on Sunday*. He has written three
previous books: *Test of Greatness: Britain's Struggle for the Atom Bomb*
(1994), *Were You Still Up for Portillo?* (1997) and *The Case of Stephen
Lawrence* (1999), which won the 1999 Crime Writers' Association Award
for Non-Fiction. Brian Cathcart lives in north London.

BRIAN CATHCART

JILL DANDO

HER LIFE AND DEATH

PENGUIN BOOKS

PENGUIN BOOKS

Published by the Penguin Group
Penguin Books Ltd, 80 Strand, London WC2R ORL, England
Penguin Putnam Inc., 375 Hudson Street, New York, New York 10014, USA
Penguin Books Australia Ltd, Ringwood, Victoria, Australia
Penguin Books Canada Ltd, 10 Alcorn Avenue, Toronto, Ontario, Canada M4V 3B2
Penguin Books India (P) Ltd, 11 Community Centre, Panchsheel Park,
New Delhi – 110 017, India
Penguin Books (NZ) Ltd, Cnr Rosedale and Airborne Roads,
Albany, New Zealand
Penguin Books (South Africa) (Pty) Ltd, 24 Sturdee Avenue,
Rosebank 2196, South Africa

Penguin Books Ltd, Registered Offices: 80 Strand, London WC2R ORL, England

www.penguin.com

First published 2001
1

PICTURE CREDITS

P A Photos, Alpha Photographic Press Agency (© Steve Finn, Ashley Knotek,
Dave Benett, Richard Chambury), Dove/Donovan, Express Newspapers,
Guardian Newspapers Limited, Times Newspapers Limited 1999, News Group
Newspapers Limited 1999, Frank Spooner Pictures

The moral right of the author has been asserted

Set in Bembo
Typeset by Rowland Phototypesetting Ltd, Bury St Edmunds, Suffolk
Printed in England by Clays Ltd, St Ives plc

*To Geoffrey and Jean*

# Contents

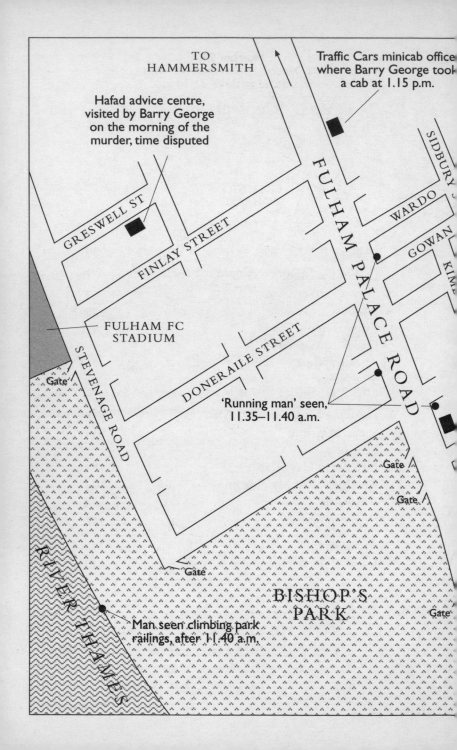

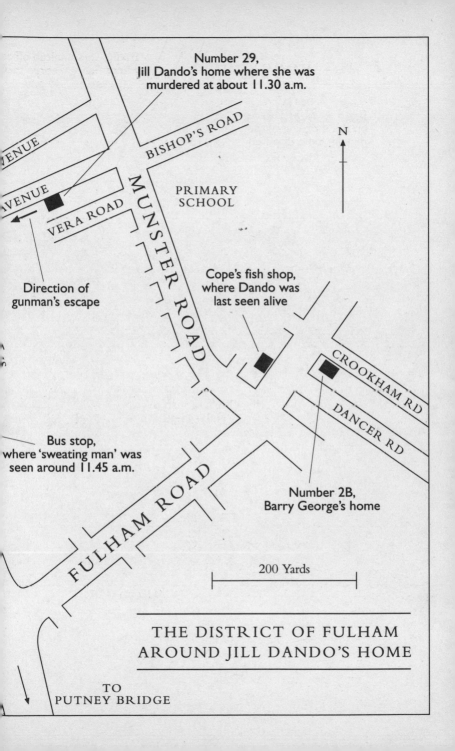

Number 29,
Jill Dando's home where she was
murdered at about 11.30 a.m.

BISHOP'S ROAD

N

VENUE

AVENUE

VERA ROAD

MUNSTER ROAD

PRIMARY
SCHOOL

Direction of
gunman's escape

Cope's fish shop,
where Dando was
last seen alive

CROOKHAM RD

DANCER RD

Bus stop,
where 'sweating man' was
seen around 11.45 a.m.

FULHAM ROAD

Number 2B,
Barry George's home

200 Yards

THE DISTRICT OF FULHAM
AROUND JILL DANDO'S HOME

TO
PUTNEY BRIDGE

# 1. Out of the Blue

*'The news was best when read by Jill. None of us could have believed it would, one day, be about her.'*

Monday 26 April 1999 was already a busy news day. The bombing in Kosovo and Serbia had been going on for five weeks and Nato spokesmen were claiming that morning that the latest raids had destroyed the last remaining bridge over the Danube inside Serbia. There was still plenty of fallout from a meeting of Western leaders the previous day in Washington, which brought to the fore disagreements about the wisdom of a ground invasion of Kosovo. And in Belgrade itself a senior Serb leader had hinted at the possibility of a peace deal. On the home front, meanwhile, the big story was the horrific nail bombings in London: the first of these had happened in Brixton a fortnight earlier and the second in Brick Lane at the weekend. After the black and Asian communities, everyone was wondering, who would be the next target? The police, working day and night to catch the perpetrator, had just extended their warnings to minority groups outside the capital. In the business world the Bradford and Bingley building society was balloting its members on whether to convert to a bank, while in sport England were preparing for a big Euro 2000 qualifying tie against Hungary. There was more than enough, in short, to keep the newsdesks occupied.

Between noon and 12.30 p.m., however, crime correspondents with national papers and broadcasting organizations in London began receiving calls or bleeper messages telling them of another potential story. Something had apparently happened to Jill Dando, the messages said. These were confidential tip-offs – from friendly police officers, from people eavesdropping on official radio traffic or from others who had just picked the information up by chance – and at this stage they were vague. Dando had been in an accident, said some. She had been attacked, said others. She was injured; perhaps she was even dead. Scotland Yard press officers were being very vague so the reporters turned elsewhere in the hope of learning something. Dando's agent, Jon Roseman, took several calls from reporters at his London office but he had heard nothing and could not help. Her brother Nigel, a journalist in Bristol, was contacted, but he too was in the dark. Both men were naturally alarmed and immediately began making calls on their own account to Dando's private phone numbers and to whomever else they could think of, but without result. No one, it seemed, could confirm anything.

By one o'clock the rumour was much stronger: Dando had been killed. As word spread through the huge BBC television newsroom in west London, where she still worked and had many friends, people were left astonished and distressed. Some wept. The news travelled up through the corporation's hierarchy of editors, managers and controllers until it reached John Birt, the director-general. Dando was one of his big stars and he knew her personally. Meetings were interrupted and executives made their way to the newsroom. Was it true? Although there was still no firm confirmation, all the signs suggested that it was. By now the BBC's lunchtime news bulletin was on air but in the absence of hard facts this story was not reported. Dando was a public figure and her death – assuming she really was dead – would inevitably be big news, but she was also a BBC employee and the corporation had obligations to her and to her family and friends. Could they go with an off-the-record confirmation or must they wait for something official and formal, which might not come for an hour or more? And even when they had the official word, should they delay further until those closest to her had all been informed? They had to be careful to do the right thing. As the editors paced the floor and the journalists pestered Scotland Yard, camera crews and reporters were taking up positions around Gowan Avenue, the Fulham street where Dando lived and which had been cordoned off by police. The lunchtime bulletin, meanwhile, worked its way steadily through Kosovo, the nail bombs and the Bradford and Bingley, according to script.

Others were busy too. Among the crime correspondents who had picked up the rumour before 1 p.m. was Martin Brunt of *Sky News*, who quickly called his news editor to tell him. 'What, *the* Jill Dando?' came the reply. 'Yes, *the* Jill Dando,' Brunt said. He was on his way to Fulham. Soon after 1 p.m. he called in again: he had received confirmation that Dando had definitely been attacked, that it was not an accident. This came, not from an official Scotland Yard spokesman, but from a police source whom Brunt could not identify on air. There was a hurried consultation in the Sky newsroom and the decision was taken. It was now 1.22 p.m. and a sports correspondent was on air discussing Kevin Keegan's selection for the Hungary game when news presenter Paula Fenech broke in to announce 'some news we're just getting'. Sky, she said, 'has just learned that the BBC presenter Jill Dando has been attacked at her home in west London. She has been taken to hospital. We have no other details.' It was a scoop, the first public word of the attack. Sky returned immediately to the sports report but four minutes later, at 1.26 p.m., they had an update on the Dando story: 'She has died in hospital following an attack at her London home.'

The Sky reports were seen by staff at the *Bristol Evening Post*, who broke the news to their colleague Nigel Dando. Jon Roseman also saw them. And so did people at the BBC, many of whom felt Sky had jumped the gun. Then at 1.37 p.m. the Press Association news agency ran the 'snap' that gave the story to every significant news outlet in the country: 'BBC presenter Jill Dando, thirty-eight, has died after being attacked in the street outside her London home today, police sources said.' Another snap followed: 'Found by a friend with multiple injuries just before noon. Pronounced dead at Charing Cross Hospital just after 1 p.m.' Moments later, at 1.41 p.m., the BBC finally ran a brief insert in the local London news report: 'We're getting news that the news presenter Jill Dando has been stabbed. More on that later.' Soon afterwards senior executives approved a newsflash, which was read by Jennie Bond. It was now hard fact, and it was sensational. Across London that lunchtime bleepers and mobile phones rang out, bringing editors back to their desks to rearrange television and radio news schedules and tear up planned newspaper layouts. Kosovo was downgraded; out of nowhere this was the top story of the day and the hunt was on for material – facts, comment and background – to fill the airwaves and the pages.

Among the first to give his reaction was Tony Hall, the BBC's head of news and current affairs. 'Everyone in BBC News is devastated,' he said. 'She was a wonderful person to work with and was respected and trusted by millions. All our thoughts are with her loved ones and family.' Others soon followed. Hall's colleague Alan Yentob, the BBC's director of television, spoke of an 'evil and inexplicable act'. Dando had been modest and professional, he said, with a rare gift for putting people at their ease. 'She was a very uncomplicated star, and there aren't many of those around.' Nick Ross, her co-presenter on *Crimewatch UK*, stepped outside BBC Television Centre to say: 'It's hit us like lightning, like a bolt out of the blue. It's astonishing. It really is astonishing.' And he paid his tribute to her: 'People say treacly things in these situations but the truth is that everybody got on with Jill. She was just a generous, open, friendly person; there was no side to her at all.' Nicholas Witchell, another colleague, said the loss was 'unspeakably dreadful'; Desmond Lynam was 'totally stunned and shattered'; John Humphrys said the news took the breath away.

Within an hour came word from Downing Street: 'The Prime Minister was told of Jill Dando's murder as he was preparing his statement on the Nato summit. He was deeply shocked. He had met her both professionally and socially at Downing Street and in common with many other people he found her totally charming and highly talented. He thinks it appalling that anybody could do such a thing.' Later in the day William Hague, the Conservative leader, declared: 'I am shocked and horrified by this senseless and brutal murder. Our first thoughts are with Jill's family on this tragic day. Jill Dando made a great contribution to popular broadcasting. She will be missed by millions.' The murder was raised in the House of Commons, where word reached the Conservative frontbencher Sir Norman Fowler during Home Office questions. 'On behalf of the Opposition,' he said, 'can I say that we have all been appalled to hear the news of the murder of Jill Dando?' Over murmurs of assent Jack Straw, the Home Secretary, replied: 'May I associate myself and the Government with your remarks? Jill Dando was someone who was known to virtually everybody in this country, if not personally. She was someone who was at the height of her powers. She had done a huge amount personally in the fight against crime by her role not least in *Crimewatch UK* and therefore this makes her death all the more poignant. I'm sure I speak for the whole House when I say that our deepest sympathy goes to her loved ones, her family and her friends at this terrible, tragic and appalling loss.'

People from her past emerged to talk in bewildered tones of their thoughts and memories. The deputy head of the comprehensive she attended in Weston-super-Mare described the shock of staff and pupils, while someone from her sixth form college recalled her returning there recently to open a new library: 'She came across as such a lovely person . . .' Her editor at the local paper where she had her first job said he just couldn't believe it. Former colleagues in Radio Devon, where she began her career in broadcasting, professed themselves stunned. At BBC regional television in Plymouth someone said: 'She was so bubbly and happy-go-lucky. . . It is just tragic.' At twenty-eight minutes past five a spokesman for Buckingham Palace declared that the Queen was 'shocked and saddened' by the news. The Duke of York, who had known Dando personally, was particularly saddened, the spokesman added. It turned out that she had helped the duke to promote a charity for the blind of which he was patron, and this proved to be only one aspect of her charitable work. Someone from the British Heart Foundation came on air to say that Dando had been a tireless fundraiser and campaigner, while the chairman of a hospice in Weston-super-Mare described the generous support she had given.

Many noted that the timing had a particular poignancy, for Dando had only recently announced that she was to be married to a London surgeon, Alan Farthing. In the past she was said to have been unlucky in love but this latest romance, everyone agreed, had proved blissfully happy and she was looking forward to a big wedding later in the year. 'That was the only thing that had been missing in her life up to now,' said Nick Ross. 'She desperately wanted to really fall in love, head over heels, and get married, and it *was* happening. And now this.' Her career was also on the move: the previous night had seen the screening of the first programme in a new series for her, *Antiques Inspectors*, and there were apparently plans for several other ventures. In particular she was reported to be in line to present the BBC's special millennium-night programme, a plum job for a presenter, marking her out as the best in her field. As Jon Roseman put it: 'Jill was at the pinnacle of her career.'

Who could have done such a thing? The picture was confused, and no one even knew how she had died – it was said she had been found outside her door with serious head injuries and that she died in hospital, but that was about it. Though reporters and camera crews were now at Gowan Avenue in force they could do little to clarify matters. The pictures showed the narrow residential street cordoned off with blue-and-white tape, and dozens of police officers at work. One rumour at the scene spoke of a gunshot but the general assumption was that Dando had been stabbed, indeed the Press Association was not alone in reporting she had been the victim of a 'frenzied stabbing attack'. The police, for their part, were insisting there would be no announcement about the cause of death until the post mortem was completed that evening.

Reporters were struggling. Was this a robbery or mugging gone wrong, or had Dando been the chosen target? Was there more than one attacker? Was she leaving or entering her house? While the answers were awaited most minds turned to the possibility that, like John Lennon, she had been killed by someone with an insane obsession, perhaps someone who had been following her – a stalker. Perhaps some madman took the announcement of her engagement as reason to kill. Reporters also pointed out that she appeared on the cover of that week's issue of *Radio Times* in an uncharacteristic pose, dressed head to foot in black leather and standing in front of a sports car beneath large letters that said: 'VROOOOOM'. Might this have outraged a deranged admirer? Or could she have been killed by a professional criminal because of her involvement with *Crimewatch*? There just wasn't enough to go on. In time the police revealed a little more: a well-dressed white man had been seen after the attack walking briskly or running from the scene and possibly carrying a mobile phone. They appealed for further information.

The tributes and expressions of shock flowed in a torrent. The chairman of the Police Federation spoke of the 'cruel irony that someone who cared so much for the victims of crime should be killed in this tragic way'. John Birt spoke of Dando as an accomplished professional with enormous versatility and a sweet, unaffected elegance. 'She was loved by her audiences,' he said. Martyn Lewis described 'bewilderment, tears and anger' in the BBC newsroom and Jennie Bond said that in twenty-two years at the corporation she had never seen such shock. Sophie Rhys-Jones, who knew Dando socially, was 'deeply shocked and upset'.

The *Six O'Clock News* on BBC1 that evening, read by Martyn Lewis, opened with the headline: 'One of Britain's most popular television presenters, our BBC colleague Jill Dando, has died after being attacked outside her London home.' Kate Adie, a journalist associated by most viewers with war, presented the main report. Standing in Gowan Avenue against a background of busy police officers, she linked together the clips: a neighbour told of finding the body; a doctor at the hospital stated the times of arrival and death; a detective described the man seen running away and appealed again for help. Then came tributes from Straw, Yentob and others. Adie observed: 'It is rare that a reporter can say a murder victim was the kind of woman who had no enemies. I can say that about Jill Dando.' There were more reports looking at her career, possible motives and the distress of friends and family before the bulletin moved on to other matters, notably war in the Balkans. Then at the end Lewis returned to the big story: 'Tonight's news is dominated by the murder of our friend and colleague, Jill Dando. Jill was special – not only to the millions of you who watched, admired and loved her over the years – but to all of us who had the privilege and delight of working with her. The news was best when read by Jill. None of us could have believed it would, one day, be about her. Good night.'

Both BBC1 and ITV changed their schedules that evening to accommodate tribute programmes, mixing clips from Dando's many television appearances with reminiscences from colleagues and friends. ITN's Trevor McDonald interviewed Lewis, who described the mood at the BBC as he had presented the *Six O'Clock News*: 'We felt in many ways, Trevor, that there was an empty chair beside us because Jill had shared so many bulletins with me and my colleagues on the programme.'

It was the BBC's main evening bulletin at nine o'clock that brought the coverage to its climax. Read this time by Peter Sissons, it began: 'Jill Dando, known and loved by millions, has been brutally murdered.' Once again Adie reported the story, ending her report with the same observation about Dando being 'the kind of woman who had no enemies'. And this time Michael Buerk presented a husky-voiced profile: 'The camera loved her even before she wore the gloss of stardom,' he said. 'It's the *Holiday* programme we'll remember. The gorgeous girl next door freed from the straitjacket of news, on permanent location. It looked the easiest and most fun job in the world. That was her special talent. The crushing schedule, the endless travelling never showed.' He went on: 'A golden career and the hopes of future happiness ended bloodily just before midday. A terrible price to pay for being lovely and famous, a terrible shock for you and me who knew her.' And to the series of reaction clips was now added the response of Alan Farthing, Dando's fiancé. 'I am totally devastated and unable to comprehend what has happened,' he said. 'Jill was respected for her professional abilities, admired by all who met her and adored by anyone who got to know her.' Again, after dealing with the rest of the news, the programme ended with a word from the presenter. 'That's the main news tonight: the brutal killing that today stunned everyone here at the BBC Television Centre,' said Sissons. 'At the age of thirty-seven, in her prime as the nation's most popular presenter, and radiantly looking forward to marriage in the autumn, Jill Dando was shot down by an attacker outside her home not two miles from here. A senseless murder that leaves this newsroom in which she worked a darker place and makes a lot poorer the medium which she graced. Good night.'

*Shot down* – she had been shot. Not long before the bulletin began, this further sensational element had been added to the story: the post mortem showed that Dando died from a single bullet to the head, fired from close range. This was no frenzied attack; if anything it seemed cruel and emotionless. The newspapers for the following morning had their headlines and now they were going to press.

One summer afternoon a little more than two years later, long after the initial shock had passed, a barrister rose to his feet in court number one of the Old Bailey and invited the jury to look back on the day that Jill Dando died. The murder was, he said, one of those rare events which are so shocking and so sensational that many people are able to remember long afterwards what they were doing when the news reached them. He cited as other examples the climax of the Cuban missile crisis (he was a man in his fifties) and the death of the Princess of Wales. So popular was the television presenter, said the barrister, so central was she to the lives of many people that her death, which he described as an atrocity, eclipsed at the time even the conflict in the Balkans.

Extraordinary as it may appear, this was no exaggeration. Jill Dando was not a royal princess, nor did her death alter the course of history or even topple a minor government minister, but for many, many people it was a great shock. Eleven million viewers tuned in to see Martyn Lewis present the *Six O'Clock News* that night, a record for the programme exceeding even the numbers who watched on the night of the Dunblane tragedy, or at the height of the Gulf War, or during the week that followed the death of Diana. And in the press the next morning the story swamped all else – the *Daily Mail*, to pick just one, devoted its whole front page to a photograph of Dando and carried reports and comment on pages two, three, four, five, six, seven, eight, nine, twenty and twenty-one. Such was the public appetite for information in the days and weeks that followed that the smallest development in the murder inquiry was certain to command front-page headlines while the most inconsequential insights into Dando's life and career merited full-page spreads inside. Her funeral was lavishly covered and when her memorial service took place in London months later questions were raised in the editorial columns about why it was not carried live on national television. This was not mere hype or media self-indulgence, for the public reaction was instant and visceral. Viewers of the *Six O'Clock News* that first evening, for example, had not had time to be exposed to hype; they were simply turning on the first available bulletin so that they could learn more about what had happened, and they did so in unprecedented numbers.

As Dando herself might well have observed, she was only a television presenter, so why was her death greeted in this way? No doubt there were many reasons. Nerves were still raw after the death of Diana twenty months earlier, so the media and the public may have been jumpy or excitable in the face of an event which bore at least some similarities. It is certainly hard to believe that Buckingham Palace and Downing Street would have reacted so promptly had Dando died three years earlier. Another feature of that day's events which made them compelling was that this was a celebrity story that caught celebrities off guard. For a generation familiar with the thrill of fly-on-the-wall programmes it was like a glimpse inside the world of television, enabling us to see well-known people who normally appear composed and in control suddenly experiencing real emotion on camera. But these are surely marginal factors and they scarcely begin to explain the rawness and breadth of a response which was, as that barrister indicated, a genuine phenomenon. The true explanations must lie in the rare character of the fame that Jill Dando had built up over ten years in national television and in the extraordinary nature of her murder that morning in Gowan Avenue.

By her death Jill Dando acquired the dismal distinction of being the most famous and the most popular person ever to have been murdered in Britain. It is true that John Lennon and Earl Mountbatten of Burma, two notable murder victims who come to mind, both happen to have been killed in other countries, but the point is not a pedantic, geographical one. Jill Dando had a familiarity, even an intimacy with the viewing public of a kind that is not available to movie stars or pop singers, let alone politicians or royalty. People – millions of people – felt in a way that they knew this woman almost as they would a neighbour or friend. How she achieved this, how she made the journey from awkward West Country schoolgirl to queen of prime time, is a complex and fascinating story that belongs exclusively in the modern television age. Her bond with her audience was exceptional and the sudden breaking of that bond was inevitably a cause of distress. The circumstances in which it was broken – that bullet out of the blue on her doorstep, just as she was preparing for marriage – greatly amplified the response. Nothing about her popular persona could explain such a violent end, and the more that was revealed about what happened in Gowan

Avenue the more inexplicable it all became. It was a crime that, if it had not actually happened, would have been dismissed as an outlandish, tasteless fiction. 'What, *the* Jill Dando?' said the editor at Sky, and his words summed it up.

## 2. West Country Girl

*'When I was eight I used to get Ladybird books out of the library about newspapers and TV.'*

Jill Wendy Dando was born on 9 November 1961 at Ashcombe House maternity home in the Somerset seaside town of Weston-super-Mare. A strapping baby at nine pounds and four ounces, the new addition completed the Dando family – father Jack, a printer then in his mid-forties, mother Jean, a housewife ten years younger than her husband, and nine-year-old brother Nigel. They lived in a three-bedroomed bungalow semi on Madam Lane in Worle, a district of Weston that stretches eastwards towards Bristol.

Later in life Jill Dando would describe her childhood as 'very ordinary, but quite idyllic' and this was no doubt a fair description, but what she did not remark upon was the striking stability of her background. It was evident even in the family name: Dandos may be rare in Britain as a whole but in Somerset the surname is both familiar – the Weston phone book lists almost 100 of them – and old, dating back by some accounts to the Conquest. Jack Dando, then, came of long-established local stock, as did the woman he married, and he also spent almost the whole of his working life with one long-established local firm, the *Weston Mercury* newspaper, where from soon after the war until the early 1980s he was a senior figure on the printing side. As for Weston-super-Mare itself, the town was not so much standing still as going backwards. Once among the more stately resorts – in its early years it was touched by the elegance of nearby Bath – it had since suffered the successive ravages of German bombing and British postwar planning, so that by 1961 it was reduced to a very sleepy place, literally: on the one hand it was a home for the retired and on the other a dormitory town for people working in Bristol and further afield. The sixties, by and large, passed it by; Pearl Carr and Teddy Johnson topped the bill, the donkeys continued to ply the beach and low tide still stubbornly left mud-brown sand stretching almost to the horizon.

If the world Jill Dando entered was quiet, it was also as cosy and loving as could be. When she was three or four months old she was the centre of attention as the family posed together for a black-and-white group photograph, a little scene that says a good deal. The baby is in Jean's arms, gripping a motherly finger and scowling, as babies will when they are expected to look happy. The others are gazing happily down at her. Jean, seated, wears a bright floral dress, a bead necklace, spectacles and a Celia Johnson perm. Nigel, looking over her shoulder, is neatly coiffed and, with a V-necked sweater over a shirt and tie, very much the well-groomed schoolboy. And Jack sits to the side, a lean man with a face that might have come from the 1930s – horn-rimmed spectacles, trim moustache and close-cropped black hair receding at the top. His pinstriped suit has wide lapels, again suggesting an earlier decade, and under it he too wears sweater, shirt and tie. There is nothing forced about their smiles; the Dandos are evidently delighted with their baby and amused by the grumpy face she has pulled.

There was, however, a worry, for soon after the birth a murmur was detected in Jill's heartbeat. This did not mean her life was necessarily in danger – such problems often correct themselves as a baby grows – but it was grounds for concern. In fact while she was a baby she seemed to develop reasonably well and it was only when she became a toddler that the problems showed. 'I couldn't walk across a room without getting out of breath,' she said later, 'and I certainly couldn't run around with other children my age.' The fault was in her heart and time was not healing it, indeed the bigger she grew the worse things became, until eventually she was sent to Bristol Royal Infirmary for tests which showed she had a hole in the heart and a blocked artery. This was disastrous news, for the prognosis was bleak. In the early 1960s it was almost unheard-of to conduct open-heart surgery on an infant and surgeons tended to wait until the patient was six or seven, but in this case it seems they held out little hope she would survive that long. If they operated straight away, however, the chances of something going wrong were high, indeed Jill's parents were told there was a 70 per cent likelihood of failure – in other words, she was more than twice as likely to die as to survive. However bad the odds, Jean and Jack had no choice but to gamble with their daughter's life, and the operation was performed in Bristol in January 1965, when Jill was just three years and two months old. It took eight hours, throughout which her little body was kept chilled to a temperature of fourteen degrees centigrade. She survived that day, which was a relief in itself, but then came the wait to see whether the heart would function properly. Jack and Jean shuttled up and down from Weston in the family Ford Prefect.

The first sign was a small one, but promising. A nurse drew back the bedclothes a little to reveal Jill's fingernails and for the first time in her life they were really pink, rather than white or blue. So, it proved, were her toenails. A few days later the Dandos turned up in the ward and were alarmed to find their daughter's bed empty. Looking around, they saw a nurse coming in and they were about to ask what had happened when they realized there was a child with her. It was Jill and she was walking; a full recovery had begun. Years later she looked back: 'I don't remember being ill or any recovery period, but I do recall being in hospital. All the little things have stuck in my mind, such as being pushed around the ward in a pedal car by my father, eating disgusting tomato soup and watching *Crackerjack* on television. I remember it as being fun.' The return to Weston, when it came, found her bursting with new-found energy and life: sitting beside Nigel in the back of the car with her new teddy-bear on her lap, she sang 'Puff the Magic Dragon' at the top of her voice all the way.

The operation left her with a scar from her throat to her navel. Broad and livid at first, it faded with the years but could still be seen at her neckline when she was an adult, particularly if she had a tan – television viewers would sometimes write to her, asking how she came by it. And although from her mid-twenties she complained of occasional palpitations, her heart was strong. Inevitably, however, the childhood drama had profound effects. By the standards of the time Jill had come along fairly late – her parents had waited nearly ten years after Nigel was born – and in some respects, with her brother so much older, she was like an only child. That alone made her precious. Now she was doubly so. It was as if she had been taken away and then miraculously given back again. The scar and the annual check-ups were steady reminders of this narrow escape, this second birth, and it is hardly surprising that Jean Dando was, to use Jill's own words, 'extremely protective' of her daughter. Jill would always remember being fussed over in childhood, for example being pestered to wear vests even on warm summer days, and a neighbour of the time recalls that, quite understandably, the little girl was 'mollycoddled'.

Most only daughters are close to their mothers but circumstances were conspiring to create a bond between Jill and Jean that was especially tight. Jean Dando was a strong woman, the dominant personality in the home. Though Jack was a figure of authority at work, like most Englishmen of his generation he was not inclined to show his emotions with his family or to be too involved in day-to-day family matters. Every week he brought home his wages in a brown envelope and watched his wife divide it into piles – the coal money, the holiday money, the food money and so forth. Every day, whatever the weather, he cycled the three miles to the *Mercury* offices in the centre of town, leaving the car for his wife to use. For her part Jean was heavily involved in church affairs – the Dandos were Baptists, attending

Milton church every Sunday – and in the Women's Institute, as well as in raising her children, running the house and keeping an eye on her own mother, who lived near by. In all of this Jill liked to play whatever part she could; if she was at home, likely as not she was helping Jean.

Not that she was always at home. There were other children to play with in the neighbourhood and they tended to congregate in the quiet cul-de-sac of Orchard Close, around the corner. There, safe from traffic, they could fight their wars, act out their dramas and ride their tricycles and bicycles. When they tired of that they could roam in the fields and play in the local stream, for they were on the edge of the countryside, with a dairy farm just across the way whose cows occasionally strayed into the gardens. When Jill spoke of the idyll of her childhood, it was probably of this that she was thinking. Weston beach was not part of her everyday stomping ground. For a start it was miles away on the other side of town, and then there were the tourists, some of whom could be pretty rough and ready. Only at weekends with her parents, or occasionally with Nigel during school holidays, did she get to paddle and make sandcastles among the summer throng.

For her education little Jill went first to Mendip Infants and then to Greenwood Junior School, where Betty Jones, a teacher, found her a 'star pupil, always volunteering'. Jones said much later: 'I taught Jill for two years from the age of six. She was always very good at anything you asked her; she was really very clever. By the time she left my class at seven she was a fluent reader. She was rather giggly but never naughty.' From Greenwood Jill graduated to Worle Comprehensive, a new, concrete establishment with some 1,000 pupils, built to accommodate the children of the new commuter families whose streets of homes were covering over the fields eastward from Worle.

Even in the most settled and loving surroundings adolescence is difficult, and Jill Dando's was no exception. When she spoke later of the years between the ages of eleven and sixteen the usual

warmth and enthusiasm were missing, and the principal reason
seems to have been what happened to her looks. The photographs
of the growing girl tell the story. At eight or nine she was pretty,
with long, blonde hair, bright eyes and a winning smile. One
picture shows her sitting at an electric piano at home, her fingers
on the keys (although she is not playing), and her eyes turned
into the camera. She is wearing a smart little summer dress, has a
fashionable clip in her hair and a ring on one finger. You sense
that she cares about her appearance and likes being a nice-looking
girl. A few years later, perhaps aged thirteen, she posed for
another photograph, this time a head-and-shoulders shot. She is
obviously very thin, her eyes are half-shut and her hair is short,
shapeless and no longer blonde. Her mouth, slightly open, shows
uneven teeth and she is wearing spectacles with lenses so big and
thick they distort and obscure half her face. As she was to say, in
her own eyes at least she had become 'rather an ugly little girl'.
This affected her deeply, and in lasting ways.

The spectacles had been the worst of it. 'I was the only child
in my class who wore glasses. When the school optician broke
the news that there was no alternative I went home in tears and
my mother had to comfort me.' Teased by schoolmates, she
became introverted, competitive about her work and extremely
neat – as she put it, 'a bit of an anorak'. Once, much later, she
was asked to name the best gift she had ever received, and the
answer was revealing: 'A sewing machine when I was thirteen.
My parents sacrificed a lot to buy me a brand-new electric one
for Christmas, and I remember bursting into tears of joy . . .' A
sewing machine was not something to be shared with friends.

She was now even more of a home bird, sticking closely to
the mother who never let her down and avoiding situations
where she had to fend for herself. Only once, for example, did
she go on a school trip, staying in a youth hostel on Exmoor,
and then she was so miserable she swore never to repeat the
experience. She kept the vow, remaining stubbornly in Weston
even when the rest of her class went off on holiday exchanges to

France. The one exception was a camping weekend in Budleigh Salterton with her church youth club, and on that occasion she took a sun lounger to sleep on because she was afraid of creepy-crawlies on the ground. In all of this she was following her mother, who didn't like travel. Not for the Dandos the new holiday destinations in Spain; Jean, for one thing, hated aeroplanes. So when they took their summer holidays in the late 1960s and 1970s it was in Bournemouth or Torquay – some years they never left Weston. And by her own account Jill was fourteen before she visited London for the first time, on discount rail tickets with her parents. 'We went to see *My Fair Lady*, walked along the Embankment, visited the Tower of London and all the usual tourist spots,' she recalled. 'There was an anxious moment on the Underground when my mother and I boarded the train but the doors closed before my father could get on and he was left behind on the platform. We got off at the next stop and went back, and thankfully we found him.'

When David Cassidy came along she fell for him hook, line and sinker, listening for his songs on the radio, buying the singles, pinning up the posters, writing fan letters. She was eleven and she would say later that he was the first man she gave her heart to. It didn't last. After Cassidy came a similar devotion to Donny Osmond and after him she developed the pop passion that remained with her for the rest of her life, for Cliff Richard. She even wanted to sing the sentimental songs herself and persuaded her parents to use their Green Shield Stamps to buy a guitar, but that phase soon passed – playing, she found, gave her calluses on her fingers and she didn't like that.

The ugly duckling phase came to an end in the summer of 1978, when she was sixteen. Most girls and boys change in important ways at this time but it is not usually so sudden as it was with Jill, and she would later present it as a deliberate and conscious act – 'I decided to reinvent myself,' she said. Perhaps it was simply that she saw the opportunity: she was leaving Worle school and going to Broadoak sixth-form school, on the other

side of town, and may have thought that since she was turning
one page she might as well turn two. Whatever the explanation,
the action she took was radical: her bottle-end glasses were
exchanged for contact lenses, her drab hair was permed and
tinted blonde and her old wardrobe was simply dumped. Out
went the once-loved school uniform and the home-made clothes
of her 'anorak' years, and in came a fashionable 1970s look that
included clogs, skinny-ribbed sweaters and bell-bottomed jeans
(always worn with a crease). By now her body had also changed
and she proved to have a figure to do justice to the clothes.
The combined effect, as she recalled, was remarkable: 'Nobody
recognized me. I couldn't believe it when the heart-throb at the
church youth group asked me out.' This was something new
and thrilling. 'Previously I had always been the one to get
broken-hearted and suddenly I found I could turn the tables,
which gave me a sense of power and excitement.'

There were other signs of a new leaf being turned. She took a
Saturday job working in Weston library, which meant dealing
with the public there. 'She was certainly shy when she first came,'
recalls Lyn Tanner, who worked with her. 'She would blush
easily when people asked her questions or if there was a problem,
and sometimes she got the giggles. But she was very positive
about it and wanted to get on.' The job paid £6 per week,
money which gave her a little independence. At school, too, she
came out of her shell. Pupils at Broadoak attended for five terms,
with the sixth devoted to study leave and A levels, and the
experience was supposed not only to raise their academic standards but also to stimulate responsibility and self-reliance. Every
year in the spring a head boy and girl were elected by secret
ballot, and in 1979 Jill Dando put herself forward and was voted
in. 'She had just two terms to impress her peers before that,' says
Graham Max, a Broadoak teacher of the time, 'it speaks for itself.'
This was clearly a period when confidence was running strong
in her. Max remembers her carrying off her responsibilities in
style. 'The head girl bit was done professionally, with a consider-

ation that it should be done well,' he says. 'And I recall that she put a lot of effort into the rag week, organizing and motivating people, making sure things were done rather than just sitting and talking about it.'

While the ugly duckling was becoming a swan, liked and admired by both pupils and staff, she could not become a clever swan, and when the A level results came through in the summer of 1980 they were less than impressive. It did not matter, for by then she had decided exactly what job she wanted to do and she knew her qualifications were good enough: she would be a journalist at the *Weston Mercury*. She laid the groundwork while still at school by doing a spell of work experience on the paper and when the time came she applied to the *Mercury*'s editor, John Bailey. He set her a test: to write an essay on 'My thoughts on the year 2000'. Whatever she wrote it was good enough and she was in, starting on a weekly wage of £41.36, paid in cash in a brown envelope.

Often, later in life, she would be asked about this career choice and she had a couple of stock answers. This was one: 'It was the smell that did it for me. Every Thursday Dad would bring home a stack of papers hot off the press and the newsprint gave off this wonderful, warm smell.' The other was that she was inspired by the example of her brother, by then a reporter on a Bristol-based paper. As a schoolgirl, she would say, she liked the look of Nigel's job because 'you never know from one day to the next what you're going to be doing'. Both these answers have charm, and no doubt a grain of truth, although her father for one had a more prosaic memory – 'It seemed the natural thing to do. She had been very good at English at school.' Yet none, of course, is the whole story. And since this is such an important moment in her life – the first step on her path to success and fame – it is worth looking a little more closely at what was going on.

On the one hand it's clear that journalism at the *Mercury* was a cautious choice, in some ways the most cautious she could have made. While most of her classmates were seizing the chance to

leave sleepy Weston, Jill Dando stayed put and took a job that
allowed her to continue living at home with the mother she
doted on. Not only that but she joined what in many respects
was the family firm. Jack Dando, after all, had been a fixture at
the paper for more than thirty years, while Nigel had done his
training there, so even before her spell of work experience she
knew some of the staff by name and was familiar with many of
the rhythms and patterns of local newspaper life. And though
journalism is by most standards an exciting profession there can
have been few less challenging places to join it, for the *Mercury*
was a newspaper very much in the mould of the dull, conservative
town it served. By 1980 it had been in the hands of the same
family, the Framptons, for well over a century and its office, a
Victorian-Gothic building on Weston's main street, was a local
landmark. John Bailey, who had been editor for almost twenty
years, described it as 'a clean, good-standard family paper' and
no one would have argued with him. Then still a broadsheet, it
was quintessentially small-time, carrying headlines ranging from
'Avon drive to aid young jobless' and 'Caravan site plans to
extend activities' to 'Fire destroys donkey food' and 'Award for
Uphill dog' (Uphill is a village). One week in 1980 the front
page led with the story: 'Winter Gardens future – no immediate
change'.

But if Jill Dando's first career choice suggests a girl who, for
all her ability to reinvent herself, had yet to discover a real spirit
of adventure, there is something else to be considered as well.
She was ultimately to become a television celebrity and in 1980
the shortest route to that position, apart from becoming an actor,
was probably through journalism. At that time, too, the vast
majority of journalists started their careers on local papers. If
she had been deliberately aiming for the result she achieved,
therefore, she might well have chosen this as a first step. So is
there any evidence that she was following a bigger plan? The
answer, perhaps surprisingly, is yes, there is some.

When Jill Dando, the successful celebrity, was asked about the origins of her interest in television she once again supplied a variety of answers but they all pointed back towards her child-hood. 'I had a cousin who was a production secretary on *Jackanory* and I thought it was the height of glamour,' she was to tell the *Daily Telegraph*. In *OK!* she said that once, while on holiday as a child at Butlin's in Minehead, she had seen a BBC crew filming for the *Holiday* programme and had jumped up and down behind the presenter, as kids do. 'From then on I kept telling my mother I wanted to work on the *Holiday* programme.' And to the *Today* newspaper she said: 'When I was eight I used to get Ladybird books out of the library about newspapers and TV. I was fasci-nated about what went on behind the scenes.' Which of these, if any, was the true genesis of her interest doesn't matter much, and she was probably stretching memory too far in trying to locate it. What does matter is that it was a recurring thought for the young Jill Dando, one that lodged in her head from an early age – an age, perhaps significantly, before her 'anorak' period. Her brother Nigel confirms this, saying it was her 'stock phrase' as a girl that she wanted to work behind the scenes in television.

Many girls and boys have the same thought – television is an attractive and familiar thing to them – and most of them grow out of it, so it would be wrong to give such a childhood fantasy great weight. Yet in the case of Jill Dando it would also be equally wrong to discount it entirely, for as we shall see it was a curious fact about her that at almost every point in her life when she has to make a choice relating to her career, whether it be major or minor, she chooses the shortest path towards the goal she ulti-mately achieved. So although she certainly did not select the job of local newspaper reporter because she had a clear-sighted plan to progress from there to presenting *Holiday* on BBC1, it is equally certain that the notion of a career in television was somewhere in her head at the time. And there it remained, a voice that over the years would sometimes speak to her in whispers and sometimes sing out loud. Like many other people who become successful performers, therefore, Jill Dando formed her ambition early. By the same token, like many such people she also experienced strong contrary emotions, in her case most notably the desire to stay at home with her mother and hide from the world beyond Weston. These two sides of her character, the ambitious performer and the shy hometown girl, were to jostle and compete with one another all her life, and in curious ways the tension between them contributed significantly to her popular success.

For the moment, however, we are still in Weston-super-Mare and she is starting out as a cub reporter on the *Mercury*. According to the practice of the time she was required to complete a two-and-a-half-year traineeship before qualifying and so it was that she discovered in Weston the full range of local news staples: council meetings, magistrates' courts, Rotary gatherings, planning disputes, golden weddings, agricultural fairs, local history and so forth. By all accounts she found it easy. She could write well enough and she knew the area and many of its people, so she had assets to draw on. John Bailey remembers her as shy, but also determined. As with the library job of her schooldays she was meeting and talking to strangers, and while this ran against her instincts she learned to cope with it and even, for the first time, to enjoy it. For their part Weston folk were more than willing to spare time for this pretty, slightly giggly local girl from the *Mercury* who took such an interest in everything. She also proved equal to the discipline of the job. Local reporting may not usually involve earth-shattering events but you need to get it right because the people who are mentioned or quoted will read the paper and challenge forcefully anything that is contentious. Dando, however, was diligent and thoughtful. Years later a local magistrate whose court cases she covered would say: 'I never read a report from her that was factually untrue or written for sensational effect.'

In addition to her on-the-job experience she had to attend two residential college courses in Cardiff, covering such topics as typing, shorthand and media law. This meant, among other things, that for the first time she lived away from home, albeit for just two months each time. The experience proved a pleasant one, partly because she was placed in digs which provided what a contemporary remembers as 'a real home from home'. And she shone on the course: most students, for example, needed to sit through both phases before their shorthand came up to scratch, but she went from nothing to 100 words per minute in her first course alone.

In the *Mercury* offices she was popular, just as she was wherever she worked for the rest of her life. On the one hand colleagues were attracted by her unaffected eagerness about the job and on the other they responded to her interest in them. She was the sort of person who remembered what you told her about yourself, was concerned about your worries and shared your moments of happiness. And she had little sense of hierarchy, looking everyone in the eye in exactly the same way. Chris Wiltshire, who joined the *Mercury* a few months after her, remembers that she was such a hit he found her a very hard act to follow. One photograph of the newsroom at the time shows Dando at her desk in the centre of the room with a typewriter in front of her and heaps of paper piled around. Her permed hair, parted on the left, tumbles down to her shoulders and she is wearing her trademark smile. Pinned to the wall at her side is her large Cliff Richard calendar. Another picture from the same period has her on the telephone, taking notes. She is demurely dressed in a dark woollen skirt reaching below the knee, a short-sleeved top and a rope of pearls wound twice around her neck – a poised and businesslike young woman.

She had plenty of boyfriends in this period but few lasted very long, something that had been true since her schooldays. She would say later that she had her first kiss as a fourteen-year-old, with a boy called Roy whom she knew from the church youth club, but the romance was over in three weeks. Then there was Steve, who played 'Annie's Song' for her on the guitar. At Broadoak there were more boyfriends, and in her early years at the *Mercury* still more, including a couple of young colleagues, but these were not great passions. One man she dated over quite a long period was Andrew Ray, a young official in the local magistrates' court whom she met through work. She visited him at his home in Bristol where they watched *Brideshead Revisited* together; they made a trip to London and when she went to Cardiff he drove her over in his MG. But though they became close he was conscious that this was not, for her, an exclusive relationship – she was seeing other 'chaps', as she called them. Ultimately it was he who ended it, although they remained friends for years afterwards. There seems to have been a diffidence in her: the girl who had lost her heart to David Cassidy was shy of giving it to lesser men, even when, as happened, they were very keen on her. And there was another odd thing: friends noticed, and she would later talk about, her particular fondness for older men. Roy at the youth club was three or four years older, as were some of the other boys, and, somewhat to the bafflement of her contemporaries, after leaving school she dated a number of men who were more than ten years her senior, one of them a man in his forties. It was also a standing joke that she was especially attractive to her girlfriends' fathers – 'All our dads were in love with her,' said one contemporary.

Her social life now acquired a new dimension, for she joined the Weston amateur dramatic society. Because of the summer trade the town had several theatres and since childhood Jill had attended plays and shows with her parents. At school she had done a little acting but once she entered the adult world it became a real enthusiasm. The society was glad to have her – there were always parts for pretty young women – and as ever she took to it well. One part she played would much later attract national newspaper attention: it was in a farce called *Pardon me, Prime Minister*, when she was required to be caught with a politician in a compromising position and a state of undress. Others in the cast recall her being shy about appearing in her underwear, and although she later spoke of having 'nothing to cover her modesty apart from a couple of copies of Hansard', she seems to have revealed very little. In the production photographs she is to be seen wearing a substantial undergarment which, perhaps significantly, had the effect of covering her scar. But she was not restricted to bimbo parts and landed lead roles in such plays as *Berkeley Square* and *A Murder is Announced*. In *Johnny Belinda* she starred as a deaf girl and had to learn some sign language for the part, and according to Gerard White, the society's president, her performance was 'truly excellent'.

Another sideline that absorbed her, if only for a while, was radio. Weston General Hospital ran an in-house station called Sunshine Radio which was strongly supported by staff at the *Mercury*, and the young Jill was drawn in. 'It was fun,' she said later. 'I started off doing the ward round, when you go out and collect the requests . . . We took a Uher, which is the recorder, around with us chatting to the patients and getting interesting stories from them. They [Sunshine Radio] asked me to do something they hadn't done before, which was a local news bulletin. I went on to do, for a little while, co-presenting on a Saturday afternoon programme, including sports reports. I was awfully nervous; it was awful. Luckily there was somebody else there to prop me up . . .' For a while this was a passion. One colleague recalls her carrying the heavy tape recorder with her on assignments for the paper just in case there was an opportunity to record an item for the station. Another felt the need to advise her against spending so much time on radio in case she jeopardized her chances of qualification as a journalist. It was advice which, eventually, she had to heed, and she gave it up. 'I couldn't commit myself every week,' she would say.

Late in 1982 she completed her professional training, passed her proficiency test and became a fully qualified journalist. When Nigel Dando had reached this stage he immediately moved on to a bigger paper. So, after Jill, did Chris Wiltshire. So did most young reporters. The *Mercury* was a good, solid paper of its kind but it was very small-time and it was only natural for bright journalists to put the golden weddings and Uphill dogs behind them as soon as they could and reach for the next rung on the professional ladder. Not so Jill Dando, who watched as her contemporaries graduated to better-paid and more challenging jobs elsewhere, but stayed where she was. Why? It is certainly tempting to put it down to timidity. She remained, after all, the 'home bird' she had always been, still living with her parents and still very close to her mother. (One *Mercury* colleague recalls that, even though they saw each other every morning and evening, Jill and Jean often chatted on the telephone during the working day – lively, gossipy conversations full of exclamations and laughter.) And at twenty-one years of age Jill had still not travelled abroad or flown in an aeroplane, so her horizons remained very near. But while the ties to home remained strong she did, in fact, have ambition and she did try to get out of Weston; the reason she stayed was that she could not get the sort of job she wanted.

Inspired by her hospital experience, she had set her sights on working in radio and after qualifying she applied for two or three jobs, first at Radio Bristol, her local station, and then farther afield. She even went for a couple of interviews, but was rejected. 'It was the same old story: they say, well, either you're too young, you haven't had enough journalistic experience, or you haven't had broadcasting experience yet.' From then, she said a few years later, it was 'a case of just waiting and seeing', of staying on at the *Mercury* and acquiring experience. Curiously, though, she did not return to Sunshine Radio, nor did she apply for jobs at other newspapers. Perhaps she lost confidence or perhaps she was merely patient. Whichever it was, two more years passed before she left Weston.

It was spring 1985 when she spotted in the *UK Press Gazette* an advertisement for a job as a broadcast assistant at BBC Radio Devon. She would say later that she applied because she could no longer stomach the fêtes and planning meetings which remained her daily bread at the *Mercury* – 'I thought, "I've had enough of this."' It's easy to see how that would happen, but other things had changed. By now Jill Dando was twenty-three and had lived a little more. She was on top of her work and knew everybody who counted in Weston. She had even been abroad, albeit only on a short trip to Strasbourg for the paper to report on the work of the local Euro-MP. And she had acquired some experience in love, including one long-term involvement. Through her reporting work she met and fell for John Crockford-Hawley, a local councillor then in his mid-thirties, and they became an item. When he was made mayor of the town she would often accompany him at formal occasions – as his consort, they would joke. The relationship lasted some time and friends say she was very keen on him – it was presumably this she was thinking of when much later she said she had once thought she would marry in Weston and settle there for life. But it did not lead anywhere and in due course they parted. 'You could say I was her first love,' Crockford-Hawley would tell a reporter; he seems also to have been her first real romantic disappointment.

If she had no romantic ties, however, her family ties were tighter than ever, for in 1984 Jean Dando was diagnosed as suffering from leukaemia. For a while she had good days when hopes rose, but over time they were increasingly outnumbered by the bad. She was dying, slowly. It is all the more striking, then, that at this time Jill should have applied for a job based sixty miles away in Exeter, but she did, and when it was offered to her she accepted it, although not without a great deal of soul-searching. Both she and Nigel would later recall how difficult the decision was. 'She agonized over leaving Weston,' Nigel said. 'It was Mum who told her she had to go for it.' Jill explained: 'She knew how much the job meant to me . . . She was incredibly selfless.' It may have eased her mind that her father, by now retired, was at home full-time, and that she herself would be only a couple of hours away by car, but it was still a decision full of meaning. Jill was a devoted daughter; her desire to make this career move must have been powerful indeed.

John Lilley, acting manager of Radio Devon at the time, had been 'bowled over' by the bright young woman from Weston who turned up for interview. 'She was so full of life and energy, absolutely vivacious,' he said. His confidence was to be quickly rewarded, for just as she had taken readily to newspaper work, so she proved a radio natural. She spent two or three months in Exeter and in Radio Devon's district offices learning the ropes of professional radio: how to edit tape, how to conduct interviews, how to use her own voice and so on. Then she was allowed on air to read short bulletins. Her first effort was a disaster – she missed her cue and after a long pause asked anxiously: 'Is anybody there?' – but it was just a hiccup and before long she was co-presenting the station's breakfast show, *Good Morning Devon*, running from 6 a.m. to 9 a.m. every weekday. This was the usual magazine of local and national news, short features, traffic, sport and other useful information. One of the station's most popular programmes, it required its presenters to be quick-thinking, well informed and fluent, and Jill Dando, now turning twenty-four, was all of these. The job also required something extra, a measure of self-projection, and this too was something she took in her stride. In the summer after the joined, the station had the idea of mounting a light-hearted promotion for the show to tour the many carnivals staged in Devon's villages. After some discussion it was decided to send the two lead presenters, Dando and Alan Dedicote, out in a float in the shape of a four-poster bed, a stunt to evoke the idea of listening in bed in the morning. John Lilley recalls that he was uncertain whether Dando would agree, since he knew she saw herself as a serious journalist, but she loved the idea and threw herself into the tour with gusto.

This happy spell was broken when, on 7 January 1986, her mother died at the age of fifty-eight. The end, when it came, was expected. Two weeks earlier the doctors, acknowledging that there was no more that they could do, had allowed Jean to spend her last Christmas in Worle with her family. Jill said later: 'It was lovely to have her at home again, but . . . she was in a dreadful way, so weak and frail. It was awful to see her like that.' This was an ordeal for everyone. 'I must have cooked the Christmas lunch but I don't really remember any of that – just the crying and trying not to let her see me in tears.' With Jean's death Jill lost her closest confidante, her most trusted critic and her best friend. She had adored her mother, as she once explained: 'She was everything I wanted to be. It was she who encouraged me in my career when I was starting out in local radio. And she was always there when something went wrong, telling me, "You can do it, Jill."' Theirs, she said, had been a 'synergistic' bond – each seemed to know what the other was thinking, and they found the same things funny. On another occasion she said: 'I put my mother on a pedestal, for the best of reasons: she gave me as much love as any mother could possibly give, and I gave back as good as I got. I always knew she was there. She was my rock.' A great vacuum now appeared in her life and her father and brother, both reserved characters, were not the kind to fill it. Nigel had left home when Jill was ten and had since married, and the two siblings had drifted apart. She told later how it was she who broke the news to him, by phone. 'It's happened,' she said. 'All right. OK,' Nigel replied, quietly. And they never spoke about it again.

She had been brought up a Christian, baptized by immersion according to the ritual of her church soon after her fifteenth birthday. Although by the time of her mother's death she had ceased to be a regular churchgoer she remained a believer and that belief was not shaken by the death. Instead, she would say, it was her ambition that wavered as she paused to reassess her priorities. 'I felt my life had been turned upside down,' she told an interviewer years later. 'I wondered whether I should give up broadcasting and give something back to life that was more tangibly useful to others.' She went so far as to consider becoming a missionary. But the doubts did not last long and the pull of her chosen profession was too strong. She chose instead to immerse herself in her work and over the ensuing year, amid the hurly-burly of early-morning radio, she was able not only to survive that first shock of grief but also to turn her eyes to her next career step.

When John Lilley had first interviewed her as a job applicant he asked a question which is a commonplace in such situations and received an answer which in retrospect is powerfully revealing. What, he inquired, did she see herself doing in five or ten years' time? As he recalls she answered with some hesitation that, although she did not know whether she would have the ability, she would like to think that in due course she might become a television reporter. Ever so tentatively, then, she was expressing her recurring thought, and this was even before she had got into radio. Once she had been at Radio Devon about a year she began expressing it again. As a favour to a friend, Howard James, she did a guest appearance on his programme on the in-house radio station at the Royal Devon and Exeter Hospital, and she talked about herself, her work and her short life. As a breakfast show presenter she was by then a recognized local name and James asked her about her plans and hopes for the future. This is what she said: 'There are thoughts, and in Radio Devon you can diversify. I mentioned news producers earlier. They are more deskbound, but they're paid more. There's that to do, although I think I would prefer to be out and about more. That's why I joined, to meet people and do interviewing. I have thought about branching out to London, but London has always terrified me in some way, because I've always been a home bird I suppose and I think to move to London is such a big step. I don't know that at the moment I would like that. I would love to do television work; I would like to do television reporting, perhaps.'

Again she was almost embarrassed to admit to it, but there it was: her ambition. Most of her colleagues had no doubt that she would make the transition; she had too much ability to stay long in local radio and her looks and manner seemed perfect for television. Lilley was one of those who encouraged her. The regional BBC TV station was based in Plymouth, forty-five miles from Exeter, and Lilley visited frequently. He recalls bringing Jill with him more than once and introducing her to staff from the television newsroom so that she could make contacts, find out about the work and put down a marker for future jobs. But this was a small pond and although the local news chiefs showed interest they had to tell her they had no vacancies. She seemed content to let the matter drop for the moment, but then early in 1987 one of her co-presenters on *Good Morning Devon*, Mike Allen, spotted an advertisement for reporting jobs at Television South West, the region's ITV company of the time. TSW was then beefing up its news coverage and wanted four junior reporters; television experience was not necessary. Allen showed it to Jill and suggested that she should apply, but her first reaction, he recalled later, was a loss of nerve. 'No, I can't do television,' she said. 'I really can't do television.' He stood her in front of a mirror and challenged her: didn't she think that face belonged on television? She applied.

She was interviewed by, among others, David Atkins, the company's news chief. 'I think I knew almost from the moment she walked in,' he says. 'She was confident, had lots of ideas – which is so important in regional news – and she had a wonderful personality. She sat forward in her seat and was really engaged and lively. After about half an hour she left and I don't think we even needed to discuss her; she was guaranteed to get one of the jobs.' It meant leaving Radio Devon, a small, cosy outfit where she had made friends, and it meant leaving Exeter, where she had lodged very happily with a colleague, had a lively social life and once again performed with the local amateur dramatic society. But she wanted a television job and there were none in Exeter and none, for that matter, in the BBC, so she moved on.

She spent only a few months with TSW and a good deal of that time was devoted to learning television skills. Atkins recalls her as a quick learner who asked a lot of questions and showed a lot of promise. In time she was given small on-screen reporting jobs and she acquitted herself well. Then one day, when he was abroad, Atkins received a call from her to say that she had been offered a job as presenter of BBC South West's evening television news show, *Spotlight*. 'She was very apologetic. She didn't particularly want to go and she wondered how long it would be before she might become a presenter at TSW. I had no vacancies and I told her so. I said there might be an opening in the not too distant future and that it might do her no harm to wait and spend a bit more time learning the ropes, but it was up to her.'

The *Spotlight* story is another tale of hesitation accompanied by brilliance at interview. Simon Willis was among those who assessed her. 'The word had gone around that she was quite a talent,' he recalled, and her audition did not disappoint. She read a few news stories for the camera, talked over some pictures, and conducted an interview. It was 'quite amazing', he thought. 'For a first audition it was the best I've ever seen.' Would she take the job? While she rang Atkins to find out what future she might have at TSW, the *Spotlight* producers recruited Roy Corlett, a former boss at Radio Devon, to persuade her to accept. In the end she made the move and *Spotlight* got exactly what they hoped for. Though she was nervous before her first show, once the cameras were on her she was so assured and so word-perfect that after the sign-off her new colleagues gave her a round of applause. One remarked: 'It seemed as though she had been doing it for years.' This was late 1987 and she was just turning twenty-six.

In becoming a television presenter she had crossed an important professional line. No longer primarily involved in gathering news, she now devoted herself mainly to delivery. The jobs and their demands, even in regional television, are very different. She was less and less involved in the sort of work she had been doing since 1980 – phoning, chasing, observing and generally chipping away at the quarry of daily events – and more and more bound up in presentation. Her days became shorter, more studio-bound and more regular, tuned to the rhythm of presenting a half-hour show every evening at 6.30 p.m. She didn't have to find the stories, others would do that. Her job was to deliver them, to link them together smoothly, conduct short interviews in the studio and paper over the cracks if anything went wrong. Her looks – face, hair, clothes – counted for more and her reporting skills for less. Above all, for thirty minutes each evening she had to appear poised and in control, no matter what was going on around her. After just a few days with *Spotlight* she spoke about this: 'When you're on air it is quite calm because you've got the orders coming through your earpiece telling you what's next and how many seconds there are to go . . . You are calm because you know that everything's going to work all right. At the same time you're still very nervous waiting for something to go wrong.' The contradiction in this – you are nervous but you are calm – is characteristic of the way she spoke, and honest in its way. She was *acting* calm.

Jill Dando had realized her childhood dream: she was on television. Up to this point she might easily have married and settled down in Weston or in Exeter, or her career could have taken a small but simple turn into production, public relations, small-time acting or something in the tourist industry. The opportunities were there. That she did not do any of these things can be explained by innate talent and the ability to learn quickly and well, but it must also owe a good deal to ambition and the determination that goes with it. It would be fanciful to trace these in a continuous line to childhood, to *Crackerjack* and *Blue Peter*, but the seed was probably sown then. It appears to have become a clear aim in her life while she was at the *Mercury*, where she learned to be a journalist, dabbled in radio and the theatre, met other journalists who had moved on to television, and encountered a few real television personalities. She was sufficiently determined about it to leave Weston on the first step of her journey at a time when her mother was gravely ill, to stay with broadcasting thereafter despite the shock of her mother's death and to uproot herself and switch jobs twice in a few months so that she could complete the journey and establish herself on

*Spotlight.* This was not a ruthless ambition, not a story like the film *To Die For*, in which a provincial nobody tries to claw her way into the television world with a demonic disregard for all others. Jill Dando had a solid hinterland of friends, family and interests, and she was a loyal woman who would never have treated a colleague dishonourably – the proof being that everywhere she went she made friends who remained her friends. But at the same time she knew what she wanted, worked hard, positioned herself well to progress and seized her opportunities.

This point needs to be made because she herself was coy about it: from her early days in the southwest until her death she insisted that she had never expected anything, that she had just been in the right place at the right time. Her career was, she liked to say, 'in the lap of the gods'. This coyness owes much, no doubt, to her sex: even today many people have difficulties with ambition in women. Nice girls were not ambitious and Jill Dando always tried to be a nice girl. She wanted, for example, to be modest, but real ambition entails a degree of presumption that you are better than others, that you have a right to a place in the sun. And she wanted, especially later on, to be homely and unthreatening, with none of the aggression that usually goes with ambition. Finally, she lacked confidence. This was not a chronic condition but one of occasional spasms, and it almost certainly owed something to her sheltered upbringing and her ugly duckling adolescence. Now and again she would contemplate the next rung on the ladder and be seized by terror. Was she good enough? Would she make a hash of it? Would people laugh at her? Was it worth the risk? Without her mother around to sustain and reassure her these crises could be quite profound, and she found such feelings hard to reconcile with her own idea of ambition. And yet she was not falling upwards by accident; she had the talent for success and in her heart she really wanted it.

# 3. London

*'I'm a poor innocent girl from the West Country – I don't understand these things.'*

She had been in her new job at *Spotlight* for only three or four months when it happened to her again. *Breakfast Time* was the BBC's national early-morning show, broadcast from London. Its finest hour had been its launch in 1983, when it took on ITV's all-star TV-am and won hands down, but since then its fortunes had been uneven. TV-am relaunched and, famously with the aid of Roland Rat, fought its way into the ratings lead. The BBC formula, with the presenters dressed casually and sitting on a sofa while a coffee machine bubbled in the background, came to look stale and was revamped and then revamped again. The launch presenters, Frank Bough and Selina Scott, moved on, to be replaced over time by very different personalities, notably Jeremy Paxman, Kirsty Wark and Gavin Esler. The programme was hardening up, and this was in the spirit of the times – in 1987 John Birt had arrived at the corporation as deputy director-general with a mission to reform news and current affairs output. The shape of these reforms took some time to emerge, but it was soon apparent that news was gaining in importance.

Early in 1988 the *Breakfast Time* editor, Dave Stanford, decided to tweak the programme formula again. Instead of having Wark or Paxman read the news headlines as they had been doing, he wanted a dedicated newsreader at a desk in the studio. On the half-hour the presenters would hand over and there would follow a conventional bulletin, with the newsreader introducing items and linking reports from the field. This would be more formal, giving 'focus' to the news, Stanford thought, but it would still be a part of the show, with a friendly handover to the presenters at the end of each bulletin and a little eye contact. Since he wanted it to be the same person every day he needed to hire a newsreader of his own and so he called around his contacts in regional television for their suggestions. Someone mentioned the name of Jill Dando. Stanford rang Plymouth, had some tapes of *Spotlight* sent up and liked what he saw. 'She had an infectious warmth that seemed to radiate from the screen, and she had authority.' He invited her to come and see him. When she turned up, wearing a specially bought outfit, Stanford experienced exactly what all those other interviewers at Radio Devon, TSW and BBC Plymouth had felt before him. 'It was immediately clear that this was someone special,' he recalls. 'I had no doubts. I asked her there and then if she would like the job and she was really very enthusiastic and keen.' Once back in Plymouth, however, she had second thoughts.

So quickly was she climbing the ladder that she barely had time to feel the rungs beneath her feet. Five quiet years as a junior reporter on the *Mercury* had ended in mid-1985. The three years that followed – in fact less than three – saw her rise from apprentice at a county radio station to *Spotlight* presenter. Now, after just a few months in television, she was being offered a job on national BBC1. Just as it had when she heard of the vacancy at TSW, her nerve failed her; it was all too quick. In her own words, she thought she had 'a lot more growing to do'. She was happy in Plymouth and had just bought her first house, a £38,000 cottage in the village of Ivybridge. She liked *Spotlight* and the people at BBC Plymouth and she was daunted by this next career step. She didn't like what she had heard about London and London people, and about national television, where everybody was supposed to be stabbing everybody else in the back. Friends of the time recall her mood. 'She was gobsmacked,' says Chris Wiltshire. Another, *Spotlight* reporter Wendy Robbins, could see how torn she was: 'She was surprised and not surprised.

She had a sense of destiny, as if it was inevitable. But beside the knowingness there was also a feeling of "Me?" '

Dave Stanford, for his part, was not inclined to give up. He did his best to persuade her and when that failed he passed her on to one of his bosses in BBC News, Robin Walsh. Exerting all his charm, Walsh spoke of the wider career possibilities that would open up for Jill if she took the job – the BBC was a big organization, constantly changing and needing fresh talent, and she would be at its heart. He spoke of Stanford's confidence in her abilities and of the need to grasp opportunities when they came along. After an hour of this she could resist no longer and Walsh was able to call Stanford to say that she was definitely coming to London. A press release was issued to announce the new signing and it prompted a little piece in the *Daily Mirror*. 'Top TV job's news to Jill', ran the headline, above a short interview in which she expressed her astonishment at it all. 'I had a telephone call out of the blue from the editor,' she said. 'They must have watched my tapes secretly because I didn't apply.' On Friday 16 August 1988 she presented her last *Spotlight* programme and was given flowers on air as a farewell gesture, and the following Monday she appeared for the first time on national television.

She now figured in the *Radio Times* daily listings, up there at the top of the page in the early morning slot: *Breakfast Time* with Jeremy Paxman and Kirsty Wark and 'national and international news and analysis on the hour and half-hour, read by Jill Dando'. In advance of her first appearance the *Mirror* asked for an interview, this time to talk about clothes. 'I've spent hours sorting out my existing wardrobe and hoping I have enough outfits to last until I can get around to a proper shopping trip,' she said. She explained that she bought most of her clothes in Next and Principles, 'where I always find something to suit me', but for her first day on *Breakfast Time* she had gone to 'a smashing boutique' in Plymouth and splashed out £150 on a taupe and navy check jacket and another £90 on a white top and skirt.

These, she noted, would not only make her feel 'really special', but would also be practical since they would go with other clothes she had and they were machine washable and crease resistant. Out of its context – the *Mirror*'s style page – this all seems trivial and naïve. She was reading the news, after all, not modelling clothes, and even if she had been modelling, her taste was hardly remarkable. But this was the first of many newspaper and magazine interviews in a similar vein, and although in the years that followed her technique would become more refined, the approach she took with the *Mirror* in 1988 contained ingredients that would last. She was open and frank, ready to name the price of everything down to her shoes (£9.99 in Debenham's). Her story included simple, homely details – 'I've spent hours sorting out my wardrobe' – which gave the readers a picture of her as real and ordinary. She was unpretentious and she had a steady line of self-deprecation. 'It really is a case of country girl heading for the big city,' she said, and 'I love scarves but have yet to work out how to wear them with style.' And finally she was a little defensive: she felt, for example, that she had to justify spending the money by saying she would get plenty of wear out of the clothes. All of this was to have a strong appeal to newspaper readers.

At the end of the *Mirror* interview she was asked to name a favourite television personality and her choice was interesting: Sue Lawley. Lawley was at that time at the peak of her career on the small screen, the first woman journalist, interviewer and presenter to join the top flight of BBC 1 names. There had been newsreaders, such as Angela Rippon and Jan Leeming, and there had been Esther Rantzen, who bridged consumer journalism and light entertainment, but there had been no woman in the news and current affairs field with Lawley's breadth and depth. In a quite novel way she combined authority and determination with femininity and even glamour and it was natural, in 1988, that a young woman in Dando's position should have regarded her as a role model. This took practical form: when she wanted a

London hairdresser Dando asked the BBC who Lawley used and was told Martyn Maxey at Michaeljohn; that was where she went. Lawley for her part would certainly have recognized Dando's approach to the media at this stage in her career, for she too was very open in her early years. In more ways than one the names Lawley and Dando would become linked.

It was not just her wardrobe and hair that Dando changed when she reached London. She sold the Ivybridge cottage and together with a cousin, Judith Dando, who already lived in London, bought a four-bedroomed terraced house in Southfields, near Wimbledon. The price was £158,000. She also swapped her Ford Fiesta for a Honda CRX, her first new car, at a price of £10,000. Her income had clearly jumped and she was making use of it.

But as the months passed in London and she grew accustomed to her new life she began to feel that something was wrong. It was, by media standards, a hard life, much harder than she had known. Presenters such as Wark and Paxman shared their role with others and rarely worked more than three mornings in a week, but Dave Stanford's idea was that Dando should be *the* face of *Breakfast Time* news, and so she carried it pretty well alone. The show ran from 7 a.m. to 8.35, meaning that she had to be in the office at 5 a.m. at the latest every weekday, which in turn required her to go to bed in mid-evening to be ready for a 3.30 a.m. start, night after night. It was, says Stanford (who worked similar hours), 'like having permanent jet lag'. And the work itself was limited, once she was used to it. She played a part as a journalist in the preparation of the bulletin, alongside the editors, sub-editors and reporters, but it was only a small part. And when the approved script was eventually placed before her she was allowed to change it only in minor ways to fit her speech style. On air she read the headlines and introduced the sequence of news packages, but there were no interviews or one-to-ones with reporters. It was plain fare.

She was not the sort to complain, indeed once she was used

to the idea of speaking to a national audience she was content to bide her time, but she knew she was not being stretched. It was the lifestyle, or rather the lack of it, that wore her down. As she said later: 'When I came to London the first thing I thought was "Wow! With all these restaurants and theatres and cinemas to go to, what a wonderful life I'm going to have!" But it didn't turn out like that. I hated the noise; I hated how long it took to get anywhere to see people.' As she had feared, having left all her friends behind in the southwest she was not making new ones. Partly it was the different culture of national television, which was more competitive and less amiable than in the regions, but besides that, few people can sustain a social life when they have to be in bed at 9.30 p.m. every night. There was also a problem of background: she had come along the traditional journalistic career path of school followed by local and provincial reporting, but now she found herself in an environment dominated by graduates, many of whom, she felt, tended to look down upon her. Her few attempts at romance in this period seem to have been limited to *Breakfast Time* colleagues, and they were generally short-lived.

For the first time in her adult life things were going wrong and she had no one really close to turn to. She missed her mother and she was regretting Plymouth – 'In terms of my personal life, I felt I'd made a big mistake.' She didn't quit but she found another way of expressing her distress. 'I'd get home at 10 a.m., sit down and eat a packet of biscuits. Then I got depressed about putting on weight and the whole problem escalated, with me eating to console myself.' The effect was not instant, but over the months her weight rose from nine stone seven pounds to well over eleven stone. 'I felt like a lump. I was comfort eating because when I first came to London I hated it and hated the hours I was working.'

In the BBC newsroom, however, she remained the positive, smiling Jill she had always been at work, from the *Mercury* onwards. Every colleague paints the same picture of a young woman with apparently limitless charm who never failed to be bright-eyed and upbeat even in the dark early hours of the grimmest January morning. Stanford was one of many who recalled her characteristic laugh, constantly ringing across the newsroom – her loneliness and her insecurities were tucked away. Another senior BBC figure who noticed her in her early months in London was Bob Wheaton, then editor of the *Six O'Clock News*. She first caught his attention on screen: 'I saw her and thought, "*She's* talented, a total natural from day one, totally at ease with lights, camera and autocue." She had so much talent; it just needed marshalling.' When their paths crossed he spoke to her. 'She was very naïve, young, delightful, Christian, uncomplicated, nice, well-brought-up,' he recalls, and he was struck by her vulnerability – too nice and too naïve for her own good, he thought. 'I said to her, "You'll need to acquire a sharper edge here. You'll need to look out for yourself a little more, look out for the sharks and charlatans."'

In December 1988, after Jill Dando had been with *Breakfast Time* about six months, Dave Stanford moved on and it was Wheaton who replaced him. A Rhodesian who had worked his way up from sub-editing on the World Service, Wheaton was a hard news man and had been responsible for relaunching the six o'clock evening bulletin in an extended form designed to give it more authority and urgency. He now turned his mind to a similar overhaul of the breakfast show. Within a few months the decision had been taken not just to relaunch but to bin the whole *Breakfast Time* format and start again, creating a longer and more formal programme providing 'rolling news' for the morning audience. Once again the influence of John Birt was probably at work here, since he saw news as an area where the BBC should be displaying its strength to the maximum. More distantly, too, Rupert Murdoch may have played a part – Sky TV had just launched, with a twenty-four-hour news service among its selling points. Wheaton's new programme would be 'hard' where the old show was 'soft'. The last vestiges of the old sofa-and-coffee regime were to disappear, to be replaced by smartly dressed presenters, usually a man and a woman, sitting behind a desk on a sharp, blue-tinted set. And it would have a new, straightforward name: *BBC Breakfast News*.

On the face of it this was bad news for Dando, since there would no longer be any need for a mere newsreader. It proved otherwise. Paxman was leaving the programme and Wark was due to follow him before long, so Wheaton knew he needed to recruit new talent. For his principal anchorman he brought in Nicholas Witchell, whom he had known on the *Six O'Clock News*, while for his lead woman the obvious candidate was Sally Magnusson, already on the breakfast programme. But Wheaton also saw great promise in Jill. He was impressed by her ability to 'see straight through to the viewer' – the autocue did not seem to intervene – and to move naturally while on camera. He decided to give her a chance. Both women, Dando and Magnusson, were signed up for the team and on the day of the launch, 2 October 1989, it was Dando who appeared alongside Witchell. In Wheaton's words, 'She was in the hot spot from day one.' It would often be said later, by Dando herself among others, that she got her break because Magnusson was pregnant at the time. While it is true that Magnusson would shortly take leave to have a baby, it was not immediate; she was a full member of the *Breakfast News* team at launch. Dando, once again, was not simply lucky.

Where she was fortunate was with the turn of world events. The launch fell in the middle of the most dramatic period for international affairs in a generation, as the communist regimes of Europe wobbled and fell one by one and Western leaders proclaimed a new world order. Breakfast television news was often the first to bring these developments to the British public, so ratings were healthy and she was involved to the full. This was a particular challenge for her since she did not regard herself as naturally a hard news journalist – given the choice, as she had observed a couple of years earlier, she would always prefer a human interest story. She lacked confidence in her own ability to conduct interviews with politicians and to get the best from exchanges with senior reporters in the field, and her inclination was to play second fiddle to Witchell or to Laurie Mayer, another of the presenters. Wheaton had to push her, and he had to push his editors into giving her more responsibility.

She was also struggling with her weight, for that extra stone and a half was still there. In fact Wheaton, when he took over as her boss, asked a colleague to have a word with her on the basis that being overweight was a sure passport out of the business. By the end of 1989, after her big promotion, she had given up the biscuit binges but by her own account she simply lacked the willpower to shake off the pounds. 'About seventeen times I decided I was going on a diet on Monday morning, but it didn't get me anywhere,' she said later. 'I spent about £91 on a weight-loss plan, but touched only two of the packed meals . . . You know how people say, "I've tried umpteen diets and nothing worked"? Well, that was me.' On the whole, however, she was feeling better. It was around this time that she finally got rid of the curly perm she had had since her 'reinvention' at sixteen. After moving to London she had let it grow longer, but now her hairdresser persuaded her to make a radical change. 'As soon as I wore it shorter and left it straight, people commented on how much younger I looked,' she said. At the same time the new job paid more, gave her more satisfaction and allowed her more days off, so she was able to shake off the jet lag, make friends and enjoy life. And the press was taking an interest in her once again: there was, for example, some fleeting gossip to the effect that she had taken a fancy to Jeremy Paxman, and every time her name came up in print now she would be described as 'the new Sue Lawley'. On Christmas Day in 1989 she read the national evening news on BBC1, replacing Moira Stuart, who had done it for five years. 'Many of the other newsreaders are married but I'm not,' Dando explained in the BBC's press release. 'So when they were drawing up the rotas, I kind of volunteered for the job.'

★

On Saturday 29 September 1990 the *Sun* carried a cheeky full-page exclusive under the headline: 'Good Lawley! Beeb boss is at it again', followed by the sub-head: 'Bob falls for newsgirl number two'. 'Bob' was Bob Wheaton, and the *Sun* was linking an old story about him with a new one. The old story was an allegation the same paper had made back in 1987: that Wheaton 'shocked colleagues by secretly wooing' Sue Lawley at a time when he was editing the *Six O'Clock News* and she was reading it – something he 'categorically' denied at the time. The new story was that he was now having an affair with another woman on his staff, 'the pretty newsreader being groomed to follow her [Lawley's] footsteps' – Jill Dando.

This new element, at least, was true and the paper could prove it, having gone to the trouble of sending a reporter to hang around outside Dando's house at night so that he could confront the couple in the early hours as they left together for the *Breakfast News* studios. They were taken by surprise and it was a fair cop. Wheaton, who had been furious over the Lawley story, was in favour of saying nothing to the reporter – usually the prudent approach – but Dando took a different line. 'Bob and I are in love,' she announced firmly. 'It's an office relationship which developed. We are both single so I can't see any harm in it.' She went on: 'We don't live together. It's early days yet. We're just seeing how it goes.' And finally: 'I'm a poor innocent girl from the West Country – I don't understand these things.'

Those last words seem disingenuous, even twee. Dando was no man-eater but when it came to sex and romance she was not a wide-eyed schoolgirl either; she had some experience. That, however, was not what she was talking about. What she was claiming not to understand was why the *Sun* should bother to have a reporter on her doorstep at 3 a.m. The reason, as the tenor of the story was to show, was not really to do with her, but with Bob. The *Sun* had never made the Lawley story stick in the face of Wheaton's denials but now, thanks to a tip-off that presumably came from inside the BBC, it had caught him red-handed with another newsreader. Jill Dando was incidental, indeed the presentation of the story when it appeared tended to lend weight to her 'innocent girl' line: large photographs bracketed the page, one showing a laughing Lawley in feathery ball gown, bejewelled and manifestly sophisticated, and the other Dando in simple floral blouse and plain skirt with her hands folded on her knees. Above the two women, in a third picture, a moustachioed Wheaton appeared to be smirking. Throw in the fourteen-year disparity in ages between him and his new girlfriend – which the *Sun* did with glee – and the impression of the 'Beeb boss' as the Big Bad Wolf was complete. 'Gotcha!' was the *Sun*'s subtext.

Wheaton, forty-three at the time, had been married and then divorced, but though he was single and available, the newsroom gossips had never considered him a natural match for Dando. A thickset man with salt-and-pepper hair, he was always carefully groomed and had picked up the unaffectionate nickname of 'Man at C & A' among his staff (the label was not his exclusively, for the BBC is rich in such types). Besides being a good deal older than Jill – who knew of the nickname – he was also regarded as a workaholic, a man so absorbed by television he didn't seem to have much of a life. By her own subsequent account, however, Jill had been attracted to him even before he became her boss. 'I used to see this dishy chap in the newsroom and made a few discreet inquiries,' she was to tell the *Daily Mail*. 'It seems he was similarly taken, but it took a while to get off the ground. We casually passed the time of day for a while and when things took off we kept it quiet to start with.' This is a little misleading, since almost two years elapsed between their first encounters in the newsroom and the moment when 'things took off'. A girlfriend of the time recalls how the relationship began. In the early summer of 1990 Dando revealed to her friend that Wheaton had invited her on a boat trip, complete with picnic. She accepted and found herself spending the day on a cruiser on some Home Counties waterway, being plied with strawberries and cream and not talking once about television or work. Dando was 'bowled over by the sophistication of it', said the friend. 'He's really nice,' Dando reported back. 'Not what you would expect.' Now, three months later, she was telling the *Sun*: 'Bob and I are in love.'

This was the beginning of what was to prove the most important relationship of her adult life. The six years that the couple were together saw her move from behind a newsdesk in an obscure corner of the broadcasting schedule into prime time, where she was soon established as one of the defining faces and personalities of BBC 1. In that journey Wheaton played a vital role; not for nothing did he become known in the BBC as her Svengali.

It was, for the first two years in particular, a relationship of great intensity. Bob, the divorcee, lived in a two-bedroomed flat above a shop on the high street in Cookham, a picturesque village by the Thames west of London, and the couple divided their time between that and the Southfields house. They were, of course, colleagues, so by and large they did the same shifts, worked the same odd hours and had many of the same day-to-day experiences and human contacts. They talked, lived, ate, drank and breathed television. It's easy to picture them driving into work together before dawn, listening to the radio news and chatting about the breaking stories and how they should be presented on the programme, and then sometimes driving home after work later in the day, mulling over what they had done. This lifestyle they shared cut them off socially from others, throwing them together all the more, and what they talked about more than anything else was Jill's career. Wheaton is a man fascinated by the curious chemistry of television stardom – what makes one presenter succeed while another fails and the many devices that can increase the appeal to viewers. He had seen Dando's potential and had given her the big break on *Breakfast News* but he believed that she would go much, much further if she played her cards right. So he set about teaching her the deck.

'We had a very close personal and professional relationship,' he says. 'Twenty-four hours a day, when we weren't actually sleeping, we were talking about work. From hair to clothes to shoes to voice I advised her – I was fourteen years older; I wasn't worrying about *my* career.' One of the first things to change was her weight. For something like a year she had been over eleven stone and unable to do anything about it, but now, suddenly, she managed to change her eating habits and take exercise, and that was largely down to Bob. He was strict about his own diet, having followed the same regime for many years, and he persuaded her to follow his example. She acquired an exercise bicycle and for a while did six miles a day on it, and at weekends he would take her for long walks in the country around Cookham. It worked, and in time she was back under ten stone and delighted with the change. 'I feel so much better about myself,' she told an interviewer. 'I used to wear trousers and never tuck anything in, but now I feel quite happy tucking a blouse into my jeans. It has given me back my confidence.'

And confidence, as far as Wheaton was concerned, was at the heart of the matter. 'I had to build her confidence,' he says. 'She needed constant reassurance.' This meant overcoming her reluctance to take the lead in the studio, but it also meant convincing others that she could handle it. 'Things were still rocky, still uncertain,' he recalls. 'People would come up to me and say, "Should we give Jill this interview?" and I would say, "Yes, but make sure she is briefed properly."' Meanwhile, the change in her hairstyle was completed. She had long ago begun the journey from brunette to blonde, and she had switched to the shorter cut. Now Wheaton encouraged a bit of 'fine-tuning' – more blonde highlights – and the look that came to be her trademark was established. Her wardrobe, too, underwent a transformation: 'When you are on screen like that you've got to define what you are,' says Wheaton. 'Are you, say, Next, or Louis Féraud? We chose Louis Féraud.' While she also wore other clothes on air, for some time Féraud dominated and the choice was illuminating. It was a mature French style not normally associated with English women of twenty-nine, but

Wheaton knew it suited a newsreader well. It was simple and
bare of frills but still elegant in a way understood by much of her
audience. 'Jill likes the effortlessly chic way that French women
look and aims to dress in a similar style,' gushed the *Daily Star*'s
fashion editor in 1991.

She had said it was 'an office relationship that developed', but
it could not be that simple. That the editor of *BBC Breakfast
News* should be living with a young member of his own staff and
devoting so much thought and effort to promoting her interests
was something which, at the very least, raised professional and
ethical questions. Besides the short-lived and hollow indignation
of the *Sun*, however, those questions do not seem to have been
asked in public. The couple themselves had few anxieties. 'I was
her boss, but we were just a very good team,' he says. 'The BBC
is a very big organization and nobody has total control in any
area.' He alone, in other words, did not have power over her
career. She took a similar line. 'When our relationship started
I'm sure there were a few whispered comments behind hands,
but I'm thankful the romance began after we had been working
together so we couldn't be accused of nepotism.' This was true
so far as it went – she had been given the *Breakfast News* 'hot
spot' alongside Witchell almost a year before the Wheaton
romance began – but there are more subtle ways than hiring
and firing in which such a relationship could intrude on the
workplace. If nothing else, however, Dando was matter-of-fact
and open: 'He's the editor of *Breakfast News*, so he's my boss.
Bob criticizes me in a fair and honest way. He'll also tell me if an
outfit doesn't look right or my expression is too miserable. If I
disagree I'll say so, but he's often right.'

Svengalis have a bad name. The prototype is to be found in
George du Maurier's novel *Trilby*, about a penniless young model
in nineteenth-century Paris who is taken up by a much older
man – Svengali – and transformed into a sensationally popular
singer. While the word is now attached to almost any male
mentor with a younger protégée it tends to carry sinister conno-

tations, some of which derive from the book. Du Maurier's Svengali is a grotesque Jewish stereotype and his relationship with Trilby, whom he claims as his wife, is cruel and abusive. Her talent for singing, moreover, emerges only when she is hypnotized by him and deserts her the moment he dies, leaving her in turn broken and dying. This notion that a Svengali partnership is likely to be unhealthy survives, and attached to it is a more general suspicion of relationships between older men and young women, particularly where the woman is attractive and successful. This probably owes something to sexist assumptions – that the woman could not and would not make it on her own or that a man should not benefit from the success of a younger woman partner.

Bob Wheaton certainly had ambitions for Dando and in their relationship it might just about be possible to see elements of obsession, but he scarcely qualifies as a Svengali. They were in love, and she was no victim but a willing and eager participant in her own remaking. 'A lot of people who are successful have decided they are going to be there, and she knew it inside,' he says. 'She had so much talent . . . I gave her advice, but she was the one who did it.' As he says, she lacked confidence – she had that native ability and desire to succeed before they met, but perhaps not the self-belief necessary for real success in national television. The innocent girl from the West Country, as she saw herself, had probably gone as far as she was likely to go under her own steam. Wheaton equipped her to go much further. One friend of hers said simply: 'She blossomed. He grew her like a flower.' And Dando herself acknowledged the debt: 'Bob's in his forties and he has influenced me a great deal. He made me feel more confident about myself and the job I do. He's a great rock in my life.' A rock: it was the same word she used when she talked about her mother.

In 1990 the news agenda moved from the new world order to crisis in the Middle East, as Iraq overran Kuwait and the US led preparations for war. At home Margaret Thatcher was ousted as prime minister after eleven years. With so much that was unpredictable happening, often in Britain's hours of darkness, it was a perfect time to be presenting a gritty, factual programme first thing in the morning. Ratings remained good, the show was exciting and Dando was playing an ever-bigger part. For the first time she found herself conducting important interviews, live on air, with such people as Cabinet ministers. She would never be an inquisitor in the Paxman or Humphrys mode but she was able to elicit answers and information smoothly and competently, and there is a school of thought which says that is just as valuable.

On Monday 19 August 1991 came the high point of her *Breakfast News* career, a momentous breaking overnight story that left even the latest editions of the national newspapers looking out of date. At 6.15 a.m. Moscow time – 3.15 a.m. in the BBC newsroom at Shepherd's Bush – Soviet radio and television began broadcasting an announcement by a body calling itself the State Committee for the State of Emergency, stating that 'for health reasons' President Mikhail Gorbachev had transferred his powers to a deputy who intended, it was said, to tackle the chaos and anarchy that had overwhelmed the country. Soon word came through that tanks were on the move from the Moscow suburbs. News stories do not come any bigger. Jill Dando was the anchor presenter that morning for an edition that was specially extended. 'There is just one story this morning,' she told the viewers as the programme opened, 'the dramatic end of the Gorbachev era in the Soviet Union. He's been removed as president of the Soviet Union in what appears to have been a right-wing coup.' Amid all the turmoil and uncertainty she produced what was regarded within the BBC as a consummately professional performance, and one of which she always remained proud. She felt she had proved herself capable of handling even the biggest, hardest and most complex news story the world could throw at her. Soon, perhaps, she would be ready for a new challenge.

# 4. Prime Time

*'I'm in a place for three days, back for a couple, and off again.'*

*Holiday* is the oldest travel programme on British television, dating back to 1969 when Cliff Michelmore began his long run. Michelmore was eventually replaced in the early 1980s by Frank Bough, who had graduated to prime time from *Grandstand* and *Breakfast Time*. An amiable and fatherly presence, complemented on many trips by his wife Nesta, Bough proved a very popular presenter until his astonishing disgrace in 1988, when a Sunday newspaper revealed his involvement in cocaine and sex parties. He left the show and an unsettled period began. Des Lynam stepped in but lasted just a year – 'It clashed with too many sports commitments,' he said later. And then Anne Gregg, who had been a reporter on the show for several years, was promoted to the lead spot, but there were problems. With the ratings flagging a new producer, Jane Lush, was appointed with a brief to relaunch the programme. Gregg was blonde and attractive, with a strong women's-magazine appeal, but she was also fifty-one. She was invited to return to a reporter's role to make room for a new lead presenter and she refused, quitting the show and complaining publicly that she was a victim of ageism. The affair caused a fuss and the *Daily Mail*, among others, rallied to her support, but to no avail.

Lush wanted to revitalize *Holiday*. From the Michelmore days it had been based in the studio, with the lead presenter introducing the reports (as well as appearing in some of them) and explaining the practical details afterwards, while others joined in to discuss current issues in the travel world. It was at heart a professional consumer programme with a journalistic air – one of the founding reporters, John Carter, had been travel editor of *The Times*, and Michelmore himself was best known as a *Tonight* and *Panorama* man. Lush transformed the formula. The name would change: it would no longer be *Holiday 91, 92* or *93*, which was like advertising the show's advanced years, but simply *Holiday*. And there would be no more studio: the links would be spoken by the show's presenter from a location in the field – and preferably a sunny one – while a proportion of the reports would be presented by guest celebrities such as soap or sitcom stars. The new lead presenter, moreover, came from a completely different mould; she was Anneka Rice. Blonde, bright and cheerful, Rice had become popular as the helicopter-borne action-woman in *Treasure Hunt*, one of Channel Four's early successes. She had no news background and no track record in the field of travel journalism; her role, it seemed, was to be a representative ordinary person, albeit an attractive, articulate and youthful one, on the holiday road.

It didn't work. The new-model programmes began transmission in January 1992 and in a few weeks it was clear that something was wrong. The show was losing viewers and trailing its long-time ITV rival, *Wish You Were Here* (presented by Judith Chalmers, a figure much more in the Anne Gregg mould than Rice), by a mile. Rice was blamed: there were complaints that she was too glamorous, that she changed her clothes too often and that she lacked authority. The main problem, however, was that her manner was uneasy and she seemed to be trying too hard; apparently she was better at rushing around for the cameras than communicating the notion of leisure. Although the series ran its full three months with Rice at the helm it was clear long before it was over that she would be replaced. Enter Jill Dando. By her own account, Dando read or heard that spring that Anneka Rice would not be doing another series 'and a couple of colleagues suggested I should go for it'. She wrote a short letter to the head of features, Mark Thompson, expressing an interest.

'I knew he'd be inundated with applications from people wanting the job, but asked him to bear me in mind.' She would later say, as we have seen, that it had been a dream of hers to work on the show ever since that incident in her childhood when she saw it being filmed in Minehead. But now the reasons for her interest were apparently a little more sophisticated: 'It wasn't so much the glamour and the sun. It was a way of using a bit of journalism – being honest about places we visit. And also the consumer angle.'

There is no doubt that by the spring of 1992 she was ready. Breakfast television, for all its demands, remains to this day on the fringe of the schedule and success there alone does not make a star, although it can provide a stepping stone. Dando had been stretching for the next stone for some time. Newsreading had given her a number of opportunities to break out of the cornflake zone. She had read the Christmas Day bulletins, in time she became a reserve reader for the *Six O'Clock News*, appearing when Anna Ford or Moira Stuart was on leave, and during the general election campaign of 1992 she made the occasional appearance on the *Nine O'Clock News*. She was also stepping out from behind the desk, occasionally presenting *Songs of Praise* and, in the summer of 1991, co-presenting *Safari UK*, a ten-part natural history series broadcast early on Sunday evenings. There was some irony in this last, since this was the girl whose teenage camping trip was spoiled by fear of creepy-crawlies, but it was expertise in front of the camera rather than empathy with the subject that made Dando suitable for the job.

Her ambition was there, unhidden. She wanted, she said, to show the viewers she could walk and talk at the same time, and she had already told the *Daily Mail*: 'I'd like something like *Crimewatch* or a consumer programme, something with a bit of a hard edge to it.' *Holiday*, a half-hour show broadcast at 7 p.m. on Tuesday, didn't have much of an edge but it would take her into weekday prime time, a whole new league in television terms. Attractive as it was, however, this was not an obvious next step for someone who was still being described as 'the new Sue Lawley'; for one thing the real Sue Lawley would probably not have taken it on. Even in the early 1990s, fifteen years after Angela Rippon made headlines by dancing bare-legged on *The Morecambe and Wise Show*, it was unusual for a BBC newsreader to enter such a 'soft' area of broadcasting. And *Holiday* didn't just involve bare flesh; besides the swimsuits and sarongs there was the matter of joining in. A presenter was required to swim and ski, climb and dive, drink and eat, and even sing and dance. More, the job very often entailed doing these potentially undignified things alongside those most unpredictable of creatures, members of the public. From her days on *Spotlight* back in Plymouth Dando had been a news presenter; this would be something different.

Thompson and Lush chose her. 'I couldn't believe it when I was offered the job,' she said later. The appointment was confirmed in a news release in July which also reported that she would begin filming for the next series straight away in Bournemouth before heading on to more exotic locations. And so it began. The pace of work proved brisk indeed, a taste of things to come. In those days *Holiday* was broadcast over about fourteen weeks between New Year and Easter, the time of year when most people booked their summer holidays. Much of the filming, necessarily, was done over the previous six months, often during the summer, and since Jill Dando was the show's anchor she provided a report virtually every week. Besides Bournemouth, then, between July and December 1992 she visited Florida, the South of France, the Canary Islands, EuroDisney in Paris, India (a round trip taking in Delhi, Agra and Goa), St Lucia in the Caribbean, South Africa, Nepal (for an 'environmental adventure holiday'), France again, Pontin's at Prestatyn and Cyprus. That was twelve trips in all, of which ten took her abroad and five involved long-haul flights.

In January 1993, to coincide with the start of the series, she made what was to be the first of several appearances on the cover of *Radio Times*, the country's most popular magazine. In bright summer garb, with her broad smile and gleaming white teeth, she gazed out at the reader holding aloft a lurid cocktail adorned with a paper umbrella. 'I know this little place . . .' read the teasing copy line, introducing 'Jill Dando and the *Holiday* team's hotspots'. Inside, she recalled her own childhood holidays, which were 'very down to earth, but exciting for me as a child. I remember the cliff lifts at Bournemouth, which I rode at the age of ten; they took you straight up a perpendicular drop.' The other members of the team tended to talk about places farther afield.

To a degree that was unusual even for television entertainment shows, the appointment of Jill Dando to *Holiday* was a gamble. One popular young blonde presenter was perceived to have failed, so why would another who was less well-known succeed? The press reception for the new series was mixed. In the London *Evening Standard* Victor Lewis-Smith found her trite: 'Sadly for Jill, beaches are always sun-kissed, lakes are like mirrors, food is always sumptuous and islands are always paradise.' But if her language left something to be desired her style was more successful and the public seemed to warm to her. The ratings were good, if not spectacular: where in the previous year *Holiday* had attracted audiences of between eight and nine million, now it was often well above the nine million mark. This was enough, and by the end of the run there was no doubt that Dando would front the show for a second series.

More than that, the series was extended – instead of starting in the New Year and running to April it returned in mid-November. This was partly a reflection of changes in the travel industry, where brochures were being published earlier and earlier and customers were bringing forward their choices correspondingly. It was also among the first signs of a strategic shift at BBC1, where consumer programmes of various kinds were gradually given a prominence they had not enjoyed before. As an audience-winner it proved a clever move, and it gave Dando even more exposure. This second series began with her in the Seychelles, then Disneyworld in Florida, Turkey, the Italian lakes, London and Singapore. January 1994 brought the twenty-fifth anniversary of the programme and a special edition from Torremolinos, which had been the setting for the first ever *Holiday* programme report. Cliff Michelmore was on hand with his memories, and he and Dando were likened in *Radio Times* (not the cover story this time, but a big inside feature) to Winston Churchill and Princess Diana. The remainder of the season took her to a CenterParc in Suffolk, Washington DC, the west of Scotland (sailing), the Zambezi (canoeing), Grenada in the Caribbean, Iceland, France (camping), Florida, the Algarve, Hawaii, Cyprus, Blackpool and New Orleans – in all, twenty assignments, sixteen of them abroad, and nine long haul.

Her success was confirmed. The ratings had once again edged upwards and were drawing closer to *Wish You Were Here*. Dando's manner and looks, her bright, cheerful style and her straight-in-the-eye delivery were winning over the viewers. In millions of homes, it was obvious, they liked her. Jane Lush, the show's producer, was keen to make the most of this, as were Dando and the bosses of BBC1. After stretching the series in one direction, they now decided to stretch it in the other. The show would acquire a summer season of seven programmes running through June and July, when many people were making last-minute bookings. Both seasons would continue to occupy the same 7 p.m. slot on Tuesdays and both would be anchored by Jill Dando. It was another coup for her: her prime time slot now ran through roughly thirty weeks of the year. There was just one problem: Dando's workload, combining all the travelling for *Holiday* with routine 3 a.m. starts on *Breakfast News*, was already extremely demanding. 'Sometimes I'd arrive back in the country and within a few hours I'd be at the studio for *Breakfast News*,' she would say later. 'Occasionally I caught sight of myself on the monitor and realized early evenings were catching up with me.' She did not like what was happening to her. 'I was getting tired and snappy and saw myself turning into a workaholic.' Something had to give.

In April 1994 it was announced that she was leaving *Breakfast News* and transferring to the *Six O'Clock News*, where she would read sixty bulletins a year and work alongside Anna Ford and Martyn Lewis. 'It's time to move on,' she said in the press release. While this was a break from the programme that had established her (and meant that she was no longer working for Bob Wheaton), it was in most other respects another important step up for her in its own right, for the *'Six'* was the most watched news bulletin on BBC and the timing placed her in that part of the schedule which *Holiday* had proved was her natural home.

The new *Summer Holiday* series began screening on the last day of May and was supposed to have a more nitty-gritty approach. 'The winter run of *Holiday* is about giving people ideas,' said *Radio Times*, 'but *Summer Holiday* reports on what's actually happening this year.' Dando, for her part, did not travel abroad but provided the links from a location in Britain. The reason was simple: she was by now already on the road filming for the winter series, a process that ran from May through to the following March, overlapping with the broadcasts. These trips were spread out over the period, rather than squashed together, because otherwise, she said, 'towards the end I would look pretty ragged – hardly the right image when you're hoping to put people in a relaxed, holiday frame of mind'. These were the datelines: Mauritius ('we like to start each series with a tempting, exotic location'), Skiathos in Greece, by Concorde to Jordan, Northern Ireland, Boston, Thailand, Kenya, Israel, Florence, Colorado (skiing), France (canoeing), South Carolina, the Lake District, Rome, the Gower peninsula in South Wales, Spain (tennis), a cruise in the Caribbean, Torquay, Majorca, Orkney, the Bahamas and Venezuela. In all, this time, there were twenty-two assignments, of which seventeen took her abroad and eleven involved long-haul flights.

As with her *Safari UK* role, the incongruity of it all is striking.

Jill Dando may have grown up in a holiday resort but travel was hardly in her blood – she was in her mid-teens before she saw London and in her twenties before she first left Britain (to fly to Strasbourg). Now she had become a professional on the road, and someone envied as a jet-setter. This envy is a permanent feature of the *Holiday* programme – Cliff Michelmore was once told by the BBC director-general of his day that he had 'the best job in the whole of television'. And Dando received plenty of letters expressing the same view, some of them quite aggressive. 'There's one regular,' she once said, 'who's always telling me to get off the gravy train and do some proper work instead of wasting the licence fee.' Often in interviews she would try to dispel the impression that she spent her life swanning around the globe. 'It's a good job, but not as luxurious as people think.'

It was a fair point. For about ten months of the year Jill Dando's life was now dominated by travel. Her normal *Holiday* items ran for about eight minutes, and everything in the planning was geared to minimum wastage of time and money. As far as possible items were researched, planned and even partly scripted in advance, and when it came to execution the comfort of crew and presenter was not a high priority. Close to home a trip might be completed in three days, but some long-haul assignments took more than a week. A typical journey would begin at Heathrow, where the team would gather with luggage and equipment at some unpleasant hour of the day. It became a running joke that Dando's suitcases took up more hold space than the cameras, and there was an element of truth to it – she alone, after all, had to be prepared to look good at all times and in all conditions, and that meant bringing rather more clothes and grooming kit than the average traveller. Her approach to long-haul flights evolved over the years. In that first *Radio Times* cover story she suggested she was taking it in her stride: 'My experience in breakfast news prepared me for this kind of schedule, so jet lag hasn't been as much of a problem as it might have been.' By early 1994 she was saying: 'I take a travelling pillow with me and just try and sleep as much as I can on long-haul flights, either with the assistance of a couple of glasses of in-flight champagne or, if necessary, a sleeping pill. I try and avoid taking pills if possible, as I don't want to become reliant on them.' In mid-1997, however, the pills were a fixture. 'I take one as soon as I get on the plane and it knocks me out for five hours. Because I usually have to start work not long after landing I have to be fresh for the cameras. The last thing viewers want to see is a washed-out face.'

Once on location she rarely stopped thinking about her appearance. 'Even when I come up out of the sea my make-up has to be perfect,' she said. Hair, wardrobe and make-up were her own responsibility and with limited resources on location she had to develop effective routines – in fact she wore her hair shorter after joining *Holiday* so that it would be more manageable on the road. Even then, it seems, it was not exactly quick. 'I've got my getting-ready routine down to a fine art,' she boasted after a few years in the job. 'It takes me forty-five minutes from getting up to leaving my hotel room to face the camera.' Once a scene was done, moreover, there was rarely time to linger. 'Whenever there's a shot of me relaxing on the beach, the scene's over in a flash and we're rushing off in the bus to the next location. It's a hectic schedule, particularly as we work fifteen-hour days.'

Of course the locations were usually more than agreeable and of course there was fun to be had. She loved the walking holiday in Nepal and the Zambezi canoe trip, for example – both of them, perhaps significantly, journeys that the planners in London were powerless to abbreviate. Very often, however, the pleasures had a snatched quality. A late night of merriment with the crew in a beachfront bar would very often be followed the next morning by a 6 a.m. start in a minibus. This was not conducive to relaxation. As often as not, moreover, things would go wrong and there would be delays, usually in airports; she would joke later that her specialist subject for *Mastermind* would be airport departure lounges of the world. And since the trips had to be scheduled alongside her other television work, notably on the

*Six* (newsreaders were identified in advance in *Radio Times* and *TV Times*, so they were not simply interchangeable), delays could be stressful and there were close shaves. More than once she landed at Heathrow and travelled straight to the television news studio. This was less than ideal, since by her own admission she would go on air without having followed recent news events closely (even though she always travelled with a short-wave radio to pick up the World Service). Still, she carried it off.

As for her private life, that undoubtedly suffered. 'The hardest thing,' she said in 1992 after her short first season, 'is to deal with the practical side, like when to get your laundry done, how to catch up with your mail and when to see your friends.' Over the years she was asked many times by interviewers how she coped and it was clear there was much more involved than the washing. In 1995, speaking to the *Mail*, she looked back on the first three seasons and reflected on the effect on her relationship with Bob. 'When I started doing the *Holiday* programme we did have our ups and downs because we had been together constantly for the previous eighteen months and then suddenly we were apart so long. I know that I do demand more from him than I'm prepared to give, and because I'm away a lot I expect everything to be hunky-dory when I come home. But we have both made sacrifices and it's a little easier now.' She evidently knew she was taking risks, but despite the difficulties that arose she told people that things were fine and that she had Bob's support. He 'appreciates what I'm doing and encourages me', she said. 'We manage.' One casualty was their own holidays. Early in their relationship they had the habit of taking off abroad fairly often, perhaps three or four times a year, but now it was down to one trip. During the summer months in particular she hardly seemed to stop: 'I'm in a place for three days, back for a couple, and off again.' One August she calculated that she had slept in her own bed four times in the month.

If she was straining her relationship with Bob, worse was happening with her friendships. A few of her friends from

Plymouth days had followed her to London over time and remained close, while she had acquired more in the capital, most of them BBC people; she remained a warm and charming companion who attracted friends easily. But being on the road half the year made it difficult to keep in touch, particularly when her domestic life claimed priority. And there was a further difficulty: Bob and many of her friends did not mix. In a way this was hardly surprising, since they were mostly single women of around thirty and he was a workaholic newsman of forty-five, but there was more to it than that. As Jill became more successful some of her friends felt excluded, and they suspected Bob of monopolizing her. Although when they met her she remained the same delightful person, they felt they met her less often. Rightly or wrongly they placed some of the responsibility on him.

Jill Dando was paying the price of success. She had undoubtedly changed, becoming a more adventurous and dedicated woman, and the result was a blossoming career. But it meant making sacrifices and taking risks and she knew that. One close friend from this time recalls that she seemed constantly in a rush and under pressure, and that when they talked about the pleasures of life she would say briskly that she 'didn't have time for that at the moment'. It was as if, the friend said, she had placed that side of her life on hold while she built her career.

Material rewards, meanwhile, were accumulating. By nature Jill Dando was a hoarder of money – as a child she had kept a cash book to record her finances and in later life she was the sort who always dutifully checked her bank statements when they arrived in the mail. Until 1992 she simply kept what money she had in the Halifax, but with the jump in her income that accompanied the *Holiday* job she acquired a financial adviser who in the years that followed found her useful ways of investing what she earned. This prudence wasn't all a matter of choice. Her opportunities to spend were restricted since she was on the road much of the time with all expenses paid, and when she was in London and still working on *Breakfast News* she had to go to bed early three nights a week – not a recipe for the high life. As for accommodation, up to 1994 she shared the house in Southfields with Judith Dando and spent the rest of her time in Bob's little flat in Cookham, so she was not stretched by a big mortgage. In that year, however, they made a few changes.

Bob bought a house in Maidenhead, a pretty period property with a big balcony that directly overlooked the Thames. The price was high and he borrowed a substantial sum from Jill to put towards the deposit. A few months later Jill and Judith sold the Southfields house. This was the middle of the property slump and they had to accept a price £20,000 lower than they had paid in 1988. That she could lend Bob money and shoulder such a loss in the same year shows just how liquid she was. After the sale she moved into the Maidenhead house full-time. While she and Bob were no longer working together, in other words, they were now living together. Maidenhead was handy enough for the BBC in west London (many other BBC staff lived in the area and commuted) and the odd hours they both worked enabled them to escape the notorious M4 rush hours. The new home, moreover, was also extremely handy for Heathrow.

Did she intend to stay there? The bond with Bob Wheaton was very strong; they were two people who shared a profession, a drive for success and a dedication to work. She regarded him as the architect of her success, who had taught her how to realize her ambitions, and she clearly felt she still needed his advice and support. More than that, they were in love. She was always happy and proud to speak of him in interviews – the phrases 'my boyfriend Bob' and 'my partner Bob' turn up again and again, with observations on their shared tastes and pleasures, insights into their domestic happiness and acknowledgements of her debt to him. Often in those same interviews she would be asked about whether or when she would have children, and the response was usually the same: she wanted to but there was plenty of time, and for the moment her career came first. But she and Bob were not even married, she was a conventional woman and while she could live with a man she would never have contemplated having children out of wedlock. Would they marry? Would they have children? With both her and him there is a sense in these days of matters left undiscussed, of decisions deferred, partly because of career pressures and the rush of success and partly, perhaps, because of some deeply buried reluctance to commit.

It may be, however, that she always intended to buy a home of her own, and that the Maidenhead interval came about mainly for practical reasons. When the Southfields buyer finally came along it was early summer and Dando by then was deep into her *Holiday* travels and unable, even if willing, to go house-hunting. Whatever her original intentions, the following spring, after something over six months sharing with Bob, she began looking for a home in London, much nearer to BBC Television Centre. And before long she found it. Gowan Avenue in Fulham is a long street of late-Victorian houses about fifteen or twenty minutes from Shepherd's Bush. The houses, red brick but mostly painted pastel shades, are modest in size and, though their earliest occupants would have been equally modest in income, by the 1990s the area had been comprehensively taken over by the professional classes. Number 29, painted magnolia, stands near the quieter, eastern end of the road. A friendly estate agent tipped her off immediately it came on the market and it proved to match Dando's requirements. 'I knew it was right as soon as I walked in,' she said later, when the house featured in *OK!* magazine. 'What really made up my mind, though, was when my partner, Bob, and I went to talk to the owners. They showed us into the sitting room and we spent the evening relaxing in front of the fire, sipping wine. It felt so homely.' It was also handy, in good condition and would require little maintenance (the lawn at the back was not grass, but Astroturf). The price was £265,000 and she bought it, borrowing 'about two-thirds' of the price – something like £175,000 – and putting up the remaining £90,000 or so herself.

This further expression of her newfound wealth was soon followed by yet another: the purchase of a brand-new dark blue BMW 320 convertible. An uncharacteristic piece of ostentation – 'my greatest extravagance', she once called it – this suggested that her money was by now burning a hole in her pocket. But buying the Gowan Avenue house also said something more about her relationship with Bob. Both would later suggest that it was a symptom of uncertainty on her part, but in the *OK!* interview, published in April 1996, she appeared to stress that the house was a joint enterprise. Bob had helped her choose it and Bob was helping her to choose the furniture: 'I know what I'm looking for and Bob's the same, so weekends are spent in antique shops.' Bob and she were spending their weekdays in London and weekends at Maidenhead: 'I love relaxing in the countryside at the end of a hard week, but I also enjoy returning to my new home, because this house is the realization of something I've wanted since moving to London,' she said.

In the spring of 1995 something else she had wanted for a long time came her way: *Crimewatch*. Launched in 1984, *Crimewatch UK* was essentially a programme-length version of *Police Five*, the 'filler' items Shaw Taylor had presented for years, but with a new element that had been copied from a German TV series. This 'magical ingredient', as the creators saw it, was that viewers could give information as they watched, by phoning police officers whom they could see, live, in the *Crimewatch* studio. Broadcast monthly on BBC1 in a 10 p.m. slot, with a short follow-up last thing at night, it was a ratings success from day one. It is public service television at its most straightforward – the BBC simply broadcasting police appeals to a large national audience – and the corporation is extremely proud of the number of crimes that have been solved as a result. But *Crimewatch* is also, without doubt, entertainment. The crimes are reconstructed with such care and to such high production standards that the result is often a piece of action drama to rival what can be seen in *The Bill* or in a Lynda la Plante series. And there is more than one ethical problem. Those viewers who do not get a thrill from the programme, for example, might easily get a fright, so there is a risk of contributing to the fear of crime. The programme-makers have always been alive to these questions and have tended to rely on the style of the show to deal with them. From the outset the presenters were Nick Ross and Sue Cook, pleasant young people with a background on *Nationwide*, who had a low-key manner and were generally trusted by the viewers. The build-ups to the filmed reconstructions tended to be methodical and untheatrical, and the commentaries were relatively deadpan. Cook and Ross also laid stress on the wickedness of the criminals and on the suffering of the victims and their families. In short, though the films were high drama an effort was made, through the presenters, to dampen the sense of excitement or danger they generated and to focus attention on the practical ways in which viewers could help. This effort was summed up by the words with which Ross usually closed the show: 'Don't have nightmares.' Whether the balance has always been successfully maintained is probably a matter of opinion, but the popularity of the pro-gramme is not and over the years it has become a jewel in the BBC's crown.

In 1995, after eleven years, Sue Cook announced that she was leaving the show – she said she 'felt she had had enough of crime' – and that June the BBC announced that Jill Dando would replace her. Press reports said the job paid £60,000 a year and that she had landed it 'without even having to go through an audition'. She was quoted as saying: 'I always wanted to do it when it became free,' while a BBC source declared: 'She has authority on screen but has a friendly face, and she is very popular with the viewers.' Asked how her new show would fit in with her schedule, she replied: 'I hope the fact that I have three jobs doesn't confuse the viewers too much.' Nick Ross later described how she was chosen: 'She had often told me how keen she was to work on *Crimewatch*. It was a programme she hugely admired and, with her typical modesty, she wondered if we would consider her if ever there was a chance. Consider her? We leapt at the opportunity. There was simply no one else. As soon as the vacancy came up on *Crimewatch*, it was plain as sunlight to me that Jill must be first choice. It was obvious to the rest of the team too.' And the long-standing ambition is there on the record, since she had spoken of it in a newspaper interview as far back as 1991, before she had even joined *Holiday*.

She first appeared on *Crimewatch* on 5 September 1995, in a programme that led with a brutal attempted murder in Edinburgh and also covered a million-pound armed robbery. It was immediately clear, as the producers had anticipated, that she was perfect for the part, and in time, though it was only a monthly show, it became the part of her working life she most enjoyed. '*Crimewatch* gives me the biggest buzz professionally,' she said. 'It's live, which I love, and I know it's doing some good.'

## 5. Ordinary Woman

*'I don't sit at home fretting about life and the universe. Maybe this comes across.'*

*Holiday*, *Crimewatch* and the *Six O'Clock News*, plus a variety of high-profile one-off assignments such as the D–Day anniversary broadcasts in 1994 or as a guest on the annual *Children in Need* telethon – on average Jill Dando was appearing on a high-ratings BBC1 programme twice a week. The corporate work, too, was rolling in, so that as often as she liked she was hosting company events and presenting company videos. This was an upward spiral: the more popular and famous she became, the more work she was offered, which in turn made her more popular and famous, and more sought-after by programme-makers and others. She had joined the absolute élite of television presenters, the handful of people in whose company the great majority of British viewers felt completely relaxed. Des Lynam was one, Trevor McDonald another, and then there was Jill – polished performers who added something of their own to the show they presented but without putting viewers off. It is a very rare talent and it is worth pausing to ask how it worked and how Jill Dando, the ordinary girl with ordinary ideas and an ordinary background, came to have it. There are hundreds of television presenters, even hundreds of women presenters; what made her special?

The best way of telling what qualities the viewers liked in her is through the many messages sent to the BBC and other bodies after her death and subsequently displayed on website tribute pages. These took a variety of forms, from general expressions of anger at her murder to personal reminiscences by people who had encountered her. A Fulham man wrote, for example: 'My sincerest sympathies and regrets go out to all her friends and family. Let's hope whoever did it gets caught . . . No doubt she will be watching over us all. She brightened all our days.' Someone from Bury St Edmunds sent this: 'I am devastated by this news. I have met Jill briefly three times . . . Beautiful, intelligent but above all else sincere, she was totally unaffected by the trappings of her fame. She was for me a perfect woman and so in control of her life . . .' A Londoner wrote: 'How dare someone take such an amazing person from us. To the person who has done this terrible thing, you are soul-less. My deepest sympathy to her fiancé and family. Jill was a fantastic woman and will be sadly missed by all who know of her.' Such messages, all from the BBC website, are no doubt coloured by the immediacy of her death, but since they are also spontaneous and manifestly sincere they may surely be taken as a good indication of why people liked Jill Dando. And they are all the more telling as evidence because they paint a remarkably consistent picture, with large numbers of viewers drawing attention to a small number of qualities.

A great many messages, for example – and by no means all of them from men – commented on her beauty. She was 'a beautiful, gentle lady', 'such a beautiful woman', 'a truly beautiful person', a 'successful, beautiful lady'. One writer asked: 'How could anybody harm a beautiful woman like yourself?' As many messages, perhaps more, drew attention to her smile, her cheerfulness and her freshness. 'Jill brought sunshine into our home when she was on the screen,' wrote one. 'Your smile lit up the evening news, and made even the worst news seem more bearable.' 'I will miss the rays of sunshine and warmth that she brought to my life every time I watched the *Holiday* programme.' She was 'a breath of fresh air', with 'a great smile' and 'a cheerful approach to everything'. 'She always looked as though she really enjoyed life.'

She was seen as especially good at her job, 'a brilliant journalist, both in the field of news presenting and in leisure programmes', 'a true professional in every sense of the word' and 'a versatile presenter in the prime of her illustrious career'. 'This lady,' wrote one admirer, 'juggled an extensive number of presenting jobs and still made it look like she had all the time in the world.' So accomplished was she, in fact, that she was an example to others, 'a model of professionalism and a true inspiration to millions who want to aspire to greatness and diligence' and 'a role model for all would-be presenters'.

One thread that ran through almost every message was the conviction that Jill Dando was genuine. She was 'such a natural and warm person'; 'she came across the screen as genuine and warm'. One message declared: 'You always felt that you got the "real" Jill on the programmes – she would have been the same if she was working in a shop or anywhere.' Another said: 'She cared about everything she covered – genuinely upset over sad world events, genuinely happy over the good things in life.' And a third said: 'I shall miss her natural style of delivering news and her so-natural manner.' This led to other thoughts. She was perceived as kind: 'She always exuded a certain warmth which revealed her to be a compassionate, caring person who I think genuinely cared.' She 'always came across as a caring and compassionate person', and was 'the essence of humanity, a great comfort and provider of help in many lives, known and admired by millions'. And she was unspoiled – stardom had not turned her head or made her remote. 'Whilst many celebrities become tainted by fame, it was refreshing to see one who was so unpretentious and a genuine, friendly, lovely person.' And: 'Jill's basic decency and warmth was always apparent whenever she appeared on our TV screens. In today's media world those qualities seem all too rare and precious.' Many of the messages described her as 'down-to-earth'. 'Her great gift was that she seemed to be of flesh and blood,' wrote one admirer. 'On the flat telly screen she was three-dimensional. Jill illuminated our lives, not through position, but because she made every viewer feel that she was

speaking to us directly.' Another explained: 'Too many times
the *Holiday* presenter is upper-class or not in touch with reality.
Jill was very much the person that everyone could relate to and
not feel as though they were being condescended to.'

The sum of this, of the Jill who was natural, unspoiled, beautiful, cheerful and down-to-earth, was something distinct and very
rare: a presenter who was the viewers' trusted friend. 'Jill,' said a
message, 'was one of those broadcasters who one felt an immediate affinity with; she was such an approachable person.' 'I do not
know Jill personally,' said another, 'but she was in our lounge on
so many programmes, and seemed such a lovely person.' Several
viewers expressed the same feeling: 'It's like losing a personal
friend'; 'Jill was . . . almost a family friend' and: 'Even though I
never knew her I feel like I have lost a friend.' This is a very
powerful notion. People were saying not just that they recognized Jill Dando and were familiar with her voice and manner,
but that without meeting her in the flesh they felt they knew her
as a whole person. She 'came through the screen' and was 'in
our lounge'; she did not just *seem* to be kind and cheerful, but
she *was* kind and cheerful; it was as if she was there in the room,
talking to them directly.

There is a paradox here. Television is an illusion, a *trompe
l'oeil*. Although the presenter's eyes follow you like Kitchener's
pointing finger, powerfully suggesting directness and intimacy,
we all know this is a mass medium employing artifice on a
considerable scale. Look at the work of newsreaders and presenters: when they talk they are not looking at another person and
often not even at the camera, but at the autocue machine. They
are not speaking their own words but words written for them by
others. And their minds are only half on what they say because
the remainder of their attention is on the voice coming into their
earphone. Their hair, their clothes, and even the expressions on
their faces are usually the result of careful thought. They are
sitting not in a normal room like the viewers, although it may
appear so, but in a set designed to function in only two dimen-

sions, where anything not visible to the camera is shabby and makeshift. Bright lights flood down but beyond the sunlit pool there is a semi-darkness occupied by people absorbed in their own, distinct business, moving around and talking quietly. The presenters, when the camera is on them, speak in a punchy, emphatic manner designed to communicate urgency and drama. When it is not their eagerness disappears; they are suddenly anxious; they sip water; they comb their hair; they scan the lines they will read when the red light comes on again; they listen to the voice in their ear and ask questions. Everything is geared to squeezing the maximum impact from the content, both verbal and visual, and to doing so without apparent effort and without stumbles. In short, it is a performance, and the people who do it have more in common with actors than with anyone else.

Everyone who watches television recognizes this at some level, if only because things do occasionally go wrong. We collude willingly in the deception, just as we do when we visit the theatre. So, when viewers wrote in to say that the Jill Dando they saw on television was the real Jill Dando, that they accepted her screen persona as her actual personality, they were saying something strange. They knew it was a performance but they were convinced at the same time that, unusually, it was a performance that revealed truth. How could they possibly know? Celebrity literature, after all, is full of popular personalities who behind the scenes are deeply flawed in one way or another, from the depressive Tony Hancock to the monster mother Joan Crawford. On a more modest scale the newspapers revel in tales of well-known television people engaged in behaviour that is at odds with their on-screen characters. Frank Bough is a case in point. The idea of the public nice guy who is privately naughty is as much a cliché as the tragic circus clown. If, then, the screen Jill Dando appeared to be down-to-earth, caring, cheerful and so forth, what reason had the viewers to be so sure that this was anything more than an unusually good performance?

One thing is certain: it *was* an unusually good performance, even if it was also much more. Jill Dando played her part in the television illusion with considerable and increasing skill. Take her appearance. On television, how you look and dress is important; they are important signals for the viewers about your identity. This is true in a small way about everyday life: every man knows, for example, that his choice of tie – dull or bright, patterned or plain, broad or narrow – says something about him. On television such messages are picked up by millions of people at once; if you appear frequently every tie, suit and haircut is filed away in millions of subconscious minds to form part of a subtle profile. With women this process is vastly more powerful because women are looked at more, by both sexes, and because the conventions of fashion give them a far wider variety of clothes, hairstyles and accessories from which to choose. The messages they can send through television are therefore stronger and more complex.

Jill Dando managed her own screen appearance with great care. The basics, of course, were more than adequate. Five foot eight inches tall, with full bosom and long legs, she had a size twelve figure. Her smile (her own favourite feature) was broad and winning, revealing two perfect rows of gleaming white teeth. The contact lenses she had worn since her teens left her bright blue eyes undimmed. Her hair was worn short and blonde, her skin was good and her features fine and even. In almost anybody's book this was an attractive woman. She herself had a few doubts – she thought her feet too big and worried about her chin ('I have one of those cleft chins which, when the lights hit it in a certain way on television, is accentuated') – but overall she was content. 'I don't see myself as beautiful,' she said, but 'I have some features that people would say were acceptable'. This didn't just happen.

She struggled, for example, to keep her weight below ten stone, eating a great many meals of lightweight crackers, salad and mineral water and having to fight the temptation of exotic foods while on the road for *Holiday*. (Though she owned dumb-

bells and an exercise bicycle she found them too tedious to bear.)
Television is an unforgiving medium in this department – it is
generally thought to add half a stone – so she felt she had to be
strict with herself. Her clothes, too, were carefully selected, as
we have seen. For the *Six* and, in time, *Crimewatch* she chose
suits that were crisp and unfussy, cut with straight lines but often
in surprisingly strong colours. Weaned off Next and on to Féraud
by Bob Wheaton at the beginning of the 1990s, she slowly
broadened her repertoire to include a range of suits from Marni,
Emporio Armani and Cerruti, as well as Féraud. These she would
rotate, only occasionally adding something new. For *Holiday* she
wore lower-budget clothes, often from Marks and Spencer, but
still with a certain crispness. The shorts would have their creases;
the lines were strong; while this was a relaxed look there was
nothing sloppy about it.

Grooming was a meticulous business and a time-consuming
one – this was, after all, the woman who regarded a forty-five-
minute preparation time on the road as a model of brisk efficiency.
Since *Spotlight* days she had attended the hairdresser Martyn
Maxcy – it was he who persuaded her to adopt the short cut and
he who supplied the blondeness. With the *Holiday* programme
they decided over time that natural light was not always flattering
and he developed a technique of altering the hair colour according to the light she could expect at her next destination (effort
that was acknowledged when in 1996 she was named 'head of
the year' by the National Federation of Hairdressers). Her teeth,
too, required maintenance, and she visited a hygienist frequently.
As for make-up, after all those years preparing herself for the
camera with *Holiday* she became an expert in her own right, but
for studio work she employed the BBC's make-up department
to the full and for her other commitments she had the regular
services of a private specialist.

Such attention to detail is the mark of the professional. It
would often be said that Jill Dando bore a striking resemblance
to Sophie Rhys-Jones, and the *Daily Mail* once tried to identify

what it was they had in common. Yes, it said, there were certain physical similarities, but there was more to it than that. 'What marks these women out from the hundreds of other Sophies and Jills that fill London's more modish workplaces is their attention to grooming. Look closely, and it is not only their fringes but their eyebrows that have become slimmer.' Jill Dando, in other words, was making the absolute most of what she had. This did not come cheap. In 1994 she estimated that she was spending about £6,500 a year on clothes and grooming – the BBC did not pay her a special allowance – with a 'huge' dry-cleaning bill on top of that. Four years later the figure had more than doubled to £14,000. By the standards of her profession these were not extravagant sums and they were certainly worth spending, for they undoubtedly played their part in her success.

If her screen 'look' was very carefully considered, what did it communicate to her audience? Within the limited latitude of the news and *Crimewatch* formula she was doing all she could to appeal to the core BBC1 audience. The clothes might carry foreign labels but they were very safe, slightly old for her age and without any pretension to exclusivity. Similar suits could be bought in the posher shops of most British cities. On the *Holiday* programme the approach was different but the objective the same. There was nothing flashy about her appearance – a mistake Anneka Rice was thought to have made – and the clothes had to be informal and comfortable, but she still aimed for a certain neatness. Careful never to be overtly sexy, she was happy to show off her legs but avoided bikinis, as much for reasons of reserve as because she preferred to keep her scar under wraps. The sum of it all, across the three programmes, was a look that was not adventurous but seemed elegant and attainable to most women viewers and was attractive to women and men alike. Nobody ever said: 'What on earth is Jill Dando wearing?' or 'What *has* she done to her hair?' When they thought about it they were supposed to say to themselves, simply: 'She looks nice.'

She never denied the importance of appearance. 'I am very

conscious that looks do count when you are on television, especially on a programme like *Holiday* when you are seen from head to toe in quite skimpy outfits,' she once said. 'When I first started doing the programme four years ago I was a bit obsessive about the way I looked. I was very conscious of not being shot from behind because my backside looked too big. People don't want to see a Two-Ton Tessie rolling out on to the beach.' She was aware that sex could be an issue here – from her earliest days in national television she had received letters from male viewers interested in her body and her underwear – but she was convinced that her true appeal was not a come-to-bed one. 'I don't have the Anthea Turner big eyes,' she said, 'or the Joanna Lumley sex thing. I'm just always there. I'm the reliable girl next door who would take the milk in if you went away.' Much commoner than the underwear letters, she said, were the requests from women asking: 'My husband thinks you are approachable and nice, and will you send me an autograph for his birthday?' Women did this because they did not feel threatened by her, she said. 'The men don't want to have sex with me, they just want to take me to a nice wine bar for a nice glass of wine.' While subsequent events were to show that this was not universally true, the clothes she wore and her general style were chosen with such thoughts in mind.

Like her appearance, her manner on television owed a lot to preparation and hard work. Tellingly, she once quoted the advice given by Michael Palin to people appearing on television: 'Be natural. Be natural. Be natural.' The paradox in this is evident: if you are trying that hard you can't be natural. And in live television, which was Dando's forte, you cannot be natural anyway, at least not in the sense that you can make mistakes. How did Dando, or how does any other presenter, overcome this? By acting natural. Like any actor she had to learn the techniques – no doubt her experience in amateur dramatics helped – and like a good actor she mastered it so completely that she could do it without thinking. But it was acquired, not innate. Besides which, television presenting is full of tricks. Even for a newsreader there are ways of moving the eyes, tilting the head and shifting the shoulders that are known to produce different effects, while alterations in the tone and pitch of the voice, or the speed of delivery, can change the whole meaning of a text. These tricks too must be learned, and Dando learned them very well.

One further area where she was able to influence her own public image was in press interviews, of which she gave more and more as her career developed. These offered an opportunity to add a third dimension to her screen persona, to speak directly about herself to her viewers, to send additional messages. Asked about her background, for example, she always mentioned what she called her 'small-fry roots' and the warmth of the family home. On the origins of her interest in television she had, as we have seen, a variety of attractive stories to tell. She invariably stressed that whenever anything nice had happened to her in her life she was surprised, and suggested that her big television jobs had been more or less thrust upon her. She admitted lacking confidence, suffering from nerves on camera and being awestruck by distinguished people. She was in short unpretentious and unthreatening. All this was supported by an almost breathtaking openness, for she was prepared to talk about anything from her relationship with Bob to the death of her mother, from her dieting struggles to the price of her house – it seemed that not only had she no skeletons in her cupboard, but she also endured her full share of troubles and worries. It is easy to be cynical about this, and interviewers and critics often were. One suggested she was such a goody-goody she probably ironed her bras, while another complained that she was 'screamingly pristine'; she herself once joked about herself as 'Blando'. But while she painted the picture with care, peppering interviews with self-deprecating remarks to balance any hint of starriness, it remained a broadly honest picture. She had certainly been more ambitious than she cared to admit but it was also true that she suffered from deep insecurities. And she herself probably had a limited awareness of her own strengths – as an early boss said, she found everything so easy that she didn't realize how enviable her talents were. The overall effect of the interviews was to add humility and vulnerability to the mix. She was telling the viewers that she was just like they were and she knew how powerful such a message could be in the television age. 'I think audiences like people that they can relate to,' she once said. 'Someone they can trust. Someone ordinary like me.'

None of this means she was a fake or that the viewers were mistaken in the person they perceived. What they saw besides the smartness and the polish was a very nice woman, and Jill Dando *was* a very nice woman – so nice, in fact, that it would be possible to fill whole chapters of this book with stories that prove it. Here is one, told by Andrew Ray, the magistrates' clerk who was a boyfriend for a time in Weston. Ray, who subsequently became a solicitor, was then new in his court job and rather anxious, while Dando was covering the proceedings for the *Mercury*. One day, during a case before a particularly ill-tempered chairman of the bench, Ray found himself sitting in a shaft of sunlight, and thus uncomfortably hot. Quietly he tried to inch his table towards the shade but what he did not know was that one of the legs was loose. At a sensitive moment in the case, the leg gave way and the desk cartwheeled forward, sending a carafe of water, glasses, legal books and papers crashing on to the floor. A stunned Ray sat where he was, waiting to feel the wrath of the chairman, but it was pre-empted by a giggling Dando, who leapt to her feet in the press box and, breaking the silence, asked where she could find a brush and dustpan to clear up. The tension evaporated and Ray escaped rebuke.

Here is another story, told by Wendy Robbins, a friend from Plymouth days. In the course of their friendship Dando had met Robbins's mother and the two got along very well. One summer's day in the late 1990s, when they had not seen each other for two or three years, Dando was filming an outdoor concert at Hampstead Heath. Spotting Robbins's mother in the

audience she immediately dropped what she was doing and
rushed over to greet her, obviously brimming with pleasure at
the encounter. No further filming could be done until they had
caught up on their gossip and until Dando had bought and
poured champagne for the whole party. Once the concert ended,
moreover, she returned for a second chat. Graham Max, who
taught at Broadoak school, had a similar encounter. A couple of
years after Dando had left Weston he spotted her drinking in a
local pub. She caught his eye, left her friends, came over to him
and chatted very happily for a few minutes, telling stories about
schooldays and inquiring about the other staff, a level of directness
and friendliness very rare among former pupils. Then there is the
story of the young woman television presenter who asked Dando
for some career advice and found herself being taken out to lunch
for a long tête-à-tête, after which she received an unexpected
series of follow-up calls, checking how she was getting on and
offering further help. And there was another young presenter,
not nearly as well-off as Dando, to whom she simply gave a
couple of her screen suits, unasked, by way of a leg up in the
business. And so on, and so on. None of these on its own is
especially remarkable, but replicated a hundred times – as they
could be – they make a convincing case: Jill Dando was every
bit as friendly, warm and thoughtful as her viewers thought she
was.

She was unusually loyal, too. Most of us drift in and out of
friendships over the years, losing touch with people who were
once close. Dando, despite the peripatetic character of her life,
fought this process vigorously. She kept names and numbers in
her Filofax and when the opportunity arose she would make
contact, picking up where she had left off. If she was filming in
the southwest, for example, she would invariably phone someone
from Weston, Exeter or Plymouth and see them for dinner. If
an old girlfriend became pregnant, or had a baby, she would
make a point of calling even if they had not been in touch for
some time. And she had one friendship that was particularly

unlikely and particularly durable, into which she put considerable effort. Throughout the 1990s she wrote almost weekly to an elderly lady in Weston who was a family friend, often long letters talking about her life and thoughts. Even when she was travelling she did not like to miss a week, and she carried with her the pink paper she used for these letters. Friendship was important to her, and she was usually prepared to put into it more than she took out.

It may be a cliché, but she was also a generous supporter of various charities, in ways that were both public and discreet. From her early days of fame, for example, she was involved in campaigns on behalf of the British Heart Foundation, offering herself as an example of someone who survived heart surgery and went on to success. More privately, following her mother's death, she helped leukaemia charities. And in the early 1990s she was recruited by the *Mercury* to lead a campaign to raise funds for Weston Hospicecare, and remained close to the project afterwards, paying occasional visits to the patients. Another charity she helped was a small organization in Norwich called the Matthew Project, which helps the victims of drug abuse. She was asked to become patron in 1993 by an old friend from Weston days who was involved with it, and she agreed. It proved a full-hearted commitment and thereafter anything she was asked to do she did willingly, from turning up to publicity events to compèring a fashion show. She also donated some substantial fees she had received from her corporate work.

This is the same compassionate, warm person who is described in the viewers' tributes. Despite all the artificialities of television they were able to see it, and how they did so remains a mysterious matter even after you take the process to pieces and look closely at its separate parts. It is much easier to explain how other characteristics conveyed themselves through the screen. For example, *Holiday* gave her ample opportunity to show that she was plucky and good-humoured. There seemed to be very little she would not do for the show, from eating strange foods and confronting sinister insects to riding large animals and karaoke singing. And there was an ingenuousness and spontaneity about her in many of these moments – moments which often could not have been re-filmed to get them right – that were surely expressions of her real character. She could giggle or blush and she could show alarm and irritation, and when she did so it was usually impossible to imagine that this was not the true Jill Dando.

The 'down-to-earth' quality detected by many viewers also reflected her real character. In part it was to do with her mind – Dando, though a more intelligent and cultured woman than she tended to suggest, was no intellectual. This showed in her attitude to the ethical problems occasionally cast up by her work: she had never been troubled, for example, by the fact that Bob Wheaton was both her lover and her boss, which others might have found uncomfortable. In the same way she never questioned the ethics of *Holiday*, a programme which some might say was little more than a package of advertisements for travel companies. She once said the programme was not afraid to criticize holidays but in truth this was rare; its role, as she knew, was primarily as a feel-good show – 'a half-hour winter warmer', she called it. The problems of *Crimewatch*, mixing entertainment and reality, did not interest her either. 'I don't sit at home fretting about life and the universe,' she once said. 'Maybe this comes across . . .' She was, in short, middle brow, with an uncomplicated, matter-of-fact world view.

And though she was a journalist by background and presented news programmes, viewers never thought of her as part of that world. Back in her Radio Devon days she once talked about the sort of journalist she was: 'I think ideally I'm more of a softer reporter, if you can say it like that. I'm not really turned on by the hard, punchy terrorism-political debates that are going on at the moment, although of course we do have to report them. I think I prefer the more human interest reporting.' These were instincts she had had to overcome at *Breakfast News* when she was handling big stories such as the Gulf War and the fall of

Thatcher, and in particular when she was interviewing, but even then, as we have seen, she had a relatively soft touch. Once she left breakfast television for the six o'clock bulletin she rarely conducted interviews, as these were left to the lead newsreader. On *Crimewatch*, meanwhile, her role was often a soft one, for example speaking to the victims of crime – among her most memorable moments on the programme was an interview with Danielle Cable, the young woman who saw her fiancé murdered in a 'road rage' attack that later proved to be the work of the gangster Kenneth Noye. So Dando was never the devil's advocate, nor did she put people on the spot or ask them awkward questions. She was seen to have a role that was warm and unthreatening – something, once again, that was a genuine reflection of her character.

Middle class, middle brow and middle England, Jill Dando sometimes looks like a market researcher's creation, that careful blend of qualities designed with the help of focus groups to reach the widest possible audience. She was not metropolitan but she was not provincial either; she was attractive without being overtly sexy, bright but not intellectual, lively without being silly, conservative but not out-of-date. Like many carefully targeted products she was ordinary and reassuring, but with a twist of aspiration. People admired her dress, her manners and her modesty in success and they saw her as a model, even an ideal of English womanhood. All of this could have been contrived, although it would have been difficult. What could not have been contrived was the warmth the viewers felt for her, which surely relates to her character and background and to those unusual qualities seen at first hand by her friends and by those who interviewed her and gave her jobs. And this is where the attempt to analyse her success breaks down. We can describe some of the reasons for it and identify some of the ways, contrived or otherwise, in which she attracted viewers, but in the end we cannot explain the whole phenomenon. Somehow, it is clear, viewers were able to see that this was someone they could trust, and we must leave it there.

# 6. Another Me

*'One of my philosophies in the past few months has been
"Seize the day".'*

The last couple of months of 1996 brought a turning point in
the life of Jill Dando. November of that year began with her
appearance, as recipient of the famous red book, on *This Is Your
Life*. This was the usual upbeat affair, featuring among others
her father, her brother, the surgeon who performed her heart
operation, John Lilley, Nick Ross and Cliff Richard. And sitting
beside the delighted Jill as the guests rolled in was Bob Wheaton,
'the man in your life'. They were presented as the ultimate in
busy couples, she constantly on the road with *Holiday* and he
caught up in a new job setting up the BBC's international
television news service. 'Thank you for bringing us together,'
Wheaton joked to Michael Aspel. 'We hardly ever see each
other.' The programme, broadcast in that early-evening territory
Dando had come to dominate, told the story she had recounted
so many times – her childhood, the operation, Weston, the
*Mercury*, Radio Devon, the loss of her mother and so forth. It
was, in its way, television's own acknowledgement of her arrival
as a star.

In the same month she gave an interview to *Radio Times*.
Timed to coincide with the screening of *Fasten Your Seatbelt* (a
spin-off from *Holiday* in which she was an air stewardess for a
few days) this was in its way another recognition of her standing.
No mere questionnaire tucked away in the back, it was 'The
Andrew Duncan Interview' – the big weekly feature spread over
four pages at the heart of the magazine. The article announced,

quite dramatically, the arrival of a new Jill Dando. 'I want to be raunchy now and again', said the headline, while the photographs showed her in leather jacket and mini-skirt with wet-look hair and a deep neckline. This was new all right. The content was a little less revolutionary than the presentation – no sooner had she said that at the age of thirty-five she was ready to be a bit raunchy than she added: 'I don't want to give the wrong impression . . . I'm wholesome, with none of the skeletons in the cupboard everyone assumes people on screen must have.' But none the less the questioning brought out a side of her not previously on show. Asked about the changing role of women, for example, she said she thought it left many men confused: 'I don't know if it's turned a lot of them gay through sheer frustration. What a waste if it has.' And she had a firm view on the monarchy: 'I'm sick to the back teeth of reading about what members of the royal family get up to.' She spoke of her own insecurities, about work and her 'Scorpio traits'. There was more attitude, more assertiveness and individuality in her approach than ever before, and this showed, too, when she spoke of her life with Bob. Mischievously, the interviewer quoted a remark she once made about her strong Christian faith and asked how she reconciled that with a long unmarried relationship. What was she doing living in sin? 'I'm not,' she replied firmly. She and Bob had separate homes and 'we divide our time between the two'. Then she elaborated: 'Because nothing is ever definite I've always been reluctant to put all my eggs in one basket. There are times when you might fall out and just want to get back to your own place and shut the door on everyone . . . It works well.' It was a curious answer. By any normal definition – including her own in previous interviews – this couple had lived together for most if not all of the period of their relationship. True, they owned separate houses for most of that time, but they shared them, usually on the basis of weekdays in London and weekends in Maidenhead. This new, detached formula, and the mention of 'falling out', suggested difficulties in the relationship and an ambivalence which had not been apparent in earlier years, the years when, for example, she had spoken of Bob as her 'rock'.

Between the time she gave that interview and its appearance in the magazine in early December Jill Dando went away on assignment for *Holiday*. This trip was to South Africa and it took her to the Kruger National Park where she stayed in the Sabi Sabi game reserve. Among the escorts for the BBC team on safari was a game warden called Simon Bassil and in the course of their three days together something happened which, by her account, had never happened to her on location before. Bassil and she became lovers. This was both a thrill and a shock. It was a romantic setting, he was tall and handsome and she evidently enjoyed herself; it was, she would say later, a relief after the tensions of her relationship with Wheaton. At the same time she was accustomed to monogamy and surprised at herself. This was not like her. When filming was complete she left Bassil behind and returned on schedule to London and to Bob Wheaton, but that relationship now had only a few days to run.

It happened, Wheaton says, on 6 December, after they had attended an evening reception together in Downing Street. This was a fitting prelude since it must have been a gloomy occasion – John Major, the host, was already a doomed prime minister. After the drinks at Number Ten, Dando and Wheaton made their way through the West End to the Langham Hilton Hotel, popular with BBC executives since it stands just across the road from Broadcasting House. And there, over a late-night glass of champagne in the bar, they agreed to end their relationship of six and a half years. Both would later say that it was a sad conversation rather than a bitter one. There would be arguments about who dumped whom but the truth is that the two of them recognized – as he had hinted on *This Is Your Life* and she in the *Radio Times* – that this had been coming for some time. Did she tell him about Simon Bassil? She didn't need to, says Wheaton. 'I knew she'd had a fling with someone.' It is clear that the fling was a symptom of their problems and not the cause.

Since she had joined *Holiday* in 1992 her commitments had grown relentlessly and she had spoken many times of the difficulties that constant travel caused to her private life. Bob, too, was now spending a lot of time on the road. They had begun as colleagues, sharing to an almost claustrophobic degree the disjointed lifestyle of early-morning television, and now, both professionally and in terms of time together, they shared very little. There was also the matter of marriage and children: neither had ever been quite ready to take the first step and while she often talked about 'putting her career first for the moment' that reluctance suggested an enduring ambivalence. By 1996 her friends were well aware of stresses. There were signs of rows, although she does not seem to have discussed them openly, and Jill appeared to find little joy in the relationship.

There may well have been something else behind the split, something that could be traced back to her childhood. It was probably no accident that Jill Dando's longest relationship, which took her from the age of twenty-eight to thirty-five, was with a man fourteen years her senior who was her boss when it began. She often spoke of her preference for older men, saying, for example, that she found them more courteous, more mature and more reliable, and she even claimed that this preference was so strong she had only once in her life gone out with a younger man, when she was a teenager. This was slightly misleading, since she had had a number of short relationships with men who were, if not actually younger, at least her contemporaries. Her insistence that she liked older men on principle seems to have had more to do with justifying the partnership with Wheaton – about which interviewers were often curious – than with anything else. But what the interviewers were getting at, and what she was denying, was that this was in some respects a parent-child relationship. Could that have been the case? She had been a very sheltered child, exceptionally close to her mother. With her father, a more reticent figure, there had always been a desire to please. Her mother, the 'rock' in her life, died when she was twenty-four and living away from home for the first time. Four years later, when she was at sea in London and in need of help, she found in Bob Wheaton a man who could be her new rock, an authority figure whom she could please and who gave her the affirmation and security she wanted – in a way, a parent substitute. This is not to deny that it was a genuinely loving adult relationship because it obviously was, but it offers an additional dimension. And what had been good for the naïve young woman in 1990 was no longer of interest to the successful presenter of 1996. She had grown up.

From that Christmas of 1996 onwards Jill Dando was different. The more independent and assertive woman glimpsed in the *Radio Times* interview took over and, although the charming, generous Jill so popular among colleagues and viewers did not disappear, she gained a new vigour and strength. She said later of the fling with Bassil that it 'unleashed another me'. Wheaton, who remained in close touch, saw the change. She was 'spreading her wings', he said, and 'breaking free'. Suddenly Dando was able to please herself. It was something completely new and, as so often with periods of self-discovery, it was to prove a bumpy ride.

The first bump was not long in coming. On the morning of 11 January 1997 she was on the front page of the *Sun*, a glamour photograph alongside the headline: 'TV JILL SPLITS FROM LOVER'. The story began: 'Telly's *Holiday* show golden girl Jill Dando has split from her lover – after he grew sick of her trips abroad.' And it went on: 'A close pal of the couple said last night Jill was "devastated" at the end of the six-year romance . . . As Jill's career soared, the passion fizzled out of the relationship and it finally hit the rocks last month.' The casual reader would have inferred that Wheaton ended it but a close reading of the text left a different impression. The 'close pal' went on to say that both parties had found themselves too busy and 'they decided to call it a day'. He or she explained: 'It all became too much and there were a lot of heated arguments about their future . . . It all blew up over Christmas.' The story contained just one quote from Dando, who was said to be on holiday: 'I don't talk about my private life.' This was not true, of course – she had always been open about her life with Bob – but what she was really saying was that she was not used to handling unmanaged publicity. The last time it had happened was at the beginning of the relationship, six years earlier, and that story had been less about her than him. Now she was 'TV JILL' in letters two inches tall and a stream of her old remarks about her closeness to Bob were being dredged up. It was embarrassing and surely bad for her image. Some readers would see in the story evidence that she was career-driven and perhaps a little ruthless, and she did not want that. But nor could she say that it was all Bob's fault.

In fact she was not on holiday when the story broke but on assignment, filming a ski item in France. She returned home the following day to find reporters and a photographer from the *Mail on Sunday* on her doorstep in Gowan Avenue and characteristic-ally she agreed to talk to them, at some length. Work had been a factor, she said, and it was 'just one of those things' that happens to busy people. It had not been a dramatic break-up; she and Bob remained 'the best of friends' and they were fortunate there were no children to worry about. Did she still hope for children some day? 'If it happens it happens . . . I wouldn't cry into my Horlicks if I reached seventy and didn't have children. If that's God's design, so be it.' Next morning, beneath the twin headlines 'Work killed my romance' and 'Sadness of Jill Dando, alone again after seven years', the paper devoted a page to the break-up. Although the reporter wrote that Dando was close to tears during the interview, the accompanying picture showed her more tense than tearful. She was as well-groomed as ever but her arms were folded, her face was pale and instead of the usual smile her lips were set in a thin line. And once again, down there in the middle of the text, was the statement: 'Miss Dando never shared a home with Wheaton.'

If the story looked like a two-day wonder – and that is clearly what she hoped – it was not, for within a fortnight the *Sun* delivered another unwelcome bump. 'JILL BAGS A NEW FELLA ON SAFARI', it announced. '6ft 7in hunk woos TV girl.' This was the story of Simon Bassil, who, the paper revealed, had won Dando's heart in his 'remote safari lodge'. It was 'lust at first sight' and, the paper could reveal, he had been left 'so besotted' that he had given up his job in South Africa and had flown to Britain to be with her. Once again 'close pals' were at work and they apparently laid stress on a particular point: 'Friends said Jill fell for Simon *after* splitting with long-term love Bob Wheaton.' In fact this was almost certainly Dando's own response to the *Sun*'s call, supplied either directly or through an intermediary, as was another comment: 'Jill has told pals: "We're dating, but taking it one step at a time."' Though the paper had misspelt Bassil's name and he was six foot two rather than six foot seven, the core of its story was accurate. He *had* come to Britain earlier that month – moving to Portsmouth, where he had taken a job in computers – and he and Dando *were* seeing each other. A month later the *Sunday Mirror* landed the inevitable follow-up scoop: a picture of the couple together in a Knightsbridge street. The copy made much of his 'safari guy' past: 'The only zebra might have been a zebra crossing, but tough guy Simon was always at her side when they went on a hunting trip . . . for bargains in Harrods.' The *Mirror* had spoken to someone in South Africa who gave an account of Bassil's departure from the Sabi Sabi reserve: 'He told everyone that he wanted to try something different and was taking a job as a computer programmer. But everyone knew that the real reason was that he wanted to be with Jill.' Now settled in Hampshire, the paper said, he was 'a regular visitor' at Dando's Fulham home.

Back in 1990, when she was caught by the *Sun* on her doorstep with Wheaton, she had said: 'We are both single so I can't see any harm in it.' This time, too, she and Bassil were both single, but somehow she could not adopt the same matter-of-fact approach. 'I can't see any harm in it' is another way of saying 'This isn't really a story', and while that might have been true of a liaison between a BBC executive and a minor news presenter it was hardly the case now. She was a fully fledged celebrity and whether she liked it or not her romantic life was fair game for the press. More than that, this was a story that would sell newspapers, as the follow-ups in other titles indicated. Her life to date, of which she had talked so often and so freely, had been perfect to the point of dullness. The previous spring, for example, she had shown *OK!* magazine around the Fulham house, talking happily of her work, her past and of the pleasure she and Bob found in shopping for antiques. 'Why life's just dandy for Jill' was the headline. This was predictable and unsensational. But a relationship with a former game warden, begun on safari within a couple of days of their first meeting and resumed after he gave up his job to follow her to England – that was something quite different. It had passion, romance and sex; the readers would lap it up.

All the openness she had shown in the years with Wheaton, which had been so effective in bringing her closer to the viewers, had seemed to carry no dangers. But now she wanted privacy she could not have it. There would always be somebody in the BBC who would tip off the papers, somebody in the street with a camera ready to sell the shots, some other customer in the restaurant with a big mouth. It was a harsh lesson, and particularly harsh as she and Bassil were just getting to know one another. It would be difficult now for the relationship to develop naturally. On the professional front, too, this looked like bad news. 'Lust on safari' stories were in conflict with her homely image and she was still, after all, a BBC newsreader who needed some gravitas to do her job. What could she do about it? Another celebrity might have battened down the hatches and made sure the papers found nothing more to write about for a long time, but not Dando. She decided to do what she had always done before – to talk. She went to the *Daily Mail*, the paper with which she now most closely identified, and she gave a long interview that appeared under the headline 'The truth about me and the game warden'.

'I met Simon shortly after Bob and I had agreed to go our separate ways,' she said. 'We met in one of the most romantic places in the world . . . He looked very handsome, he's intelligent, he's witty and yes, there was romance.' What had brought him to Britain? He had planned to give up the game warden's job and go back to computers long before he met her, she explained, and since he had family in Britain and had worked here before it was a natural place to come to. 'I think the fact that we had met was a factor but it was *his* decision. I didn't say: "You must come over. I want us to be together." ' As for the relationship now, they saw each other some weekends, going out for meals together. Yes, they were close friends but she did not want to rush into anything. 'I wouldn't even call him *my* boyfriend. He is *a* boyfriend.' In short, it was all less exciting and less passionate than the papers assumed. As for Bob, she and he remained friends, and in fact were probably getting on better than they had for some time.

She went on then to talk about herself, and she showed some more of the 'new Jill Dando'. She was determined not to sit at home moping, but to call her own shots. 'One of my philosophies in the past few months has been "Seize the day". It's rather new to me, not being part of a couple and I like to think I'm quite a sociable person so I am really enjoying going out on my own and meeting new people. I don't put up barriers. If I'm attracted to someone I think I show it. I'm as good a flirt as anybody.' Asked the inevitable question about children she struck another different note, no longer fatalistic. It was, she said, very important to her and she would be disappointed to reach forty without being a mother, but as long as she continued to travel with *Holiday* she knew she could not settle down. Maybe, she said, she would reassess her priorities in a year's time.

All of this was very revealing. Despite Bassil's arrival in Britain, for a start, she did not think of herself as part of a couple and she was prepared to flirt and be sociable with other men. So the idea that he was *a* boyfriend, in other words one of several, might be taken literally. She was also thinking long-term, trying to learn the lessons from the failure of her relationship with Wheaton, and consequently for the first time she was thinking about putting her private life before her career. And she wanted to seize the day, to enjoy the moment, which was something the earlier Jill Dando had not been able to do. Altogether she was talking like someone who had been reading positive-thinking manuals, someone who was consciously asserting control. Rather as she had when she was sixteen, she was reinventing herself. She knew what she wanted in her personal life – a strong, down-to-earth, intelligent man (probably not Bassil) – and she was determined to get it in the long run. In the meantime, 'I'm very much my own person at the moment and I want to keep that freedom'.

No less revealing is the small deception in her words. She stated firmly once again that she had met Bassil *after* the split with Wheaton, even though this was not the case: she visited Sabi Sabi in November and did not part with Bob until December. The old relationship may have been moribund, but it was not quite over. That she felt it necessary to tell what was a lie, and to lay stress on it, shows that there were limits even to her openness. She plainly did not want people to know something which they might construe – or the press might present – as evidence that she had been unfaithful. So she rearranged events a little. In much the same way she had already rearranged the story of her relationship with Bob by telling reporters that they had never lived together. On the scale of celebrity dishonesty this rates very low indeed, but it is another sign of the change in Jill Dando. She was a woman with a strong sense of right and wrong and she must have known what she was doing.

The relationship with Bassil survived the early bumps and for a few months they saw each other regularly. This for her was the quiet time of year, with few *Holiday* commitments, and the two

of them made the most of it. On the night of 1 May, election
night, she offered to do a reporting shift as part of the army of
people involved in the BBC's national results coverage, and she
chose Portsmouth for her dateline. For her it was a rare sortie
into straight reporting and though she appeared only once on
screen that night she was justly proud of the job she did, a clear
and polished summary of the prospects for the city's two Tory
marginals. And Portsmouth, of course, was where Bassil lived. A
few weeks later the couple went on holiday together to Anguilla
in the Caribbean.

In another way that she had not expected, the break-up with
Wheaton rebounded to her advantage. Where before, the serious
features editors had sometimes dismissed her as a *Hello!* person
with nothing to say for herself, now they were curious. After the
*Radio Times* and the *Mail* she was asked to do more big interviews,
with the *Daily Telegraph* and the *Express* magazine, and these in
turn were picked up and recycled as showbusiness news stories
in the daily papers. Her profile was rising even higher. This also
owed a good deal, no doubt, to the effects of time: by 1997 she
had been on prime time for five years and no one could imagine
that her success was a flash in the pan. She was at the top and
staying there. That spring, moreover, she won the Television
and Radio Industry Club award as BBC Personality of the Year
(she made a point of thanking Bob Wheaton at the ceremony).
The interviews covered much familiar biographical ground but
they had other striking common factors. 'What a change from
her TV persona!' exclaimed the *Express*, having heard her say
'shit' and put on an Indian accent to tell a joke. 'How very
puzzling,' mused the *Telegraph* on discovering that the supposedly
perfect Jill Dando was so nervous she bumped into a chair and
knocked over a glass. It was true: she *was* interesting. Both were
also disarmed by her self-deprecation and defensiveness and both
detected something more solid beneath it all – 'a sterling toughie',
the *Express* surmised.

As far as her love life was concerned there was an interesting progression in her public comments. To the *Telegraph* in June she said that things with Simon Bassil were still fine but they had no plans to live together. 'There is a lot of pressure on us,' she continued. 'I couldn't take him to the National Lottery with me the other day because of all the photographers, and poor Simon was disappointed. I don't know what all the fuss is about anyway.' This was clumsily put and left Bassil looking like a schoolboy denied a treat, but it also showed that she was uncomfortable about being seen with him. When she spoke to the *Express* in August she didn't answer questions about him at all, making clear instead that she lived alone and had no marriage plans. 'What I am sure about,' she went on, 'is that if the right man does come along I will know it.' In fact the relationship with Bassil was effectively over. By October she was describing herself as single and telling the *TV Times*: 'Simon's lovely but it was one of those things. Now we're just friends.' It had all been a bit of a mistake, she implied: 'I've never met anyone on location and had a relationship with them before. It's the most romantic situation in the world, two souls colliding under the stars, and it was fabulous. But when you suddenly bring it back into reality things aren't the same.'

So that autumn of 1997, punctuated though it was by another round of assignments for *Holiday*, gave her a first real experience of being single since the unhappy days after her arrival in London. She had occasionally, as she might have put it, 'wined and dined' other men while she was seeing Bassil, but now she threw herself into the dating business. It was great, she said later. 'I was my own boss. I could have dinner with three different men in a week, which was nice. There were no ties. I found a kind of youthfulness which I enjoyed. I was quite skittish.' In the words of a friend, she was 'making up for lost time'. Was this Jill Dando being promiscuous? Perhaps, but in context it is hardly significant or surprising. These were the 1990s. She was nearly thirty-six, earning a substantial six-figure salary (although not the £750,000 that was often reported) and she had looks that, as friends testified, could literally stop traffic. She was doing only what most women, or indeed men, might do in a similar position. Much later, one of the men she saw at this time talked anonymously to the *Sunday Times*. They met, he said, through work and she would call him sometimes when she was in the country to arrange meetings, but somehow he didn't talk to others about the affair at the time. It was all secretive and 'curiously unemotional' and it petered out after a couple of months.

For Dando now there was the short term and there was the long term. In the short term, she told herself, she wanted to be skittish and have fun, to be single and to be in charge. In the long term she remained a true romantic, longing for the perfect man to come along. This was a position fraught with difficulties. She didn't want to find herself in the *Sun* again, linked to a man she had just met, whose name would then be trotted out in print for years to come. And she didn't want another entanglement that wouldn't last, like the Bassil affair. If she was going to have fun, therefore, it would have to be short-term and secretive and so it probably had to be unemotional as well. And in time something was bound to go wrong.

'Why can't I find a nice fella?' she used to say to a friend in the Radio Devon canteen back in her Exeter days. Besides Wheaton she had never really found one, and she was probably never quite sure he was right for her. She had certainly made it difficult for herself, putting her career first, keeping odd hours and spending half the year on the road, but she still had that girlish dream of meeting a nice man she could settle down with. She knew it, her close friends knew it and as 1997 progressed her colleagues and even her public knew it. 'I don't want to be single for too long,' she said. 'I've always believed that I didn't want to get married until I knew it was right, and until that happens I won't.' When it did happen, when it was right, she said, everything would be different. 'I would be like a little flower and the stalk that had been holding me up this long would suddenly wither away and another would grow in its place. I'm sure it will happen one day.' So which would come along first, the perfect man or the tabloid scoop full of sleazy innuendo?

Somebody who was thinking along roughly these lines late in 1997 was Jenny Higham, an old friend of Jill's from her days in the southwest who now worked in St Mary's Hospital in London. As Jill later put it, 'She [Jenny] decided I'd met enough Mr Wrongs.' Concerned about the drift of Jill's life, Higham persuaded her friend to take part in a bit of matchmaking. 'We didn't acknowledge it was matchmaking. It was just a few casual meetings with other people around,' said Jill. One of these other people was a surgeon from St Mary's called Alan Farthing, a friend of Higham's who had separated from his wife earlier that year. Farthing, a gynaecologist specializing in keyhole surgery, was thirty-four, handsome and quietly charming, and Higham thought her friend might like him. Dando later told the story to *Hello!*: 'Jenny brought Alan along when I was standing in on Esther Rantzen's talk show when she was poorly. I was looking from behind the set knowing that she had brought this chap and I thought he looked nice – nothing more than that . . . After that the three of us went out for dinner.' At the end of the dinner, during which Farthing apparently spent much of the time merely watching as the two friends talked, Dando invited him to her birthday party, which was two weeks away. He apologized: he had been invited to a rugby match followed by a friend's party on that day and could not make it. 'Jenny decided she ought to try again and two or three weeks later we met up again, just Jenny, her husband, Alan and me; a very casual thing. After that, Alan drove me home and we arranged to see each other for dinner a couple of nights later.'

Dando may have thought it all 'very casual' – she used those words twice – but it was also a pretty determined display of friendship from Higham, who took it on herself to introduce these two not once, but twice. And this second time around it worked – 'there was no stopping us', Dando said. Weeks later they were on holiday together in Australia, watching the New

Year fireworks explode over Sydney harbour bridge. Dando was very soon convinced that this was the man she had been waiting for all her life. He was, she said, 'absolutely gorgeous'; she respected him, he had a good sense of humour and he was not 'swayed' by what she did for a living. Like her he came from the southwest – in his case Dorset – and like her he had been brought up a Baptist. They laughed a great deal and never argued, she found. Alan, as she and Higham agreed, was not just Mr Right but 'Mr So-Right'.

# 7. The News

*'Just because I'm blonde and haven't been to Bosnia doesn't mean I'm a bimbo.'*

The new Jill Dando who had been unleashed at the end of 1996 very soon began to talk openly about changes in her career, and the principal change she had in mind was leaving *Holiday*. This was the programme that had made her and it had been a perfect vehicle in many ways, but the price was high, both physically and emotionally. Professionally, too, it might have begun to work against her. This was a golden spell: *This Is Your Life*, BBC Personality of the Year, big interviews and assignments – she was being chosen to compère awards ceremonies (even one on ITV) and to present National Lottery shows. With all this going on, was it wise to spend four months of the year out of the country? Was she missing opportunities? Was she, as the agents might say, failing to maximize the product?

And there was another question: was she in danger of becoming stuck with *Holiday*? By Easter 1997 she had done five seasons and was already signed up for another; unless she wanted to take root in the slot she would surely be wise to move sooner rather than later. Age, too, was a consideration. When her first series was broadcast she was thirty-one; she was now thirty-six. The format, with its bright sunshine, bare flesh and DIY hair and make-up, was essentially unforgiving when it came to female looks (some celebrity women simply refuse ever to be filmed in direct sunlight). Yes, Judith Chalmers had got away with it for years on ITV, but Chalmers was not Jill Dando; she did not have so many other balls to keep in the air or so many other small-screen ambitions to fulfil. And for that matter Chalmers had just been replaced by Anthea Turner (a change which drew from Dando a delightfully barbed remark: 'We're both blonde and we're similar ages, although she [Turner] is a year older'). The short of it was that Dando could see that unless she was prepared to pigeonhole herself she would need to move.

Once again this was new territory for her. Hitherto she had been working her way up, landing new shows, establishing a reputation and defining an image. Now she was managing success, which was different. If she was to leave *Holiday*, a strong prime time show, she would need to be sure she could replace it with something as good, a programme that enabled her to deploy her talents and personality just as well. Such programmes did not grow on trees. This became her main professional concern as 1997 progressed and she discussed it with her agent Jon Roseman. By this time she was, he says, 'an incredibly canny and shrewd operator' when it came to her career; she consulted him (as she still occasionally consulted Bob Wheaton), but she made her own decisions. She had very clear ideas about what was right for her and what was not, what the audience expected and what it would not like. She worried about getting it wrong, and with good reason: more than one leading presenter has vanished from view after taking on a programme that did not work. Understandably then, even the new Jill Dando was cautious about her next move. She made a pilot show for a property series, but it did not take off. She was offered a daytime talk show like the Esther Rantzen programme she had worked on, but she feared the change of audience. 'They'll forget me,' she told Roseman, meaning her prime time viewers.

Late in 1997, as the time approached when she had to decide about another *Holiday* series, there was a little game of public brinkmanship with the BBC, something the old Jill Dando had never done. She had already hinted once in print that she was having doubts about her future with the programme and now she was a little more explicit. 'They want me to do another year but I am keeping my options open,' she told the *Daily Express*. 'I do like it . . . but there are times when I yearn for my front door.' Dando, the paper said, 'also revealed that she would like to front her own chat show'. When the BBC was asked to comment on this they denied everything; a spokeswoman declared: 'She is not even thinking of leaving *Holiday*.' But there was no denial from Dando herself, and other papers followed up the story. One, the *Mail on Sunday*, interpreted her remarks as a manoeuvre: 'It's probably fair to say that her public dithering is an aggressive bid for the chat show she would really like to have, and could probably be translated along the lines of, "If you don't give me what I want, I'm off to ITV."' That didn't happen, yet, for within a few days she had reached an agreement with the corporation: she would sign up for another year with *Holiday*, which would take her through to Easter 1999. Reports that she had been considering quitting were 'a little exaggerated', she now said (as though she had had nothing to do with them), and her bosses 'weren't best pleased'. In fact she had shied at the fence. There was no new vehicle for her that she thought suitable, nothing to match *Holiday*, so she opted to stay put. One more year, she said.

That was early December. We may speculate that if the timing had been a little different, if the discussions had taken place after her return from Australia a month later, she might have taken a different decision. For by then she had decided she was in love with Alan Farthing. Hardly had they got back from Sydney before they booked another holiday, this time a skiing trip to France, where they would stay with Jill's cousin Judith, now settled in the Alps. When they got to Villeneuve in mid-March, however, something unplanned but inevitable happened: they were spotted. 'TV JILL HAS A HOL NEW LOVE', announced the *News of the World* as it printed a set of pictures of the two together on the slopes, including one that showed them kissing. Some fellow-skier, it seemed, had recognized them and alerted the newspaper, which dispatched a photographer. The story was

written in the familiar style: 'TV travel beauty Jill Dando looks
on top of the world over the new love in her life. For, as our
exclusive pictures show, the thinking man's blonde has been
smooching in the snow at a top French ski resort with a dashing
doctor.' This new love 'ended a black run in her romantic
record', declared the paper, 'as she made up for a whole year
without a date in sparkling style'. There was reference to 'her
last two failed romances' and much nonsense about temperatures
soaring and ice melting because of their passion. To cap it all,
Farthing's name, age and profession were all there, as were the
additional details that he was separated from his wife, worked in
St Mary's Hospital and lived in Chiswick.

They had been comprehensively rumbled. They were just
back in London when the story appeared in print and Farthing,
who had no experience of such intrusion, was shocked. He
worked in a sober, serious profession and had a reputation to
consider – his patients, colleagues and students would be reading
this frothy stuff. In a similar situation most of us would become
alarmed. But it was also true that they could have been more
careful, as Dando must have known. The story would not have
worked nearly so well without the kiss, so they might have
avoided exposure if they had kept their embraces for private
places. Still, it had been bound to come out sooner or later, as
her experiences with Wheaton and Bassil showed, and this,
fortunately, was not too soon. The relationship survived.

Her own reaction to the story was the familiar one: she talked
about it in the press. Before the ski trip she had been to the
Dominican Republic to record another *Fasten Your Seatbelt*
special, which this time found her taking on the role of a holiday
rep who organized weddings for British visitors. While there she
posed for a series of photographs for a feature in *Hello!* The
interview took place a couple of weeks later and by that time her
romance was in the papers, so inevitably *Hello!* wanted the whole
story and just as inevitably she provided it. There was, said the
article, 'that certain radiance about Jill Dando which a woman

has when she's in love'. It shone from her eyes, said the magazine, as if to say: 'Yes I am glowing . . . and I am happy.' Dando told the story of how they had met and then described the current state of things: 'It's all very nice, but that's all I can say at the moment. Once you put your partner in the spotlight, inevitably there is an amount of interest and if someone isn't used to it it can actually throw the relationship. So that's why I'm being cautious . . . It's early days and I don't like to count any chickens.' Not too cautious, however, for the reader was left in no doubt that for her this was a big romance, and it wasn't just the *Hello!* prose style. She raved about Farthing's looks and his charm; she gushed about seeing in the New Year with him in Australia and she said how glad she was not to be single any more. Taken together with her descriptions of 'choking up' as she watched the weddings in the Dominican Republic, the message was a strong one. And this was new for Dando; she had never, for example, spoken of Simon Bassil in this way.

That she was beginning to believe that she had found her 'nice fella' at last was bound to have an impact upon her career. She never concealed, from herself or anybody else, her feeling that constant travel had undermined her relationship with Bob Wheaton and that it would make further relationships difficult. Now she had the man she wanted she was keen to scale things down. Since she had already signed up for another series of *Holiday* it was too late to get out of that, but it would be her last, and very soon she told the BBC of her decision. Word leaked out and when the papers reported that she was quitting 'to work at her new romance', Jon Roseman tried to give it a more sober spin. She would be concentrating on *Crimewatch* and other work, he said, and any decision she made would be 'based solely on professional considerations'.

It would certainly be wrong to suggest that love had gone to her head. This was still the canny Dando and if she was giving up *Holiday* she still wanted something big to replace it. Since there was nothing quite right at the BBC, for the first time she allowed herself to look elsewhere and in April she began a flirtation with ITV. How serious this was is hard to tell. She still had *Crimewatch* in her BBC portfolio and it was a show she loved. Whether she was ready to leave it obviously depended upon ITV being able to offer something even better. Perhaps they could: she had spoken, for example, of wanting an evening chat show of some kind and it might have been possible to negotiate something suitable. There were some high-level meetings to discuss the possibilities and once again the story made the press, with suggestions that she had been offered a £1 million deal. Someone speaking on her behalf, probably Roseman, was quoted that April as saying: 'She is TV's hottest property and if the ITV offer is right, Jill will walk. She wants a fresh challenge. It is going to be a big battle.'

It is difficult to imagine her 'walking' in this way, since she had developed into such a quintessentially BBC1 personality. If she was one of the defining faces of the channel it was in a double sense: she defined it and it defined her. She somehow belonged in public service broadcasting. And yet the same has been said of many others who have subsequently switched channels. In Dando's case it never happened, for by the summer she had negotiated a new contract with the corporation. The *Mirror* quoted a BBC executive as saying: 'We are very relieved she doesn't want to go to ITV even though she was offered more money. Jill is very popular with the viewers. She's one of the faces of the BBC and we can't afford to lose her.' By then she may already have spotted what it was she wanted to do next at the corporation.

In the course of 1998 the BBC was conducting a comprehensive review of its news output which was generally expected to prepare the way for the biggest upheaval in a decade. In keeping with the management style of the Birt years this review was formal, bureaucratic and long-running – by that summer, with the announcement of the findings still months off, it was a year behind schedule. There was no shortage of informed rumour, however, and this indicated that a significantly new approach would be recommended. For ten years and more the main BBC television bulletins at 6 p.m. and 9 p.m. had tried to combine punchiness with authority in their presentation. They began with urgent, thumping fanfares and dramatic headlines and were presented from imposing sets decorated in shades of blue. The stories were briskly told, very often with the help of correspondents who were experts in their field. The idea, when this formula was established, had been to claim the top of the market: the message to the viewers was that they were getting the most serious, most important and most trustworthy coverage, both national and international. From the mid-1990s on, however, the ratings and the market research began to suggest that this approach was becoming dated. Many viewers, particularly younger ones, found the 'hard news' agenda intimidating and the specialist explanations baffling. They were uncomfortable with what was seen as a 'cold' style of presentation, which was often contrasted with the human interest strengths of ITN. The news review was examining these matters.

One early rumour about its conclusions – which was to prove correct – was that there would be a new emphasis on news presenters. It was not that the BBC was short of presenters, rather the contrary: the *Six O'Clock News*, for example, had well-known lead presenters in Martyn Lewis and Anna Ford, but the problem was that they were far from alone. On a given day, in fact, the bulletin might be read by any two from a list of fourteen names, of whom Jill Dando, contracted to read sixty reports a year, was just one. The early leaks from the review suggested that in future the *Six* would be read by a single presenter, rather than two, and that person should be the accepted anchor of the show, appearing as far as possible every weekday. This, it was thought, would give the viewers a familiar face at the start of the evening's television. There were soon suggestions in the press that the BBC might poach Kirsty Young, the much-praised news presenter on the new Channel Five, to fulfil this role, and then in early August Dando's name was also linked with the job. She liked the idea. Working in the newsroom she was well aware that change was coming, and the timing seemed very good. Just as she was giving up *Holiday*, here was a big new opportunity: she might be the anchorwoman of the *Six*.

In some senior quarters in the BBC this was thought to be a very good idea indeed, and on 16 August the *Sunday Times* picked up this view. 'Dando to replace Martyn Lewis in new BBC "star news",' said a report in the paper. She had been picked, it was said, to relaunch the BBC's highest-rating bulletin, which would become more like a soft current affairs programme along the lines of the old *Nationwide*. She would be paid £400,000, including her fee for hosting *Crimewatch*, and would appear five nights a week. When an official BBC spokesman was asked about this he dismissed it as pure speculation. 'Any information about changes to the news can't be accurate, since no conclusions have yet been reached.' But there were some senior figures eager to jump the gun and the following day one of them briefed the broadsheet media correspondents, explaining the direction the review was likely to take. Sure enough, the *Six* faced the bigger changes. Instead of being simply an early evening version of the *Nine* it was to become more distinctive, with a brief to attract younger viewers who were less interested in straight politics and hard news. It was important to find the right presenter, and research had been commissioned to indicate which were most popular with the audience. Michael Buerk and Dando topped the list. The *Daily Telegraph* wrote: 'Jill Dando, who counts Sir John Birt, the BBC's director-general, as one of her greatest admirers, is expected to take over from Martyn Lewis as the face of the *Six O'Clock News*.' The *Guardian* agreed: 'Bright, blonde and – crucially – viewer-friendly . . . she is seen as right for the £400,000-a-year job.'

But this was stirring up a hornets' nest. For one thing the BBC's main news presenters, including such figures as Michael

Buerk, Anna Ford, Peter Sissons and Edward Stourton, were being held in contractual limbo pending the completion of the news review. Since no one knew exactly what format the programmes would have, let alone who would be fronting them, it was impossible to pin down terms for contracts. Instead, as a temporary arrangement, presenters were being offered a form of words which did not specify when they would do their newsreading, or even on what channel. Naturally this was causing dissatisfaction and as the speculation about the future became more public, so the presenters grew more unhappy. Several of them broke cover to complain, among them Anna Ford, who objected to press suggestions that she was thought 'snooty', and Peter Sissons, who complained of a 'beauty contest'. They blamed the corporation for allowing this undignified state of affairs to come about. 'We are part of the BBC's assets,' said Sissons. 'People don't just turn to the BBC, they also turn to its presenters. But its managers have been undermining our stature by giving the impression that we are dispensable. I think they have shot themselves in the foot.' While the corporation publicly expressed sympathy this plainly did not run very deep. 'I can understand it is frustrating and unsettling,' said a spokesman, 'but it is the trade-off for their high wages . . . Insecurity is the price they pay.' In truth the feelings of the existing presenters were low on the list of priorities. At the highest levels in the BBC the future of the *Six* was arousing strong feelings; some believed it would be an important indicator for the direction of BBC television as a whole.

One of the biggest changes brought about by John Birt after he first arrived as deputy director-general in the late 1980s was to merge the news department with the current affairs department. This may seem a minor structural matter but Birt saw it as strategic. The entity that emerged, which also swallowed up radio news, was called News and Current Affairs, or NCA, and it was given a new status so that the NCA chief became a big player in the corporation. Birt's intention was that news and journalism should be better placed to make their presence felt (something which did not necessarily enamour him to his journalists, who were suspicious of the sort of news he seemed to want). One early internal test of Birt's vision came in 1988 with a dispute over the start time for *Newsnight*. Until then the programme had drifted somewhat in the BBC2 schedule, beginning anywhere between 10.30 p.m. and 11 p.m. Birt thought this unsatisfactory and demanded a fixed start at 10.30 p.m., which other television bosses resisted. That he got his way was a sign both of his own growing power and of the new primacy of NCA.

For most of the following ten years NCA enjoyed a good run, benefiting from its senior status in terms of resources and power, but by the late 1990s things were beginning to change. The Birt years were clearly coming to an end, which meant that thoughts were turning both to the future shape of the corporation after he left and to who might succeed him. Among the contenders for the job were Tony Hall, the NCA chief, and Alan Yentob, overall head of BBC television. That Hall was in the running clearly put his department's record at the centre of the debate and many outside NCA believed it had simply lost the plot. As the establishment of the review of news showed, there were signs that the audience's taste had changed and the BBC had been left behind. Resentful programme-makers and schedulers in other departments argued that NCA was letting the side down, that their own efforts to capture viewers with comedies, dramas and consumer programmes were being undermined by dour news bulletins which simply caused people to switch channels. Inside NCA this was hotly disputed – news viewing on ITV was also in decline, it was said, so it was not just a matter of the BBC's style. They fell back, too, on Birt's old argument that while the BBC's primacy in news might not be a ratings winner on its own it was a mark of excellence which raised the standing of everything else broadcast on the two channels. And they interpreted the whole affair in terms of power politics: as the Birt era closed, the enemies of NCA were trying to put the department back in the lowly position it had occupied before he came along.

The review of news output, and ultimately the career of Jill Dando, fell into this field of battle. On 5 October the conclusions of the review were made public and they were like a cold shower for NCA. Viewers under thirty-five tended not to watch news because they did not understand it, they did not feel it was relevant to their interests and they were put off by its didactic style and its forbidding presentation. Words such as 'back-bencher', which were routinely used in the bulletins, meant nothing at all to many in the audience, while stories about international economic developments or big business might as well have been in Greek. Instead there was a strong interest in regional news, which had long been a poor relation, and in greater diversity of subject matter. Questions of public policy should no longer dominate. The review not only recommended changes of substance but also, as the rumours had long indicated, of presentation. 'We need an inviting style,' it said. 'We need a more thoughtful use of pictures and sound, warmer studio sets on television and an emphasis on consistent, familiar presenters with journalistic credibility.' The *Six* would be transformed first to give it that 'warmer' feel. It would have fewer correspondents, a cosier, more informal tone and an agenda more geared to the viewers' interests and concerns. As to the presenters there would be one rather than two, but who that might be was not specified. Press speculation, however, continued to point to Dando.

To some in the corporation the arguments in favour of giving this important job to Jill Dando were overwhelming. The viewers loved her and she was now an important part of the BBC1 brand. On screen she combined qualities of trustworthiness and integrity with a homeliness and accessibility which seemed to be just what the review demanded. And she was highly experienced – despite all the *Holiday* programmes and other commitments, she had been reading news bulletins on BBC1 on a regular basis

for a decade. A nightly 6 p.m. bulletin presented regularly by
Dando, striking a friendlier note and dealing with news in a more
appealing way, might well attract viewers to the channel. This
view was held right at the top of the organization: Peter Salmon,
controller of BBC 1, Alan Yentob and John Birt all liked the
idea. In the previous couple of years, in fact, these senior figures
had come to see in Dando something they had not noticed before.
She was not just a good presenter; she was a very important asset,
a powerful link to the audience; it was no accident that she had
begun to appear at executive and corporate events and that her
picture figured so frequently on corporate documents it was as if
she was a walking, talking BBC 1 logo. And into the bargain, as
they got to know her these senior figures inevitably learned to
like her personally. Now, they felt, they had in the new *Six* the
perfect vehicle for her talents.

   She felt the same way. This opportunity was coming along at
the perfect moment – the new format was to be launched early
in 1999, just as her commitments with *Holiday* ended – and it
had just the right profile and content. And while it would not be
a prime time chat show it promised to test her in new ways.
Since she had joined the *Six* in 1994 she had always taken the
supporting role in presentation, and she was tired of this. 'As a
second presenter I don't do interviews, which I don't resent, but
I'd sometimes like more of a challenge,' she had said. As anchor
on the new *Six* she would have ample opportunity to show her
abilities and talent. The new agenda, too, would suit her well.
She had suggested publicly in the past that 'news sometimes
neglects the human side of life', and this would be her opportunity
to help correct that failing. As for the lifestyle, it would certainly
be taxing to present the programme five nights a week, but not
nearly as taxing as *Holiday*. She would have a life, in London,
with Alan. One of the people she discussed this with was Bob
Wheaton, who had by now left the BBC to set up a company
of his own, but who was in touch with developments. The two
were still in frequent contact, and she left him in no doubt about

her hopes. 'She had decided to concentrate on news . . . She had taken a decision that that would be the mainspring of her life. It provided her with a way of coming home.'

She knew, however, that the job was not yet hers – far from it. From the moment her name had first been linked with it there had been signs that some thought her unsuitable. A quote from the *Express*, attributed to a BBC 'traditionalist', was typical: 'Jill Dando is very pleasant and well-spoken, but John Humphrys she ain't.' The review, people in NCA pointed out, had explicitly called for the *Six* to have presenters 'with journalistic credibility', and this was something they thought Dando lacked. Viewers might trust her, but even by her own admission she was not an authority figure, not somebody who could put Cabinet ministers on their mettle or infuse an important news item with gravitas. That, it was said, was why she had always been the second presenter on the old *Six*. If the BBC yielded to the pressure to have her as the new anchor it would be devaluing its own news output, giving in to a populist version of journalism and, in a phrase, 'dumbing down'. In terms of internal BBC politics this would be a strategic setback for NCA and a retreat from the notion that news excellence was at the heart of the corporation's public standing. Although not everyone in NCA took quite such an apocalyptic view, and although Dando herself was a very popular and long-standing NCA employee, the opposition to her was strong, and it went to the top. It was widely reported that Tony Hall did not want her to get the job, putting him at odds with Salmon and Yentob.

Dando herself, though she stood back from the argument, had strong views. She had long believed that NCA was infected by intellectual snobbery and she thought this was playing a part in the opposition to her appointment. Unlike, say, Jeremy Paxman or Sue Lawley or Kirsty Wark, she was not a graduate and as a result she felt she was viewed differently inside the organization. Like many people in such a position she was defensive; she argued that her own experience was no less valid. In 1992, when she

was still working on *Breakfast News*, she had questioned the
supremacy of the Oxbridge degree. 'I think experience of life is
more important,' she said. 'Those weddings and jumble sales you
cover as a trainee reporter can teach you more about people, but
there's an element of intellectual snobbery at the BBC which I
sometimes find difficult to overcome. It really annoys me.' Two
years later she complained that BBC news editors were obsessed
with heavyweight politics. 'A good human interest story can
come in but they want to concentrate on Moscow or the peace
process because they're Oxbridge, brought up with PPE.
There's nothing necessarily wrong with that, but I think there's a
certain amount of blinkered-ness.' This view was clearly strongly
held. A few years later, asked to name her pet hates, she gave
two: mobile phones in quiet areas and intellectual snobbery.
Unlike the Oxbridge types, she was saying, I speak directly to
people. Now in 1998 she and her supporters felt that her time
had come. She was professionally more than capable of carrying
the *Six*, just as she had once carried *Breakfast News*, and as an
ordinary, middle-brow person she was better equipped to make
it reach the necessary audience.

The dispute continued for two months, with the arguments
finely balanced and the public language growing steadily more
unpleasant. The *Mail* liked her – 'a friendly face with a down-to-
earth and classless style' – but her critics had the ear of the
*Guardian*, which quoted an insider as saying: 'Whoever presents
the *Six O'Clock News* will ultimately be the choice of Tony Hall.
And it isn't going to be Jill Dando.' Peter Sissons was quoted as
saying that the BBC seemed to be obsessed with blondes. 'If
you're a brunette, you'd have to do something about it,' he said,
as news presenters were seen as mere 'fashion goods' in a market
where looks were more important than brains. But it was only
when her name began to appear in lists of blondes alongside
Ulrika Jonsson, Gaby Roslin and Denise van Outen that Dando
felt obliged to speak out herself. She was a qualified journalist
with nineteen years' unbroken service in the news world and it

was simply unfair to place her in this company. 'Just because I'm blonde and haven't been to Bosnia,' she declared, 'doesn't mean I'm a bimbo.' The whole affair, she could see, was beginning to damage her in a completely unforeseen fashion. She was proud to be a journalist and had always taken enormous care to protect her standing and to keep her distance from the growing army of frothy young women presenters. Yes, she did the *Holiday* programme and yes she wore summer clothes on it and giggled, but she believed that she had always ensured her behaviour was compatible with newsreading.

In mid-December, after returning from a *Holiday* assignment in Australia, she met the NCA management to talk about this and find out whether she was still in the running. When she was told that, though the final decision had not been taken, she was unlikely to get the job, she was not so much disappointed as furious. Tony Hall had a perfect right to give it to someone else, she felt, but the corporation should not have allowed her to be humiliated in the course of its internal battles. First she had been presented as a shoo-in and then, while the outcome hung in the balance, she had been portrayed as empty-headed and journalistically incapable. All for nothing. Deciding that she had had enough, she served notice that she would leave NCA at the end of her current contract and stop reading the news altogether. An agreed statement put the best gloss on it for both sides.

Dando, it said, had decided she no longer wished to be considered for the anchor role. 'I am relieved to put an end to the incessant speculation surrounding my involvement with the *Six O'Clock News*,' she was quoted as saying, and she was looking forward to new opportunities elsewhere in the BBC. Jon Roseman said it was for the best, but left no doubt that in her view the BBC had made a poor fist of things: 'She, in common with a number of other senior BBC presenters, was somewhat disenchanted with the length of time things were taking. To undertake such a significant new series via a split decision would not be a great career move.'

It was a big setback, by far the worst she had known in her professional life, and she was very upset by it. Nine months earlier she had had three good strings to her bow, *Holiday*, *Crimewatch* and the news; now she had only *Crimewatch*, a show which went out once a month. If this was managing success it did not seem to be going well and for a woman constantly concerned that she was about to fall off the tightrope it was a bad time. That she came through it without great difficulty says something both about her relationship with Alan Farthing and about her own personal strength. But though she may have believed it at times, she was not looking oblivion in the face. Outside N C A, people in the B B C were falling over each other for a piece of her, and all the way to the top, to John Birt, there was a determination not to lose her but to find the right new programmes for her to present. There was no shortage of work on offer; it was still just a matter of finding the right show.

Early in January 1999, while they were spending a weekend together in a country house hotel in Sussex, Alan proposed and she said yes. They bought a ring together at Asprey's but for the moment told only immediate family and their closest friends, who were sworn to secrecy. The announcement was held back for a party they had already arranged for the end of the month at the Pier restaurant in Chiswick. Sir Cliff Richard, Anna Ford, Gloria Hunniford, Nick Ross and Michael Buerk were among the guests, as were Jack Dando, Jill's cousin Judith and various of her aunts and uncles. Alan Farthing's family were there too, and a number of his friends and medical colleagues. Despite the secrecy, few of them can have been very surprised when the happy couple broke the news. The wedding was to be in September and there was planning to be done, no easy matter when Jill was still on the road a good deal for her final round of *Holiday* programmes. This would be a celebrity event, and the couple soon contracted for the photographs to appear in *OK!* magazine, for a reported fee of £200,000. There would be a dress, to be designed by Lindka Cierach, and much more. There were other arrangements to be made, too: significantly, they were to share a home. In fact Jill had been spending more and more of her time at Alan's house in Chiswick over the previous few months, but now they were to be married they had decided that they would both sell their existing properties and buy another, bigger house together in west London.

Her final series of *Holiday* was no less demanding than all the others, taking her to Zimbabwe, Vancouver, Turkey, Scotland, Cannes, Venice, Mustique, Alaska, Sydney, Tunisia, Piedmont, Cheshire, Crete, Malaysia, California, Ibiza, the Bahamas, Capri and Rio. Once again it was every continent bar Antarctica: nineteen destinations, nine of them long haul. And as a parting treat she was allowed to do the report she had wanted to present ever since she joined the programme – Weston-super-Mare. This was a nostalgic trip involving an endless chain of encounters on the street with old friends, and the result was an affectionate portrait that showed the place at its best without quite suggesting that it was Britain's answer to St Tropez – she admitted, for example, that the sea at Weston was never, ever blue. In fact, though she still loved her hometown she shared the dismay of many who lived there at the changes overtaking it. A couple of years earlier she had made these feelings plain in an introduction she wrote to a book of historic photographs of Weston. Much of the town, she said, bore little resemblance to the place where she had grown up. 'The green, open playgrounds of my child-hood in Worle have fallen prey to the apparently ever-growing need for more housing.' The Rozel bandstand on the seafront, once a favourite place of hers, had also vanished, to be replaced by a café of which she plainly disapproved. The family-run shops, too, were dwindling in number. This was, she concluded equivocally, 'a town that time has changed, for better or for worse'.

She too was changing again in these early months of 1999. Love, marriage, a new home and the possibility of children – all these altered her priorities. At work, besides winding up her *Holiday* commitments, she was engaged in several fresh projects. She was preparing a programme on royal weddings, to be broadcast around the time of the marriage that summer of Prince Edward and Sophie Rhys-Jones. She had been booked to compère the television Bafta awards in early May, alongside Michael Parkinson. There were also plans for a programme about infant heart surgery, in which she had an obvious interest, and she was still discussing her long-term future and the various possibilities for a big new show. In the short term, however, her principal commitment was a series called *Antiques Inspectors*, to be broadcast from late April. Previously presented by Carol Vorderman, this was a spin-off from the *Antiques Roadshow* which was dedicated to finding neglected treasures in the nation's attics and garages and to showing off the unsung glories of small local museums and collections. Like the *Roadshow* it toured the country and employed specialist expertise, and Dando's role was, in the words of *Radio Times*, as 'chauffeuse-cum-presenter-cum-travelogue link woman'. By way of a gimmick she drove from place to place in a silver Aston Martin DB6 that was itself something of an antique and was the badge of the show. *Inspectors* was not her big new thing but it suited her and it would have a good slot in the schedule, at 6.45 p.m. on Sundays.

For the new series, moreover, she needed a new look, since neither her *Holiday* nor her *Crimewatch* wardrobes would do, and she took advice from a fashion journalist, Hilary Alexander. The result was another minor reinvention of Jill Dando, more modern and much more eye-catching than before. Here were spike heels and tight leather trousers, satins and pinstripes, Betty Jackson and Paul Costelloe. In the words of Alexander, she had 'slipped the reins just a little' and was showing her sense of fun. The first series took in Glasgow, Shropshire, Mousehole, Portmeirion, Sherborne, St Ives, Norwich and Dublin, so once again she was living a peripatetic existence, albeit much closer to home. It was a busy spring.

# 8. A Terrible Thing

*'Today,' she told Alan, 'I'm going to be a lady who lunches.'*

Her last *Holiday* programme was broadcast on 13 April 1999, the series ending with Dando in Rio de Janeiro (although of course this had been recorded some weeks before), and twelve days later, on 25 April, the first *Antiques Inspectors* was to be screened. Between the two dates she gave some interviews. To the *Daily Mirror* she confirmed that this was a watershed year in both her private and her professional lives. 'In Alan,' she said, 'I have met the perfect partner. He is the right person, and that has never happened before.' As for work, she assured the paper that though she had left *Holiday* and resigned from newsreading she was not retiring. 'I gave up those programmes to do other things . . . There's life in the old dog yet.' To *Hello!* she talked at length about her life, the childhood heart operation, her protective parents, her mother's death and her unhappy arrival in London – 'I was pushed into the limelight before I was ready for it,' she declared. She spoke, too, of her feelings of inferiority in the company of big-name correspondents and of her struggle to assert herself. 'Some might say that my non-aggression is a quality that a lot of people don't have in this business. All the same, I do wish I could occasionally put my point across a bit more forcefully . . .' Typically, these remarks are both contradictory and expressive: on the one hand she suggests that many viewers would be more comfortable with news presenters who were interviewers rather than inquisitors, while on the other she acknowledges that she might be better off if she could be more aggressive. This was as close as she came to mentioning her disappointment over the *Six* and to a degree at least she was blaming her own deference and timidity. But she was not one to dwell on a setback: winding up with some warm thoughts about Alan Farthing and their wedding plans, she professed herself happy and successful far beyond the expectations of her youth. 'I guess at the moment,' she told the *Hello!* interviewer as he left her on her Gowan Avenue doorstep, 'I don't have a care in the world.'

On Tuesday 20 April she woke to find her picture all over the tabloids. The new edition of *Radio Times* was coming out and the papers had jumped on the cover picture. There she stood, all black leather, zips and heels, with her arms folded defiantly across her chest, a mischievous smile on her face and the Aston Martin growling behind her, its headlights on. The *Mirror*, for one, gave it a whole page. 'Stunning looks, lovely body, heavenly to be with,' it said. 'Are we talking Aston Martin or Jill Dando? Well both actually. This is TV good-girl Jill as you have never seen her before . . .' It was just the sort of publicity that *Radio Times* and the producers of *Antiques Inspectors* wanted – an excellent send-off for the series. That same evening Dando co-presented *Crimewatch UK*, which included an important appeal for help in finding the man responsible for the Brixton nail bomb. Nick Ross would later say she was 'so happy' during rehearsals and that her performance was 'electrically good'. On the Wednesday she flew to Dublin to film for the antiques programme. She was there with the show's resident experts, Hilary Kay and Lars Tharp, and it being Dublin and this being the last in the series they had a merry time – Kay and Tharp would both later recall a great deal of joking and laughter. On Friday night, when she had finished in Ireland, she returned home, and by now 'home' meant Alan Farthing's house in Chiswick, for she had been living with Alan pretty well full-time since the New Year. As often as he could when she flew in from assignments abroad Alan now met her at the airport, but this time it wasn't possible. Instead he rushed home to be there ahead of her and began preparing dinner; they spent the evening together. In the middle of the night, however, he was called out when one of his patients went into labour, so on Saturday they were both tired and had a slow, lazy start. At lunchtime he went back to the hospital to check on his patient and Dando took the opportunity to visit her own house in Fulham.

Number 29 Gowan Avenue was all but sold, and it had been a quick and painless business. She had put it on the market in February with a local estate agent who discreetly showed it to a few clients and invited bids in sealed envelopes. The winner, as it happened, was a relative of her next-door neighbour at number 31, Richard Hughes. Although by April the deal was done and contracts had been exchanged, most of her belongings were still in the house so it remained her base for work. There she kept her fax machine, since she did not want it spewing out all her business papers in Alan's house while she was away on location. And there she kept her work clothes – the sharp new wardrobe for the antiques series, the suits she wore on *Crimewatch* and her dresses for evening wear. So that Saturday afternoon, 24 April, she drove the three or four miles down to Fulham to catch up with her mail, phone messages and faxes and to sort out clothes for the dry cleaners.

The house was relatively private – the hedge at the front was five feet high and there was a small tree as well, while the ground-floor windows had net curtains. Perhaps this screen was there by design; she had been doorstepped by reporters here more than once and a stalker had called too, although she was not at home at the time. The property itself had gained nicely in value: having bought for £265,000 in 1995 she was now selling for about £350,000. She kept it very neat and cosy, the decoration fresh and smart and the style neither modern nor old-fashioned. Downstairs the two main rooms had been knocked through to make a living and dining room combined. She liked rosewood furniture and had a few antique items, although nothing particularly valuable, while her bookshelves and cupboards were of the built-in variety, painted white with brass fittings. Here she displayed her awards, her collection of theatre programmes, some of her travel books and the guitar bought with Green Shield Stamps way back when she was thirteen. The kitchen and bathroom were functional and low-maintenance while the main bedroom upstairs showed the same comfortable, conservative mixture of styles – built-in wardrobes, an antique mirror above the mantelpiece and a big brass bed. She had once been photographed for *OK!* lying on the bed in a kimono, curled up beside her teddy bear, holding open a book and smiling at the camera. On the wall above the bedhead hung a set of small, matching frames containing pressed flowers.

That Saturday afternoon she arrived at the house at 2.02 p.m. – the details of the visit were retained in the domestic alarm system and subsequently extracted by the police – and busied herself about a variety of little jobs. As she checked her fax machine she noticed that the ink cartridge was running low and paper was in short supply – she would have to restock. She also picked up a dress to wear at a formal event she was attending that evening. Then at 3.34 p.m. she let herself out and returned to Chiswick. The evening engagement was a mixture of work and play: with Alastair Stewart she played host at a ball in the Natural History Museum to raise funds for the Royal British Legion. With her at the top table was Alan, and also Lord Archer, who was then in the running to be the Conservative candidate for mayor of London. One of Archer's party tricks, mastered in his years attending Tory functions around the country and subsequently much in demand, was the charity auction: through a combination of hectoring and humour he had the knack of milking a well-disposed audience for the largest possible sums of money. On this occasion he performed with his usual aplomb. One of the items to be sold was a dance with Jill Dando and he persuaded someone to pay £400 for the privilege. She also danced with Archer himself, and of course with Alan.

Sunday was a quiet day. She was nervous about *Antiques Inspectors*. She had given it the biggest push she could on the cover of the *Radio Times*, but would it make a difference? Could she still attract the viewers? Was the show right for her? And was she right for it? In the morning Alan played a round of golf with a friend at his club in Buckinghamshire and afterwards Jill joined them for lunch followed by a drink at the friend's house. They were back in Chiswick by 6.35 p.m. and watched the programme together. This first show was set in and around the town of Ironbridge in Shropshire and the 'find' of the week was a collection of Coalport china. The experts performed well, the car looked good and she kept up the momentum and the mood of enthusiasm efficiently and stylishly. Everything seemed fine, which was a relief. Afterwards Dando took a few calls of congratulation, one of them from Alan's parents in Dorset, who had become very fond of their daughter-in-law to be. Later, she and Alan sat down to talk about the wedding plans. The date was set for 25 September, exactly five months off, and although they had considered a West Country venue they had decided in the end to marry in London, at a church in Putney. They talked about the guest list and the invitations and together they drafted a letter about their requirements to Claridge's, where the reception was to be held. Then they went to bed.

On the morning of Monday 26 April, therefore, Jill Dando awoke a happy woman. At work things were looking good; after the setback with the *Six* she was now getting back on course. The new show was up and running, work was under way on the royal weddings special and there were several other ideas in the pipeline. In a couple of weeks she would co-present the Baftas, which was a feather in her cap, and she was in line to front the BBC's Millennium Day coverage. Yes, things were definitely looking up. As for her personal life, it was just about perfect. Her friends had been telling her for months that she was like a lovestruck teenager, alternately giddy and soppy about Alan. When she was not with him, even when she was abroad, she was constantly phoning him, sending him faxes or at the very least talking about him. And he, too, phoned and faxed her, exchanging jokes, drawings and messages of love. It was a very good feeling and things were only getting better. Soon they would have a new home together – they had made an offer on a house in Maida Vale – and then there would be the wedding and after that, they both hoped, a baby.

The alarm went off at 6.45 a.m. because Alan had an early consultation at the hospital. Dando, for her part, had no reason to get up then. In fact, after several frantic months of travel for both *Holiday* and the antiques programme, she was beginning her first sustained spell in London – a fortnight – and that day was that rarest of things, a weekday without commitments. She wanted to make breakfast but Alan told her to stay where she was; she should relax for once. By the time he had showered and dressed, however, his breakfast was waiting for him on a tray on the bed; she had dutifully hopped back in. They chatted while he ate, then at 7.25 he set off and she was left to contemplate the day. Such days were useful for catching up with the chores, but she also meant to treat herself. She had arranged to see an old friend from breakfast television days, Anastasia Cooke, and they were to attend a charity lunch and fashion show at the Lanesborough Hotel. 'Today,' she had told Alan as he left, 'I'm going to be a lady who lunches.' Both of them hoped that in her new life there would be many more days like this.

At about 8 a.m. she spoke on the phone to Alan's mother Barbara, picking up where they had left off the night before. They discussed plans for the wedding – the first fitting for the dress was due the following day – and also talked about a birthday party for Alan's father, who was soon to turn sixty-five. After that she got up, had breakfast, pottered about for a while and then began preparing to go out. At 9.50 a.m. Jenny Higham called and they chatted, Dando trying but failing to persuade her to come along to the fashion show too. Higham said later: 'She was completely bog-standard normal. She'd had a great weekend and was really happy.' After that conversation Dando made one last call from the phone in the house – to a travel firm to discuss arrangements for the honeymoon – and then at about 10.10 a.m., dressed and made up to face the day, she left. She was wearing a beige raincoat over a red jacket, black trousers and ankle boots, and carrying a large black handbag of the kind that is worn slung over the shoulder. She pulled the house door shut behind her, locked it and went to her car. Using the device on her key ring, she switched off the alarm and it made a gentle 'blip' noise.

From Chiswick – Farthing's house is on a small private estate – she made her way to the Great West Road, turning east and then pulling in at a BP petrol station. A closed circuit television camera watched as she filled up the BMW. The time was now 10.20 a.m. As she paid her bill she also bought a pint of skimmed milk and before driving off she made a call on her mobile phone. Again she was making arrangements and again it was to do with Alan: his birthday was a couple of months off and she was ringing the Prince Edward Theatre to try to book tickets for the birthday night to see the show *Mamma Mia!* The call complete, she drove to Hammersmith and found a parking space in Bridge Avenue, her progress through the streets followed by a succession of cameras. As she parked she took a call from her agent – not Jon Roseman himself but Allasonne Lewis, who worked at Roseman's company and had been handling Dando's day-to-day business for some time. It was Lewis who sifted and processed the many bids for Dando's time, and once dates were fixed it was Lewis who arranged the details. The two were in frequent contact when Dando was in London – and often, too, when she was abroad – sometimes talking half a dozen times in a day. They also kept in touch through the fax in Gowan Avenue, to which Lewis would send letters, contracts, scripts, newspaper articles and so forth. That morning, however, Lewis was aware that there was something wrong with the machine because some of her faxes had not got through. Dando said she was on the case; she was on her way to buy ink and paper and would sort it all out by lunchtime. There was other shopping to be done, too, and she would do it at the same time.

From Bridge Avenue she walked to King's Street, a busy thoroughfare, and visited a branch of Ryman's where she found the paper she wanted – 500 sheets of white A4 – but no ink cartridge. She paid and left; the till receipt was timed at 10.46 a.m. Next she went into the King's Mall shopping centre, where once again cameras followed her as she called at various shops. One set of stills, subsequently released by the police, shows her in Dixons. They are a little blurred but obviously her, and they capture this much-photographed subject in a way that is both banal and telling. The calf-length raincoat is worn open; the handbag is over the right shoulder; the boots are shiny and the buttons stand out from her jacket. As she enters the shop, her eyes scanning the shelves, she transfers her Ryman's bag from right hand to left and pushes her right hand into her pocket. Then, turning to examine the display of cartridges, she shows her profile: a slender neck, a strong jawline, neatly glossed lips, hair whitened by the neon light. The face is at rest, without any trace of stress or worry but also without the familiar smile.

She didn't find the cartridge and after ten minutes or so she made her way back to the car. There was another job to be done before she called in at Gowan Avenue. Weaving her way through the one-way system using short cuts and back streets she knew well, Dando made her way to Fulham Palace Road and headed south. Near the junction with Lillie Road she was spotted in stationary traffic by another driver, Sarah Pusey. Dando caught her eye and smiled back and Pusey quickly rang a friend on her mobile phone to report this celebrity sighting. Police were later able to fix the time of the call at 11.13 a.m. At about the same time Dando herself took a short call on her own phone from a television producer who wanted to talk about the royal weddings documentary. Soon the traffic was moving again and she reached the bottom of Fulham Palace Road, where she turned left into Fulham Road and began looking for somewhere to park. She tried Dancer Road but had no luck and then found a space in the lower stretch of Munster Road, just south of the lights. From there she walked the short distance to Cope's fish shop, arriving at about 11.20 a.m., and bought two Dover sole to eat with Alan that evening. The staff in Cope's recalled later that she seemed perfectly happy, if a little worried about getting a parking ticket. She was still in the shop when her mobile phone rang again: it was the Prince Edward Theatre confirming her booking, and she was delighted. That call, the last she ever received, was timed at 11.23 a.m. Quickly now she made her way back to the BMW and drove north up Munster Road, crossing Fulham Road at the lights and continuing for about 400 yards until she reached the seventh turning on the left, opposite the school: Gowan Avenue. Number 29 was a little way along on the left and by good fortune she found a vacant parking space right in front of it. What was in her mind at this moment? She was a practical woman with the habit of planning and arranging things so she was probably juggling her movements for the day. The Lanesborough event began in an hour; how would she get there and back? Would she have another chance that day to look for the ink cartridge? If she found it she could install it at the house later, when she returned to pick up the milk and fish from the fridge. She opened her car door and stepped out, then leaned back in to extract her handbag and a Russell and Bromley bag, in which she had put some odds and ends to deliver to the house, plus the fish and the milk. Standing up straight she swung the door shut, perhaps with her elbow or knee since her hands were full, and activated the alarm, setting off that 'blip' sound again. Then she walked around the car to the pavement and across the pavement towards the house. In all likelihood as she did this she was fumbling in her handbag for her house keys, which she kept on a separate ring from the car key. Whether the little wrought-iron gate was open or shut when she reached it we do not know, but we do know that after she went through it she was confronted by a man and she let out a cry. The man put a gun to her head and pulled the trigger.

The time cannot be established with certainty but it was

probably in the minute or so after 11.30 a.m., which was thought to be the earliest time that she could have reached Gowan Avenue after her visit to the fishmonger's. Between 11.31 and 11.32 a.m. someone tried to call her on her mobile phone and there was no answer. It is possible that she failed to respond for some innocuous reason but it is also possible that by that time she had been shot. The very latest time at which the shooting could have occurred, the police would come to believe, was 11.35 a.m.

As the gunman fled, leaving Dando sprawled across her doorstep, calm descended. Everything became still in that little patch of ground and time began to pass. Gowan Avenue is not a particularly quiet street and several drivers and pedestrians passed the gate, but the hedge and tree which in the past had given Dando privacy now shielded her from view, as did the waist-high side wall. Only someone looking in directly at the gate would see her on the ground. Minutes ticked by. It was now after 11.40 a.m. and Jill Dando's famous charm was about to pay one last little dividend. Helen Doble, who lived in a neighbouring street, was making her way along Gowan Avenue intending to visit a shop on Munster Road to use the photocopier there. She knew Dando; she often passed number 29 and had encountered the television presenter on the street several times. 'She was always very friendly,' Doble would say later. 'Whenever we saw each other we would have a good chat.' When she spotted the blue BMW in the street it occurred to Doble that Dando might be paying one of her increasingly rare visits to number 29 and so it was that, as she drew level with the house, thinking that she might catch the television star going in or coming out and that they might have another of those chats, Doble glanced towards the door.

'With one step everything changed,' she would say later. Slowly she took in the scene: the body, in coat, red jacket and black trousers, crumpled on the ground; the head, with its familiar mop of blonde hair, propped up awkwardly against the door and wall, and a vivid splash of blood across the white paint. Doble knew instantly that it was Dando and felt very strongly that she was dead. Stunned, she turned to look up and down the road for help but there was no one to be seen. She remembered that she was carrying a mobile phone, got it out, dialled 999 and asked for an ambulance to be sent to 29 Gowan Avenue. She said it was for Jill Dando, who had been stabbed and appeared to be dead. Don't move anything, she was told; help is on its way. The time was 11.43 a.m. Dando had probably been lying there for ten minutes.

The interval between calling an ambulance in an emergency and its arrival at the scene, even if it is actually brief, often seems painfully long to the caller. So it was for Helen Doble. She was alone on the pavement, looking at the body, waiting. She wanted somebody there with her, and not just anybody. 'I needed to know that a friend whom I trusted could be with me and say: "Yes, this is actually happening." Because it was broad daylight in a normal street.' An idea came and she ran to a nearby house and fetched someone. This friend took one look at Dando and ran to another house on the street, number 21, which was a doctor's surgery. The doctor was not in but the receptionist came. Now there were three of them at the gate but they still did not go in; the ambulance service had rung back on Doble's phone to repeat the advice not to move anything. Their voices brought Richard Hughes to his door and, discovering what had happened, he was horrified, distraught. Still the minutes were creeping by. At 11.53 a.m. a police car arrived at speed and two officers leapt out, one of them immediately opening the gate and approaching Dando. He felt for a pulse in the neck and, finding none, was about to attempt resuscitation when an ambulance arrived. Now in a flurry of energy and activity the paramedics took charge, quickly moving Dando out from the doorway, laying her flat and cutting away some of her clothing. As they set to work a second ambulance brought more help and then a doctor arrived by helicopter – it landed in the playground of the primary school on Munster Road. At about 12.20 p.m., after a frantic half-hour, the decision was made to move Dando to Charing Cross Hospital and she was loaded into an ambulance and driven, arriving at 12.30. There a trauma team of six people struggled for a further half an hour, but in vain. At 1.05, roughly ninety minutes after the shot was fired, Jill Dando was certified dead.

In that confusing, panicky moment after she walked through her front gate a single bullet had interrupted for ever a domestic chore, a day of leisure, a career, a romance, a life. She would never make it to lunch at the Lanesborough. She would never cook the Dover sole for Alan. She would never have that fitting for the wedding dress. She would never host the Bafta awards or the millennium show, or even see the new millennium at all. She would never find that new television series which would be just the right vehicle for her. She would never marry, move into a new home, have babies, become a grandmother. She would never write another pink letter to her elderly friend in Weston. Between the car and the door the whole complex of talents, experiences, habits and emotions that made up the person called Jill Dando had ceased to be.

Detective Chief Inspector Hamish Campbell was working in his office in a bunker-like building next to the big police station on Earl's Court Road that day when a colleague put his head round the door to say a woman had been found stabbed in Fulham. Campbell was the senior officer on call that day so the case was his. He was already in a car heading towards the scene when the message came through that the victim was believed to be Jill Dando. Campbell knew her slightly; they had met when he appeared on *Crimewatch UK* to make appeals in relation to past inquiries. He was shocked. Reaching Gowan Avenue just as the ambulance pulled away to take Dando to hospital, Campbell found the usual scene-of-crime ('soc') procedures already in full swing. The road had been closed and the stretch nearest to number 29 was sealed off with blue-and-white police 'do not cross' tape. Uniformed officers were arriving by the vanload to be sent off to begin street searches and to knock on doors, while closer to the house forensic specialists in their white space-suits were soon taking the first steps in their own meticulous examinations in front of the house. Scaffolding was delivered and erected early in the afternoon and tarpaulins were stretched over the whole house-front, garden and pavement, even reaching out to cover her car. Overhead a police helicopter circled noisily. The witnesses at the scene, meanwhile, were being interviewed and two in particular stood out – the residents of numbers 30 and 31. They had seen the killer.

Richard Hughes from number 31 worked at home and had been sitting at his desk on the first floor at 11.30 that morning. He remembered hearing the blip of the BMW alarm and recognizing it as Dando's car. Besides being famous, she was a friendly neighbour and they got on well – it was she who had tipped him off that the house was coming on the market, enabling him to alert his relatives to the opportunity. On this morning he had registered the fact that she was paying a visit and nothing more when, some moments later, he heard a woman's cry. 'It was a very distinctive scream: she sounded quite surprised,' he said. He went to the window, parted the blinds and looked out. He could not see the doorstep of number 29 but he had a clear view of the gate and there was a man there, apparently turning away from the house and heading west. This man was white, well-dressed and clean-shaven with black hair and a solid build. He was wearing a dark waxed jacket, like a Barbour. He seemed to be holding something up in his hand at shoulder height, and Hughes believed this was a mobile phone. Because the man appeared respectable and unhurried the neighbour assumed that nothing untoward had happened – he must be a friend of Jill's, he thought – and so returned to his work. Before he did, however, he glimpsed another local man, Geoffrey Upfill-Brown, emerging from his house at number 30, across the road. Upfill-Brown was going out and he too spotted the dark man heading west on the other side of the street. 'He started off running fast but then he heard my gate click. He looked in my direction and saw me, and slowed down to a slower jog. He just didn't look right, he looked suspicious.' Upfill-Brown believed the man was wearing a baggy, thigh-length jacket or coat of some kind. Once the two neighbours had told their stories to detectives they were quickly put in cars and driven around the area just in case they spotted the man again, but it was too late. Soon it was clear that other witnesses in the street had glimpsed a dark, suited man that morning.

Confirmation that the victim was dead came through just after 1 p.m., but the body had still to be formally identified and that responsibility fell to Alan Farthing. Farthing had first heard that something was wrong while he was conducting a clinic at St Mary's Hospital; a pager message came through from Jon Roseman asking him to call urgently. When Roseman told him there were reports that Jill had been attacked Farthing could not imagine that anything serious had happened, but he called Fulham police station just in case and was told that somebody from Kensington station would phone him back as soon as possible. He knew immediately from the Fulham officer's formal tone that there really was something wrong. Minutes later he was asked to go down to the hospital's casualty department where a policeman was waiting to speak to him – it turned out to be a senior officer he had met socially through Jill. There, standing in the casualty corridor, Farthing learned that a woman answering Jill's description had been attacked outside 29 Gowan Avenue and had subsequently died. They could not be absolutely certain it was her, the officer explained, until someone who knew her personally identified the body.

Clinging to the hope that there had been some mistake, Farthing made the long lunchtime journey from Paddington to Charing Cross Hospital in the back of a police car. On the way he spoke by phone to Nigel Dando in Bristol, who told him about the television news reports and said he was about to leave for Weston to speak to his father. Both men must have known in their hearts that in this case of all cases identification was almost certainly a formality, for while they knew Jill the person better than anyone in the world, her face was such a familiar feature of British life it was scarcely imaginable that a mistake could have been made. For the moment, however, Farthing could not give up hope. The press were already waiting at the hospital's main entrance so he was taken to a side gate, where there was an uncomfortable delay while keys were fetched to let them in. Later he described what happened next.

'They took me down what seemed like the longest corridor in the world to the casualty department and to a side room where Jill was lying. She had a towel wrapped around her head as if she had just got out of the bath, though it was not covering all her hair. I could see it was Jill's hair. She had a wound in the back of her head that wasn't obviously visible to me. Her face was unaffected. She had drip marks in her arm where resuscitation had been attempted and a bit of blood on her teeth where a tube had obviously been inserted to try to ventilate her. She was lying in a hospital gown, looking peaceful. I held her hand, which was still warm, and confirmed to the officer it was Jill.' Farthing spoke to the consultant in charge, Hugh Millington, who explained to him, as one medical man to another, that while they had tried everything they could it had been hopeless from the start. She had not been clinically alive on arrival.

Hamish Campbell had been waiting for word that the next of kin had been informed and the body formally identified; he now went public with his witness information. While a colleague briefed print reporters he himself went on television a little after 2.30 p.m.: 'The information at this time is not very clear,' he said, 'but what we do know is that between quarter to twelve and twelve o'clock today the body of Jill Dando was found outside her home address at 29 Gowan Avenue. Two witnesses have said they saw a white male running from number 29 west in Gowan Avenue and at the moment my appeal is to anybody who saw that man to come forward to us. He was a white man, between late thirties and forties, five foot eleven with black hair. He was described as well groomed and one person described him as wearing a suit and he was carrying a mobile phone. That is the only person who was seen acting suspiciously outside number 29 and he ran away from that location.' Campbell gave an emergency phone number and then spoke of his personal sadness at the murder: it was, he said, 'a terrible thing indeed'.

One significant phone call had already been received. A school caretaker cycling through Bishop's Park, half a mile away, had seen a man in a blue jacket apparently climbing over the railing at the bank of the river Thames. He felt that something suspicious was going on so when he got home he phoned the police. Before long a separate team of officers was at work in the park, cordoning off and searching both among the shrubs and beds and along the muddy shore of the river. Reporters followed to monitor events and a rumour soon spread that Dando's attacker had drowned himself in the Thames.

As the afternoon wore on, the clamour for information increased. Reporters who had fragmentary information from witnesses at the scene were desperate for a fuller picture. How had Dando died? Did police suspect a stalker? What was going on in the park? Though even those who had found the body tended to believe she had been stabbed, Campbell knew – because word had come from the hospital – that she had died from a gunshot wound. But he did not share this information, telling reporters they would have to wait until after the post-mortem; the body was taken from Charing Cross Hospital to Fulham mortuary for that purpose during the afternoon. Police officers, meanwhile, asked ambulance and hospital staff not to divulge information about the injury or the murder scene. As for the motive, Campbell said simply that it was far too early to speculate. He appealed again to anyone who might know anything or might have seen anything to come forward, and in the course of the afternoon calls flooded in.

Besides work at the scene such as searches and door-to-door

inquiries, one of the most urgent priorities was to establish Dando's movements that day to find out whether anything unusual had happened, whether she had met or spent time with anyone or whether she had been followed. That involved interviewing those close to her and those with strong professional connections, something that had to be done rapidly but as sensitively as possible – these people had just heard the news of her death and some were in shock. It was quickly established – the Ryman's bag and receipt were at the scene – that she had been shopping in Hammersmith, and officers were soon there interviewing people and impounding security video tapes. Street cameras along her route from there were located and further CCTV tapes taken, while a number of the people who called in to the police on that day and the days that followed had recognized the television star as she walked or drove by. One mystery that lingered for some time was the fish; the bag was anonymous, so where had she bought it? Meanwhile forensic work at number 29 Gowan Avenue proceeded. The BMW was loaded on a lorry and driven off for closer examination; the front door and the little gate would follow. Over the coming days every inch of the death scene was searched, measured and photographed; every drop and speck of blood was examined; every scrap of potential evidence identified, catalogued and bagged. Early that evening Campbell gave a press conference which was subsequently televised. Summing up the available information, he once again appealed for help. Who was the dark, well-dressed man? Where had he gone? Had anybody seen anything else that might be suspicious? Did anybody know anything that might help? If they did, they should get in touch immediately. Operation Oxborough, as the investigation was now codenamed by the Metropolitan Police, was under way.

# 9. Running Man, Sweating Man

*'There are just so many sightings; they can't all be involved in*
*Jill's murder.'*

In the first days after the murder Hamish Campbell was in such
demand to give press conferences, briefings and interviews that
he could comfortably have devoted every hour of his working
day to them, but that would have left him no time to direct
the inquiry. Nor was such openness an option; criminal
investigations must always be essentially confidential affairs, if
only to keep the criminals themselves in the dark. Thus the
supply of information from the police side fell short of popular
demand, and perhaps inevitably many branches of the media
covered the shortfall by relying on speculation, rumour or worse,
while such facts as were known often assumed disproportionate
significance.

The suggestion that Dando might have been killed by a Serb
surfaced within a couple of hours of her death. The Nato war in
Kosovo had been in progress for more than a month and by
late April the Serb regime of Slobodan Milosevic had been
thoroughly demonized in the West, so it seemed that he or his
henchmen might be among the few who were capable of such
an act. Why might Dando be their target? The first thought was
to link the attack to a televised appeal she had made three weeks
earlier to raise funds to help the Kosovar refugees fleeing their
country in their tens of thousands. The appeal, made on behalf
of the Disasters Emergency Committee, had a powerful impact,
raising more than £6 million in a few days, and now it was
suggested that it might have turned Dando into a symbolic

1. Jill Dando in adolescence. Having been a pretty child she grew into, as she herself thought, 'rather an ugly little girl', with lasting effects for her self-confidence.

2. Contact lenses, a perm and blonde tinting: the look born when she 'reinvented herself' at sixteen saw her all the way through from sixth form to national television.

3, 4, 5, 6. Jill Dando the TV star. From the early nineties onwards she was in the public eye, on prime time and in newspapers and magazines. And always she insisted that her appeal lay in her ordinariness rather than any sex appeal. 'Men don't want to have sex with me, they just want to take me to a nice wine bar for a nice glass of wine.'

With Bob Wheaton. This was the most important relationship of her adult life, and while some colleagues thought of the BBC executive as a Svengali figure she regarded him as her 'rock'.

8. With Simon Bassil, whom she met on safari in South Africa. Their romance began as the Wheaton relationship ended, but though it made some unwelcome headlines for her it did not last. This was the period when she discovered, as she put it, 'another me'.

9. With Alan Farthing, whom she described as 'Mr So-Right'. Introduced to the London gynaecologist by a mutual friend, she very soon decided he was the love of her life. They announced their engagement three months before her death.

10. Final pictures of a much-photographed woman. Security-camera stills show Dando hunting for a printer cartridge in a branch of Dixons in Hammersmith just forty minutes before she was shot.

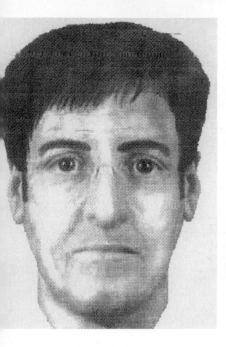

11. The police drawing of the 'sweating man' who was seen at a bus stop not far from the murder scene. Displayed on every newspaper front page, this man was often presented as 'the killer' or 'the gunman', but there were grounds to doubt his involvement.

12. The cartridge case found at the scene. Just below the rim can be seen one of the distinctive marks which suggested that the killer might have tinkered with the round. Ballistics experts had seen nothing like it before.

13. 29 Gowan Avenue after the murder. Admirers have laid their tributes against the wall, while the gate and the front door have been taken away for forensic exam-ination. The hedge and tree which helped shield Dando from view as she lay dying can be seen on the left.

## The Guardian

The return of a rebel in G2

Whatever happened to Viagra? in G2

What Notting Hill is really like in G2

...and in education the Euro quiz

Death threat peers attack police

Hitman theory after BBC Crimewatch presenter murdered with single shot last night.

# Gunman kills TV's Jill Dando

## THE EXPRESS

THE NEWSPAPER FOR THE NEW MILLENNIUM

www.express.co.uk

TUESDAY APRIL 27

TV's golden girl died from single shot in he

# WAS SHE KILLED BY A HITMAN?

## THE Sun

Jill Dan

1961-199

BOOKS FOR SCHOOLS TOKEN IS ON PAGE 14

# ASSASSINATED

## TIMES

TUESDAY APRIL 27 1999

Nato lead pounce sign of sp in Belgra

# Jill Dando killed by one bullet in the head

14. From the day of the murder the public appetite for information about the case was enormous and occasionally, when hard new facts were in short supply, speculative stories and hoaxes found their way into print.

15. Flowers at BBC Television Centre, where Dando worked from 1988 until her death. Newsroom staff wept at the news of her killing.

16. Crowds line the route of her funeral through her hometown of Weston-super-Mare. She was buried there alongside her mother.

17. Alan Farthing launches a crime-prevention charity in her memory, using the theme of 'Not for Nothing'.

18. Hamish Campbell speaks to reporters. Assigned the case by chance – he was the senior detective on call that day – for well over a year he carried a heavy burden of expectation, as both the public and his own force were impatient for the case to be cracked.

19. Barry George, also known as Barry Bulsara. The evidence seemed to point to a loner and George was certainly one of those, but did anything connect him with Dando or the murder? He was arrested and charged in the spring of 2000 and went on trial at the Old Bailey almost a year later.

target for Serb assassins. Soon another possible Serb motive was identified: on 23 April, three days before the murder, Nato bombers had struck the Belgrade television centre during the night, killing a dozen people. The Milosevic regime presented this as both an outrage against the freedom of the press and a massacre of civilians; perhaps Dando the British television star had been killed as an act of revenge. These suspicions grew when two days after the murder the story broke that Tony Hall, Director of News and Current Affairs at the BBC, had received a death threat and was under police protection. Though the details were not made public, it was true that an anonymous caller had rung Television Centre blaming Britain and in particular Tony Blair for the Belgrade deaths. 'He butchered, we butcher back,' the caller warned. 'The first one you had yesterday [evidently a reference to Dando]; the next one will be Tony Hall.' While Hall pulled out of public engagements and went into hiding with his family, security was tightened throughout the corporation and a number of other prominent figures, both on-screen and off-screen, were given protection. The following day, Thursday 29 April, brought a report on the ITV programme *Tonight with Trevor McDonald* that Dando herself had received a hostile letter after her Kosovo appeal. Someone claiming to be a Serb, it was said, had written to say that she should never have made the broadcast.

From the outset the police expressed scepticism about the Serb theory and the *Tonight* story was quickly challenged: Campbell's team confirmed that there had been a letter complaining about the appeal but said they believed it contained no threat and was not significant. But the idea of Serb involvement would not go away. Britain was effectively at war, albeit in a remote-controlled fashion, and there was both a mood of edginess and a widespread hostility towards Serbs, or at least towards the Belgrade government. Dando, moreover, had been killed in a manner that seemed to many to suggest a professional assassin or commando. And the BBC security alert was real enough; Hall was genuinely in hiding and visitors to the corporation's offices confirmed that they were being subjected to unusually close scrutiny. In the absence of any other explanation a political motive such as this seemed plausible and the headlines in the latter part of that week were dominated by talk of Serb hit-men. The *Daily Star*, in particular, backed the theory: 'Jill shot as Serbs buried TV bomb victims', it pointed out one day, and the next it reported that Israeli intelligence had warned Nato that two-man Serb teams were at large with a mission to attack 'targets of opportunity'. Echoes of this found their way into the broadsheets.

There were other speculative stories, and one concerned a woman killed in Woking in 1994. Like Dando, Karen Reed was an attractive woman in her thirties and like Dando she was shot dead on her own doorstep by someone using 9mm ammunition. What was more, Reed's sister had worked for the BBC and it had been suggested that the killer might have killed one sister in mistake for the other. On the surface there seemed to be reasons to connect the two murders but closer inspection left a different impression. Reed's murder, which occurred at night, almost certainly flowed from some criminal conflict – a close relative of hers had already been jailed for another killing. Nothing was known about Dando – so far at least – to connect her with crime in this way. Detectives on the Reed case, moreover, believed that the man responsible for the Reed murder was by 1999 in jail for another crime. If they were right he could not have killed Dando.

Another subject to fascinate reporters was that *Radio Times* cover, still on display in newsagents on the day of the murder. 'Did this picture drive a stalker to kill Jill Dando?' asked the *Mail*, and there she was again, all leather and zips, looking or trying to look dangerous. 'It emerged last night,' the paper reported, 'that she told a colleague she was worried about reaction to the picture.' The suggestion was that a man who was obsessed with her felt driven to murder by her sudden change of image. A further twist was added when someone spotted what happened when you opened up the *Radio Times* and laid it face down: on the right you had Dando in leather while on the left – the magazine's back page – was an advertisement featuring a selection of popular crime books beneath the headline, 'Couldn't you just murder?' The *Sunday Telegraph* printed the full spread and asked: 'Is this why Jill was murdered?' It reported: 'Those close to the investigation fear that, for an obsessive fan who was probably already feeling jilted over the forthcoming marriage, the *Radio Times* may have been like hearing voices telling him when to strike.'

And then there was the *Crimewatch* theory. According to this, Dando had been killed by a criminal who bore a grudge arising from the work of the programme, either someone affected by an item she had presented on the show or someone who had chosen her as the target of his revenge against *Crimewatch UK* generally. Occasional remarks she had made in interviews suggesting that she felt herself at risk seemed to support this, although from the day of the murder Nick Ross in particular strongly discouraged such speculation. A trial witness or a police informant might occasionally be threatened, he said, but 'we don't go around shooting the barristers, the police or the judges in this country, let alone television presenters'.

It is difficult to recapture the urgency and drama that attended such speculation in the days that followed the murder. The death of Jill Dando was so incongruous, so bizarre – a word Alan Farthing used – that few potential explanations could have been more outlandish than the crime itself. This was one of those events that send the compass spinning wildly and make us lose our normal reference points. The police for their part had to respond to all the theories, in some cases dismissing them or saying that they 'could not be ruled out' and in others reassuring the public that they *had* thought of this possibility and were not asleep on the job.

There were other pressures on the police. Dando was not only very well known and popular, but through *Crimewatch* she was directly associated with the fight against crime; there would inevitably be implications for public confidence in the police if it proved possible for someone to get away with murdering her on her doorstep in broad daylight. So to a degree the case was symbolic for law and order in London and nationally. Success, therefore, would have consequences bigger than the capture of one killer and the closure of one file. So would failure. And there was a political element that raised the stakes even higher.

In the spring of 1999 the standing of the Metropolitan Police was as low as it had ever been, largely as a result of the public inquiry into the case of Stephen Lawrence. After sitting for the best part of a year, the inquiry had concluded in February that shocking incompetence had blighted the investigation of the Lawrence murder in 1993 and that the Metropolitan Police as a whole suffered from institutional racism. This was a humiliation for the force, which in April and May was still struggling with the aftermath. The Dando murder and the nail bomb attacks occurred in precisely those months and were taken as public tests of the Met's ability to solve crime and protect Londoners. With the nail bombs they were able to announce an arrest on 1 May, although not before three young people had died in an explosion at a Soho pub. It had been a desperate, high-pressure investigation as well as a sensitive one – the Brixton and Brick Lane bombs were clearly racial crimes while the Soho bomb was directed against homosexuals – and the leadership of the Met was extremely relieved, even jubilant, at the outcome. This showed, senior officers believed, that the failures in the Lawrence case were untypical, or at least that the lessons had been learned. A demoralized force suddenly began to feel hope and police eyes turned eagerly to the other big challenge before them. As one Scotland Yard official put it at the time: 'If we can catch Jill Dando's killer now we will really be back on track.'

In some respects the early signs were promising. Campbell's appeals received so much publicity and the public were so eager to help that the phones scarcely stopped ringing. Taken together with extensive door-to-door inquiries this became a veritable torrent of information. It had been a normal Monday morning in a central London district and a great many people had been out and about; large numbers were able to recall something that, in the light of what happened, might be seen as suspicious. They were in cars, on foot or glancing through their bedroom windows; they were out shopping or pruning in the garden or having a cup of coffee in the front room; they saw a man, heard footsteps or might have seen the victim in her final minutes. Others rang because they believed they knew someone who might have done it, or because they had a theory or had advice for the police. There were hundreds and hundreds of them, so many that Campbell had to call for reinforcements merely to take the calls. As fast as the job could be done, the information was recorded, collated and cross-referenced by teams of police 'indexers' working around the clock, and then analysed by detectives. Some events seen as suspicious could easily be shown to have innocent explanations while others were probably too far away, too late or too early to be relevant. A great many remained, however, and from these the detectives identified a number that seemed especially interesting. Here is a selection:

A little after 10 a.m. on 26 April, just as Jill Dando was about to leave the Chiswick house, in Gowan Avenue the postman was delivering the mail. Reaching number 29 he pushed a few letters through the letter-box and when he turned towards the street again he saw a man standing in the road facing him. This man had dark hair, wore a dark suit and was generally smart in appearance, but what struck the postman was that he seemed to be looking directly at the Dando house. 'It was like he thought someone was going to receive the mail,' the postman said. When the man saw he had been noticed he moved out of sight behind a parked van.

About five minutes later a woman driver approached Gowan Avenue in her car from the east. As she paused before crossing

Munster Road she noticed a man on the corner outside the glazier's shop. He took off a hat and put it in his pocket, then he crossed the road. As he did this he looked this way and that – not to check the traffic, she thought, but as if he was searching for something, perhaps the road name. He was dark-haired and wore a suit.

Half an hour later a window cleaner working inside number 26 Gowan Avenue, almost opposite the Dando house, looked down from a skylight window and saw a man standing outside number 29 and talking into a mobile phone. This man was smartly dressed, but his hair was blond or light brown and was brushed back, and his suit was grey. The window cleaner formed the view that he was an estate agent.

At about 11 a.m. a driver heading eastwards along Gowan Avenue spotted a man standing in the road near Dando's house between two parked cars. Fifteen minutes after that a woman emerged from a reflexology session in a house near number 29 and got into her car. Before driving off she paused, making up her mind what she would do next, and as she did so she noticed a man standing in the road about a car's length away, perhaps outside number 33. He had dark hair and a dark suit, possibly dark blue, and once again he left the impression that he was an estate agent. (It was the parking space vacated by this woman that Dando took when she arrived a little later.)

At 11.29, just a minute or two before the murder, a domestic cleaner walking between jobs spotted a dark-haired man wearing a dark blue suit, possibly pinstriped, standing on the corner of Gowan Avenue and Munster Road. She thought he was agitated – very agitated – and she also noticed that he was wearing heavy, black-framed spectacles that did not fit him.

Parallel to this sequence ran another. At 10.08 a traffic warden at work in Gowan Avenue spotted a dark blue Range Rover parked illegally, facing towards Fulham Palace Road – cars in that street must show either a resident's permit or a pay-and-display docket. She had just begun to key in the car's details on her ticket machine when she noticed a man inside the car waving, either to draw attention to his presence or to indicate that he was about to move off. She thought he was talking into a mobile phone at the same time. She was, she said, 'startled and a bit embarrassed' by this, and she walked off, deleting what she had written.

About two minutes later the woman driver who had spotted a man outside the glazier's shop was driving along Gowan Avenue, heading west. As she did so she became conscious of a dark blue Range Rover behind her. It wasn't just following her, it was uncomfortably close, as if hurrying her along. Reaching the end of Gowan Avenue she paused before crossing Fulham Palace Road and she heard the Range Rover revving. She felt as though she was under pressure. It crossed directly behind her, followed her closely the full length of Doneraile Street and turned right behind her into Stevenage Road where, she was relieved to see when she checked in her mirror, it pulled over and parked near the Fulham Football Club ground.

At 11 a.m. there was another sighting of a dark blue Range Rover. A driver noticed a car of that description parked on the kerb at the corner with Munster Road; he thought there was nobody inside.

The murder took place just after 11.30 and as we have seen immediately after it Richard Hughes from number 31 and Geoffrey Upfill-Brown spotted the man walking or running westwards. This man was dark and smartly dressed, wearing a dark jacket or coat of some sort.

From this point a new sequence begins at the far end of the road. At about 11.37 or 11.38 a man who had just visited a betting shop was walking along Fulham Palace Road near the junction with Gowan Avenue. He saw a man rush across the main road in such haste that a car nearly knocked him down and then continue running down the west side of Fulham Palace Road.

Farther down the same stretch of pavement at about the same time, a woman watched a man running while talking into a mobile phone. Still farther down the road and again at roughly the same time, another woman was driving north when she saw a dark, smartly dressed man 'running for all his life' in the direction of Putney. He too was carrying a mobile phone, but her recollection was that he was on the other side of the road, the east side.

Next there is a van driver heading south towards Putney. As he drew level with Bishop's Park a man ran out in front of him, forcing him to brake. The man had come from the east side, and the driver watched as he ran on into the park itself.

Here, in the park, another sequence of sightings follows. Several witnesses noticed a man on the river side of the park acting oddly. One was a woman with a young child who saw a man sitting by the railings leaning over and talking into a mobile phone. She felt his manner was suspicious and she thought he lowered his voice as she approached so that she could not hear what he was saying. She described the man as dark-haired, wearing a dark, thigh-length coat.

It was near this same spot that the school caretaker out cycling saw a man who appeared to be climbing over the railings so as to reach steps down to the river Thames itself. This man, however, was described as wearing a royal blue windcheater – much brighter than the dark clothes seen by others.

Next, there was an important witness who waited at a bus stop on Fulham Palace Road, near the park, for five minutes at around 11.45 a.m. As he stood there eating an orange, a man approached from the south and waited with him. He noticed that this man was sweating, as if he had been running, and he took a closer look. He was five foot nine or ten inches tall, dark and 'slightly foreign' in appearance. His collar was soaked in sweat and his nose bore the dark marks left by spectacles. The witness, who was black, formed the impression that this sweating man might be a policeman. By the time a number 220 bus bound for Wandsworth drew up they had been joined at the bus stop by a few other people, including a young woman with two small children. The witness and the young woman boarded the 220, leaving the sweating man at the stop.

A minute later, however, a number 74 came along. The ticket record on the bus showed that four people boarded at the stop and according to the driver the man was one of them. He asked for a ticket to Putney Bridge station. Moments later a man roughly matching his description answered a call on his mobile phone while sitting in the bus. The passengers all got off at Putney Bridge station, but there was no sign of the dark man on the station's security tapes.

Two sightings remain. A man waiting at the pedestrian lights close to the junction of Gowan Avenue and Fulham Palace Road saw a dark blue Range Rover emerge from Doneraile Street at speed and then run the red light, heading southwards. And finally at 11.52 a.m. a traffic camera filmed a car of the same description heading south across Putney Bridge.

This file built up rapidly; much of it was to hand within twenty-four hours and the rest in a few days. The press were immediately aware of it, partly because they were hunting down witnesses on their own account and partly because the police released some information to back up their appeals for further help. As speculation about the motive subsided for want of evidence, reports and comment about the possible meaning of all these sightings took its place. It seemed that more than one person might have been involved, and possibly a getaway car, and it looked as though one of the group might have made his escape by bus. Each of these possibilities was worth headlines. Then on 30 April the police released an E-fit of the sweating man, drawn from the memory of the bus stop witness. It showed a man of around thirty with a healthy mop of dark hair, large, dark eyes, heavy eyebrows and a tense, even sad expression. Deep lines ran down from the sides of his nose to the corners of his thin-lipped mouth, while on the bridge of his nose were pinch-marks of the kind left by spectacles. Appearing on the front of almost every national paper, this man was variously described as 'the killer', 'the man who shot Jill Dando' and 'the prime suspect'. A further flood of calls and letters to the police followed, almost all of them suggesting names of men resembling the E-fit.

It was the chain of sightings, however, that was exciting most interest, both inside the investigation and outside. It was impossible to read all those descriptions of dark men in dark suits, and to follow the apparent flow of events from outside Dando's house down to Fulham Palace Road, then to the park and the bus stop, without trying to see it as a coherent whole. It could all, without too much effort, be resolved into a single scenario, one that made some sense and seemed to point the investigation in certain interesting directions. This scenario looked something like this.

Three men are involved. One is the waiting man, who later becomes the running man and the sweating man at the bus stop; he is the lookout. Then there is the gunman, who was seen by Hughes and Upfill-Brown and who wore that jacket or coat. And third, there is the driver of the blue Range Rover, which is the getaway car. They know where Dando lives and they expect to find her in the house or to intercept her as she visits that morning. The lookout is there early enough to see the post delivered and he checks whether anyone comes to the door. Nobody does. The wait that follows is probably longer than any of the group expected and this delay causes problems for the driver. He does not want to sit in a parked car in the street as that will attract attention, but at the same time he doesn't want to find himself completely adrift – finding a parking space of any kind in this area can be difficult. Once he has been disturbed by the traffic warden he over-reacts, driving off in a great hurry and waiting for a while some distance away near the football stadium. He eventually returns but as he feared has difficulty finding a space and, after parking on the corner for a time, he moves away again. The lookout, meanwhile, waits in the street and watches. Where is the gunman? His plan is to hide inside the gate to number 29 and attack Dando when she arrives, but he cannot take up position too early in case someone other than Dando goes to the door first and sees him hiding. He must wait somewhere else until he receives the signal that she is approaching, but we do not know where that is. As time passes the lookout becomes increasingly conscious that he is being seen by passers-by, and thus increasingly anxious. The driver, too, is still on edge. All three men have mobile phones; they contact each other frequently.

Jill Dando drives up. The lookout spots her in time, enabling the gunman to take up his position behind the hedge. The murder is committed and the gunman walks and then runs away from the scene westwards. He is not seen again. At this stage, however, something goes wrong: the Range Rover does not appear. Whether or not this concerns the gunman we cannot tell, but it throws the lookout into a panic. The police could be along any minute; he has to get away. To escape from the scene of the murder he runs the length of Gowan Avenue and then crosses Fulham Palace Road in such haste he is almost knocked over. Still running, and by now talking urgently into his mobile phone, he heads for the quiet of Bishop's Park. Where is the Range Rover? Perhaps it is stuck in traffic or boxed into a parking space in some way, or perhaps the driver has been caught in a conversation he cannot escape without arousing suspicion. Eventually the lookout gets through to him on the mobile phone. They need a rendezvous but it would be unwise, given the likelihood that the police are on their way, for the car simply to pick him up at the gate of the park. They choose a point a little farther on: Putney Bridge station. The lookout will have to get there by bus. They fix a time. Flustered and sweaty, the lookout heads for the bus stop, waits and then makes his journey, while the Range Rover finally extricates itself and, now travelling at speed to make up for lost time, reaches Fulham Palace Road, tearing down towards the rendezvous, running a red light on the way. What, meanwhile, has happened to the gunman? He has kept his cool and made his way more discreetly from the scene, either using a car of his own or fixing a separate rendezvous with the getaway car by mobile phone.

Variations on this scenario are possible. There might, for example, have been a fourth man, or there might have been only two. And they might have received word of Dando's movements by phone that morning from somebody who watched her leave the Chiswick house, or from somebody following her. But the broad pattern, the long wait and then the panicky movement from number 29 westward to the park and eventually Putney Bridge, is there. It seems to fit. And if it does fit, then however you look at this murder plot it is a shambles. Three men wait near the scene for some ninety minutes, at least two of them making themselves so obvious that they are each noticed by several people. The murder itself is efficiently done but the getaway is chaotic, at least so far as the driver and lookout are concerned. The lookout's panic is so complete that he loses all restraint, running across a busy road in full view of anybody passing, and making a phone call at the same time – something guaranteed to draw attention to him. The driver, too, is less than cool, and running a red light is only the final sign of his panic. They are very fortunate that the body is not found for a quarter of an hour, giving them more than enough time to overcome their panic and to escape before the alarm is raised and the first police cars reach the scene.

Furthermore, if this scenario was even half accurate then it said something not only about the character of the murder but also, perhaps, about the motive. It was difficult to imagine, for example, that an obsessive fan would or could organize an operation on this scale, involving other people. At the same time it was plainly not a very professional operation. Various possibilities suggested themselves. The first was that the killing might have been done for money, but by amateurs, people who have not killed before but are prepared to do it for cash and have been employed by someone not in a position to find anyone more expert. Or it might have been a political killing carried out by inexperienced people unfamiliar with the locality, perhaps even the country – a makeshift group of Serbs, for example. The sweating man at the bus stop, after all, was described as 'slightly foreign' in appearance, while the man seen by the postman might have been 'Mediterranean'. It was no accident that two very different crime experts who wrote about the case in the press in these early weeks, the former detective John Stalker and the former convict John McVicar, both concluded that there might well be merit to the Serb theory.

This scenario also begged a number of questions to which it seemed likely that answers could fairly easily be found. Where, for example, did the gunman wait? Surely somebody saw him. What went wrong for the driver? If he really found himself stuck at the crucial moment there were almost certainly witnesses to his predicament. Was Putney Bridge station really the rendezvous, and if so how many people met there? It was likely that someone would have noticed a Range Rover stopping to pick up one or more men. This seemed in many ways to be a strong line of inquiry, certainly the strongest available, and yet from the very outset the investigators could see grounds for caution. Perhaps the whole scenario was too seductive, too convenient. The elements, after all, were intrinsically disparate; different witnesses had seen subtly different things and they might not belong in the same narrative at all. Among them, furthermore, were a number of contradictions, large and small, which might be attributable to failures of memory among the witnesses, but might not.

The Range Rover, for example, was seen at least five times in a period of roughly two hours, twice stationary and three times on the move, three times near Gowan Avenue and twice elsewhere. Two were in a hurry, driving so quickly they attracted attention. One witness believed there might have been two people on board, two saw one, a fourth thought the car was empty, while the fifth sighting – the CCTV film from Putney Bridge – was too indistinct. In short, there was no compelling reason to assume there was just one car. And dark blue Range Rovers were common in those streets – if you sat by Fulham Palace Road for just fifteen minutes any morning in 1999 you might have seen half a dozen go by.

Look again at the man seen waiting, our lookout. One of the descriptions stands out as quite distinct; the window cleaner said he saw a fair or blond man in a grey suit while all the others involved a dark man in a dark suit. This was clearly somebody different. And the man seen on the corner at 11.29 a.m. and described as very agitated was wearing glasses while the others were not; perhaps he too was somebody different. As for the rest, dark hair and dark suits are hardly rare and only one of the men, the one seen by the postman, appeared to be directly interested in number 29. What's more, it is surely unlikely that any conspirator in a murder plot would be so casual about being seen. So perhaps these were just unconnected men who were waiting in the street for innocent reasons.

With the running man, too, there are problems. First, it would be surprising if someone trying to escape the murder scene at Dando's house ran the full length of Gowan Avenue, simply because the street is so long. The distance to Fulham Palace Road is 300 yards, all but the last fifty visible from the gate of number 29. For at least a minute after the murder, therefore, anyone coming across the body would be able to look up and see this fugitive running away. Far more likely, surely, that someone fleeing the scene in that direction would turn off into Sidbury Street, 120 yards up on the right, or Kimbell Gardens, thirty-five yards beyond that on the left. That way he would be exposed for only half as long. Yet it was at the far end of Gowan Avenue that the gambler emerging from the betting shop saw a man run across Fulham Palace Road. If that was somebody connected with the Dando murder his behaviour is surprising even for a man in panic. Then there is the further problem that this sighting by the gambler of a man crossing the road seems to be quite different from the other: the van driver reported seeing someone run diagonally across Fulham Palace Road some way farther south. Other contradictions follow: one witness saw a man running down the east side of the road, another down the west. (Could one be the lookout and the other the gunman? Not if the gunman was wearing a coat or jacket, since none of the witnesses in Fulham Palace Road reported that.) The two main witnesses in the park also see quite different things. One describes a man in a royal blue windcheater while the other, the woman with a child, saw a man on the phone wearing a dark thigh-length coat.

Finally, and most confusingly, there is the sweating man who figures in the E-fit. A great deal about his behaviour remains obscure. The bus stop at which he is seen stands on the east side of Fulham Palace Road near the corner of the park. The sweating man arrives, not from the north where Gowan Avenue lies, but from the south, so if he has left the park he has walked back in the direction of the murder scene. This is not what one would expect. About ten minutes have passed since the killing so police sirens are overdue, yet knowing that he is sweaty and looks flushed, this man remains at the stop on the main road for about five minutes, giving other people waiting there ample opportunity to inspect him. And when the 220 comes along he does not board it but stays at the stop, still with others. A minute later he boards a 74 bus and asks for Putney Bridge station – a destination to which the previous bus, the 220, would also have taken him. This is, moreover, a five-minute trip; if he had really come from the southern part of Bishop's Park he could have completed his journey more discreetly and in half the time on foot. For a man fleeing a murder, therefore, his conduct ran counter to a number of instincts. Perhaps he *was* part of the murder plot, but did not know the area and simply obeyed instructions he had received over the phone – 'Go out of the park and take a 74 bus to Putney Bridge station.' Or perhaps, on the other hand, he was entirely innocent, had a touch of flu, did not come from the park, did not know the bus routes and was just too lazy to walk to the tube station.

There is a line in detective work between fitting your theory to the evidence, which is legitimate, and fitting the evidence to your theory, which is not, but can sometimes be tempting. With this scenario there was a danger of crossing that line. And yet it remained tantalizingly possible that it was close to the truth, or at the very least that many of these sightings were indeed related to the murder; a few more nuggets from the public might decide it either way.

A fortnight after the killing, with no arrest in prospect, a question arose. The next *Crimewatch UK* programme was due to go out on 18 May, a week or so away; what should it do about Dando? This was a question both for the police and for the BBC. Naturally the programme would be presented by Nick Ross alone, and naturally it must contain an item of some sort – a prominent item – about the Dando case, but what should that be? Should there be a full reconstruction or merely a tribute to the murdered presenter? For the police there were reasons to hesitate: with this investigation, after all, publicity was the least of their problems, since every titbit of information they released was blazoned over the news bulletins and the newspapers. If there was a difficulty it was in processing and following up the mountain of data already received from the public. Might it not be better to wait until the frenzy of interest had died down, until a point where fresh publicity was needed, before playing the *Crimewatch* card? On the BBC side, too, there were doubts. The coverage of the case on the day had drawn criticism for its subjective, emotional character and some inside the corporation accepted that henceforth there should be restraint. The *Crimewatch* team, for their part, were emotionally involved in the case; perhaps it would be better to wait.

On the other hand, the list of sightings around Gowan Avenue formed a perfect basis for a *Crimewatch* reconstruction. The chain of events could be drawn together on film; actors in appropriate costume could play various witnesses and the men seen; a Range Rover could be shown moving around. Dramatized on television each of the vignettes – the running men, the men in the park, the man at the bus stop and so forth – might be capable of jogging memories in a way no printed words could ever do. And coming three weeks after the killing it might just give the case the final push of publicity it needed. If the missing nuggets were out there, *Crimewatch* offered the best hope of finding them quickly. In the end this logic was accepted and filming began. It proved to be a news item in its own right: photographs of the reconstructions under way soon appeared in print and on the night the programme was broadcast it was trailed on the evening news bulletins.

This was, inevitably, like no other edition of *Crimewatch*. It began abruptly, without opening credits or music, with Ross in dark suit and black tie standing against a black background. 'This is a sombre and for me a surreal *Crimewatch UK*,' he said quietly. 'For all of us here it can be gruelling coping with crimes against victims who are strangers. It's been almost unbearable dealing with Jill's death. Jill Dando was much more than a colleague; she was everyone's friend. *Crimewatch* is poorer without her. But this programme was her passion. And now, as Jill helped others, we hope we can do the same for her, for her family and for her fiancé, Alan.' Alan Farthing then recounted how he had heard the news at St Mary's Hospital and said that he still found it hard to believe. Next to speak was DCI Hamish Campbell, filmed at his desk. 'We've had to look at everything, but look at it in the complete 360 degrees, all sorts of things that were happening. We've been looking at facts; we've been looking at evidence. And one of the first pieces of information – real facts – is when the postman was delivering mail to Jill's house.' Thus began a lengthy narrative of that morning in and around Gowan Avenue, spoken in part by Campbell and in part by actors reading lines from the statements given by witnesses. After the postman came the traffic warden, then the woman driver, then the window cleaner and so on through the betting shop man, the woman in the park and finally the black man at the bus stop. Again and again Campbell's voice would break in to appeal for the public's help. Did you see that car? Were you that man? Were you there and did you notice anything? If so, please come forward . . .

Campbell added some interpretation to the evidence. The sightings, he said, might not all be of the same man. 'What we know about the man in Gowan Avenue is that he was wearing a dark, waxy, Barbour-type jacket to thigh length. Certainly the man running in Fulham Palace Road is not wearing a jacket or coat. We can't be sure that the man in Fulham Palace Road is the one in Gowan Avenue, and perhaps he was a lookout. Perhaps he was a man standing at the end of Gowan Avenue and following the shooting he has run away down the Fulham Palace Road.' As for the man seen climbing the railings by the Thames, he was wearing the wrong colour jacket so there was 'a strong possibility' that he had nothing to do with the case. Campbell stressed that he wanted anyone who might have appeared in the sightings to come forward so that they could be eliminated.

Once the reconstruction of the chain of sightings was complete, Ross interviewed Campbell, and the presenter's approach seemed designed to prevent people jumping to conclusions. 'There are just so many sightings; they can't all be involved in Jill's murder,' he began. 'There must have been dozens of Range Rovers in that area at that time . . .' And, 'people run down roads every day for entirely innocent reasons, without having shot someone'. Campbell agreed, and stressed that innocent people who believed they figured in any of the scenes would have nothing to fear if they contacted the police. He was keen to eliminate anything that was irrelevant to his inquiries. Ross continued: 'It's pretty clear from that reconstruction that the guy running down Fulham Palace Road was one person, and yet that description is different from the gunman, so the E-fit that you've issued of the man at the bus stop in Fulham Palace Road may very well not be the killer.' Again Campbell agreed: 'That is possible, and certainly the man in the Fulham Palace Road was not wearing a coat while the man in Gowan Avenue was. So there's a strong indication that there are two different people.

The E-fit is of the man at the bus stop. People need to focus on that. Who is that man? Was he the lookout? Was he another party to the killing?'

They moved on to talk about the murder weapon and then to discuss possible motives. Did the viewers know of anybody with an abnormal fixation for Jill Dando? Had anybody gained by this murder, either financially or emotionally? Had anybody been noticed behaving strangely on or after 26 April? Campbell stressed that there was by now a very large reward for information leading to a conviction – the *Daily Mail* had offered £100,000 and an anonymous businessman £50,000 – and that it would be possible to claim the money anonymously through Crimestoppers. 'There's a reason why Jill Dando was murdered,' said the detective, 'and people need to look now.'

The programme was watched by more than ten million people, an unusually large audience for *Crimewatch* if not a record, and it drew roughly 500 telephone calls, yet it yielded nothing of value to the investigation. Within a couple of weeks it was clear that painfully little had been added to the file of witness evidence and, worse still, nothing had been eliminated. The waiting man, the running man, the sweating man and the dark blue Range Rover remained as opaque, as teasing as ever. Four very hectic and dizzying weeks had now passed since the murder and the investigation seemed to be at a turning point. *Crimewatch* had failed to crack the case. The door-to-door inquiries, the thousands of calls and letters received since the killing, the long list of sightings, the E-fit – all of which had generated such optimism – seemed to have led nowhere. The first headlines appeared saying that police inquiries had run out of steam, that the trail had gone cold. The papers were even suggesting that Jill Dando's killer might never be caught.

# 10. Scene of Crime

*The killer left behind the bullet and the cartridge case, and each had a story to tell.*

In the more complex murder investigations one of the most important early challenges confronting the detective in charge is to separate the quick from the slow. Some ideas and some leads require swift reactions and a rapid deployment of manpower. Other jobs, however, must be done slowly and methodically; they offer no instant return but in the long term they could make the vital difference. Neglect them in those busy early days and you may never have the chance to recover what is lost. In the case of Jill Dando the scenario of the bungled escape falls into the 'quick' category: the information came in quickly and the response had to be rapid – find further witnesses and CCTV film; discover where the fugitives went next; identify the man in the E-fit. For a fortnight or more it was the strongest and most urgent lead and every muscle was strained to develop it, even though detectives were always aware of anomalies and contradictions in the sightings. Once the flow of information about the Range Rover, the running man and the sweating man had dried up, however, matters in the 'slow' category came to have precedence. This work had been going on all the time, quietly and in the background. Now it was time to step back, review what had been found and work out a long-term strategy to solve the case.

Another unchanging fact about murder investigations is that the farther you move from the crime itself, in time and place, the less likely it is that the information you are receiving is relevant.

In other words, a man leaving the murder scene moments after the shooting is probably not going about his everyday business, but a man at a bus stop half a mile away and fifteen minutes later could have a hundred innocent explanations for his behaviour. So it is evidence relating directly to the scene of the crime, where killer and victim were together, that tends to have the highest value. From the outset, therefore, some of the Oxborough detectives had been working on what exactly happened at the door of number 29 Gowan Avenue at approximately 11.30 a.m. that Monday morning. This was the core of the early 'slow' work.

The testimony of the two neighbours is pivotal. To recap, Richard Hughes at number 31 heard the sound of Dando's car alarm and then the scream. As he made his way to the window he heard the gate being closed. He saw the dark man walking away, apparently with a mobile phone in his hand. Hughes then saw Geoffrey Upfill-Brown emerging from number 30. Upfill-Brown, for his part, described a man in a thigh-length jacket with a thick mop of black hair, almost like a wig. He saw the man running westwards down the road, turning and slowing to a walk. These two witnesses, identified and interviewed in the first hour of the investigation, form a triangle with the gunman himself: Hughes sees gunman; Hughes sees Upfill-Brown; Upfill-Brown sees gunman. They are locked together, giving detectives a strong, well-corroborated framework for the killing. Not all murder investigations have as much to go on.

In another respect detectives were less fortunate: although the various passers-by who discovered Dando's body had not disturbed her, the paramedics certainly had. For good reasons, half a dozen people had spent about thirty minutes trampling over the murder scene and moving the body around before the police themselves gained control of the site. This almost certainly meant that important details were lost for ever. In the effort to make up some of this ground the police later created a replica of the door, the doorstep and the little path from the gate and, using props and a woman pretending to be Dando, asked the various

witnesses to describe in detail what they had seen. Thus from the
memories of that first woman passer-by, her friend who lived
nearby, the doctor's receptionist, Hughes, the uniformed police
officers and others they built up the picture of how the body lay,
where the bags and keys were and so forth. This in turn helped
them to imagine how she might have fallen and where the killer
had stood when he struck.

The front door to number 29 was not opened that morning;
Dando did not have the time. In fact, although Hughes had
originally estimated that thirty or forty seconds elapsed between
the blip of the alarm and Dando's cry, detectives came to believe
that it happened more quickly than that, perhaps in just ten
seconds. This was something else they reconstructed. Having
collected her bags and shut the car door, she activated the alarm,
crossed the pavement and passed through the gate. Where did
the killer come from? He was definitely not with her so he had
to have been waiting either inside the gate and behind the
hedge or outside in the street. Both carried the risk of attracting
suspicion, while if he waited too far away he ran a risk of missing
her altogether. Whichever course he chose it is clear that
he surprised his victim, since both Hughes and another near-
neighbour (not Upfill-Brown) said they heard a cry. It sounded,
Hughes said, like a cry of surprise, as though someone she knew
had suddenly popped up beside her, and it did not instantly
arouse his suspicion, but his curiosity. Significantly, Hughes did
not report hearing raised voices before or after the cry, or any
voice at all, so if words were exchanged they were spoken softly.
And they were few in number: the police formed the view that
at most a further ten seconds elapsed between the cry and the
moment the killer closed the gate on his way out. It was, after
all, the cry that brought Hughes to his feet on the first floor, and
by the time he had reached the window and parted the blinds
to look out the killer had completed his work, shut the gate
and was turning away down the street. There was no time for
conversation.

As for the shooting itself, the pathologist's report told a terrible story. Dando was shot in the head with a single bullet. The mouth of the gun barrel was pressed so firmly against the skin that a clear imprint of the muzzle and foresight remained on her scalp afterwards – in the vivid police phrase, this was 'hard contact'. The bullet entered near the top of the left ear and traversed the brain. The exit wound was above the right ear and the bullet went on to strike the lower timbers of the front door, leaving a small dent and a break in the paintwork, before dropping to the ground beside the doormat. The dent in the door was nine inches above the level of the tiled porch and close examination of the impact suggested that the bullet had been travelling at right angles to the door and almost horizontally when it struck. Dando's head, in other words, must have been close to the ground when the shot was fired, although exactly how close was not certain. On her right forearm was a small bruise which may have been caused by her assailant holding her. Two other small abrasions, on her right elbow and hand, were probably the result of her impact with the ground. There were no 'characteristic defence injuries', as they are known, so she probably did not resist. The picture that emerges from this is of a swift and very brutal act. Jill Dando was taken by surprise and let out a cry. It seems likely that she was already bending down – perhaps she was putting her bags on the ground to free her hands to open the door, or perhaps she dropped the keys and was picking them up – when the killer thrust the gun violently against her head. It is almost certain that he held her in some way with his other hand to ensure that he had control and to maintain the hard contact between gun and head. He too must have been bending low and in seizing her he probably pushed her even lower. In court much later it would be said that she was crouching when the shot was fired, but that hardly describes her position: so low was her head that she must have been kneeling or even partly lying down – crushed, as it were, by force or fear. The injuries she suffered were, to use another police phrase, 'not survivable'. No matter how quickly help had been summoned and no matter how soon the ambulance had reached the scene, she could not have been saved.

This killer, then, appeared suddenly, acted swiftly and left promptly. There was no evidence in his actions of panic or any other expression of emotion. Besides closing the gate he seemed to have made no superfluous gestures, nothing beyond the bare minimum of what was needed to ensure that Dando was dead. And the closing of the gate seemed like nothing more than a piece of tidiness, since it was wrought iron and did nothing to conceal the body. No less eloquent than the killer's actions, however, were the things he did not do that he might have done. Had he wished to hide the body and thus give himself more time to get away, for example, he might have forced Dando closer to the hedge before killing her, or he might have moved her after firing the shot. Instead he left her where she fell, across the doorstep. His getaway, on foot, was equally curious. The imperative at such a moment is to get out of sight of the murder scene as quickly as possible. Every second counts. From the gate of number 29 the fugitive has three choices: he can run right and turn into Munster Road, which is 100 yards away; he can go left and turn into Sidbury Street, 120 yards away; or he can go a little farther in the same direction, to Kimbell Gardens, 155 yards away. Distance made Munster Road the natural choice but this was not just a matter of yardage; it also *feels* closest when you stand at Dando's house. All other things being equal, then, a fugitive would be most likely to turn right at the gate, but this one turned left. This seemed to suggest that he had a reason for going that way. Since the man in the coat or jacket was not seen again detectives could not know what this reason might have been, but he may have had a car parked in a neighbouring street. If so, by the time the body was found he could have been three or four miles away. Alternatively, of course, he might simply have been careless or reckless.

He left very little behind him. There was no sign that he made any mark or left any trace on the ground, the wall, the door, the gate or his victim, and if he did it was probably obliterated when the paramedics arrived. Of course, fibres and other traces were recovered, but either they could not be shown to belong to the killer or they were not sufficiently distinctive to provide important leads. And though the killer closed the gate and neither Hughes nor Upfill-Brown noticed gloves on the man they saw, no suspicious or anomalous fingerprint survived. In short, all that work at the house by the overalled scene-of-crime specialists beneath their great protective awning produced nothing useful for the inquiry. What the killer did leave, however, was the bullet and the spent cartridge case, and they each had a story to tell.

The brass cartridge case was a commercial variety produced by the Remington company of the United States for use with 9mm semi-automatic pistols. These pistols come in two sizes, the standard and the smaller 'short' weapon, and this ammunition was for the latter. This 9mm short is a handy-sized pistol that could very easily be carried in the pocket of a Barbour-style coat. A number of firearms companies around the world, including Walther of Germany and Beretta of Italy, make them, but it could not be determined which make had been used to kill Jill Dando. The evidence would normally be there: the different makes of gun tend to leave characteristic marks on the cartridge, both from the firing pin which detonates the charge and from the mechanism which ejects the cartridge afterwards. In this case, however, though the marks were there they did not give a clear steer – the first indication that the gun was an unusual one.

On the outside of the case, close to the rim, police ballistics experts found six tiny indentations of a kind that was new to them. Never had a cartridge carrying such marks been used in any crime committed in Britain and nor, so far as they could establish, had anything of the kind ever been sold commercially or on the known illegal market in this country. It was unique. To understand what these marks were you need to know that in the shooting world a cartridge case is frequently used more than once. A standard round contains four components – the case, the primer, the propellant and the bullet itself – and of these the case, if only because it is made of brass, is the most expensive. So much so that it is worthwhile for regular gun users to buy the other components separately and assemble their own rounds, re-using their spent cartridges. There is, however, a slight difficulty. Hardly surprisingly, a cartridge case is distorted in shape when a gun is fired, so it will no longer be a perfect fit for a new, mass-produced bullet. The process of tightening the case around the bullet is known as 'crimping', and the marks on the case for the Dando bullet showed that it had been crimped in a most unusual way. In Britain the commonest form of crimping, traditionally, has been by means of a crimp die, essentially a piece of steel with a tapering hole in it of the required dimensions. The assembled round is simply placed in the hole and tapped or pressed until the tapering tightens the cartridge around the bullet to give the appropriate grip. Nothing could be simpler. The usual alternative to the die is the punch crimp, a jig in which the cartridge is held at points around its mouth and squeezed on to the bullet by tightening the grip. Both processes leave marks and the marks on the Dando cartridge resembled those from a punch crimp rather than a die. But there was a problem. Conventional punch crimps leave three marks and not six, and those three marks tend to be pretty well identical. The six marks on the Dando cartridge, however, were different from each other; each was slightly ragged. In fact the marks did not appear to have been made mechanically at all. In the police phrase, the cartridge case seemed to have been 'hand-tapped around' – someone tightened it around the bullet simply by placing the point of a nail or something similar against the side and tapping it with a hammer. By implication, then, this round was assembled by someone who did not have access to the machines employed by people who are putting together ammunition in any quantity. 'Hand-tapping' would be fiddly, slow and inefficient; nobody who was making even a batch of a dozen rounds would want to do it that way.

And this was only the beginning of the crimping mystery, for the ballistics experts at the forensic science service could find nothing to suggest that this cartridge case had been used more than once or that it had ever previously been separated from its bullet. The rim of the case showed a single faint mark of the kind left by the ejection mechanism of an automatic pistol; in other words, it seemed that this case had only ever been ejected from a gun once, after Jill Dando was shot. The bullet, for its part, showed none of the characteristic scratch marks left when bullets are extracted from cases manually or by machine. So why the crimping? Why had someone gone to the trouble of making those makeshift indentations when the round appeared to have been in one piece all along? It seemed almost perverse.

If the cartridge case was surprising, the bullet also raised questions. A piece of lead the size of a pea, it was also a standard Remington product and not, as one or two early press reports claimed, a dum-dum designed to fragment and cause greater damage. Once fired, a bullet is a plastic object and as it travels down the barrel of the gun it can pick up marks which often remain on it after impact. So it proved in this case, and the marks on the bullet that killed Jill Dando showed that the gun it was fired from had a smooth bore. Most guns are rifled, which means that the inside of the barrel is shaped in such a way as to turn the bullet on its long axis as it begins its journey – it then spins in flight, which gives it greater accuracy and range. This gun, however, had no rifling, which was unusual since no commercial manufacturer anywhere in the world makes a 9mm semi-automatic pistol with a smooth bore.

Despite this, there seemed to be no particular mystery about where such a gun might have come from. Handgun ownership has been regulated in Britain for many years and after the Dunblane attack in 1996, in which sixteen primary school children and their teacher were shot, the laws were changed to make the possession of any normal handgun effectively illegal. It was not and is not illegal, however, to own a handgun that has been

officially certified as incapable of firing bullets, and there are
many of these in existence – owned, for example, by collectors
or by former soldiers or sportsmen who keep them as souvenirs.
These guns are 'de-activated' by Home Office experts to a
specification which states that they should not be capable of
repair using ordinary tools available for home use. The usual
procedure is to dismantle the gun and cut or grind various parts
– usually including the barrel – until they can no longer function.
The weapon is then marked, reassembled and returned to its
owner with a certificate stating that it has been officially de-
activated and is thus harmless. But there is a problem. What
cannot be done using ordinary tools available for home use can
sometimes be achieved using more sophisticated machinery, and
there have always been criminal armourers with the lathes and
welding equipment necessary to rebuild de-activated weapons
for illegal use. A common part of this process is to remove the
damaged barrel and replace it with one improvised from a piece
of ordinary metal tubing. While this leaves the gun without
rifling and therefore much less accurate, it will usually be adequate
for criminal purposes. This business of buying or stealing de-
activated handguns and rebuilding them has been going on for
many years and it was possible that the gun that killed Jill Dando
was one of its products.

Two other possible explanations for the peculiar character of
the gun were put forward. The first was that it might have been
a starting pistol altered to enable it to fire real rounds and the
second that it was a pistol altered in such a way as to place it
outside the scope of normal handgun legislation. The latter would
have meant fitting a new barrel at least twenty-four inches in
length, as is known to have been done in some cases. But Dando
was not killed with such an unwieldy object, so if the weapon
was one of these it was cut down again before use. In the early
stages of the investigation both of these options were regarded as
less likely than the simple re-activated weapon.

One further point in the ballistics department: just as a spent bullet carries clues about the gun it has been fired from, so it can also show marks from a silencer if one has been used. In the aftermath of the Dando murder many assumed that the killer's gun had been silenced, principally because almost nobody within earshot remembered hearing the crack of gunfire. In particular neither of the principal witnesses, Hughes and Upfill-Brown, heard a shot, and Hughes for one had been alert enough to hear the car alarm and the cry. The obvious explanation, however, was not the correct one, for to general surprise Hamish Campbell was soon able to state that there was 'no suggestion that this firearm was fitted with a silencer'. Had one been used it would have left marks on the bullet and no such marks were found. Why, then, was the shot not heard? Although a variety of theories were aired in the press there was no mystery so far as the scientists were concerned: the shot was very efficiently muffled by the victim's head. That 'hard contact' – as the killer presumably knew – was sufficient to absorb the escape of gases from the barrel which normally causes the report of the gun.

What, then, could be deduced from the case and the bullet? The type of gun itself said very little; for this purpose any small handgun would have been suitable and short 9mm semi-automatics are not rare enough to be distinctive – they are readily available in the illegal trade. The evidence of tampering, however, was important. If the gun was altered by the killer that meant he had some knowledge of firearms, and if the cartridge case was crimped by the same hand then he was apparently someone who did not have access to specialist tools. This was a very intriguing possibility and it quickly became an important element of the investigation – whenever anyone was assessed as a suspect, for example, detectives looked hard for evidence of past knowledge, particularly technical knowledge, about guns. At the same time, however, it remained possible that the gun was produced for sale by a criminal armourer and that the cartridge case had picked up those marks long before the Dando attack, in some different context. Both, in other words, might have come into the killer's possession in some random way. (The round was after all of a design produced by Remington since 1994.) Even this second possibility was a lead in itself, and criminal armourers became an important line of inquiry.

Finally in this context of the crime scene, there was the matter of the mobile phones. Richard Hughes believed he saw the gunman holding one as he turned away, and this element of his evidence seemed all the more important because mobile phones figured in so many of the other sightings from before and after the killing. A man seen standing in the street was using one; a man in a Range Rover was using one; a man seen running in Fulham Palace Road was using one; a man in Bishop's Park was using one; the sweating man on the 74 bus used one. Nothing seemed to point more strongly to the existence of accomplices than this, since it was hardly conceivable that at such a time a killer would make or accept a call unrelated to his crime. The phone, in other words, must have had a role in the murder plot. Of all of these sightings, however, it was only Hughes's that could be linked directly to the murder, so what exactly did the neighbour see? 'I saw a phone in his hand,' Hughes was quoted as saying on the day of the murder. In fact his evidence to the police, when he sat down to give his full statement, was rather less firm. The man leaving number 29 had his hand at shoulder height as he turned away from the gate and Hughes *formed the impression* that he was holding a phone. If it was a phone, however, he was not speaking into it; it was not held against the ear. Upfill-Brown, who caught sight of the gunman a moment later, did not report seeing a phone, or even seeing the fugitive holding his hand up. Mobile phones, in short, could have played a part in the murder but it was by no means certain; what Hughes saw could even have been the gun.

Such was the positive information that could be gleaned from the scene of the crime. Taken together it confirmed two basic points. The first was that this was a deliberate murder with Dando as the chosen target and not a robbery gone wrong or a heat-of-the-moment shooting. There was no sign of an attempt to break into the house or car and nothing was stolen, not the purse from her handbag, nor the Cartier watch from her wrist, nor even the large and valuable diamond engagement ring from her finger. The second point, which was a little less obvious, was that this murder might have been committed by one man acting alone. Nothing seen or discovered at the crime scene, that all-important point where killer and victim coincided, necessitated the involvement of anyone other than the gunman. This did not mean that he definitely acted alone but it underlined the possibility that lookouts or getaway drivers might be red herrings. In this context the evidence of Hughes and Upfill-Brown about the coat was especially important. Hughes believed he had seen a shiny jacket, like a Barbour, while Upfill-Brown described something baggy and thigh-length. None of the other sightings in the area before and after the killing involved a garment of this kind, and no such coat or jacket was found dumped in Gowan Avenue or nearby.

The next question was, what sort of man did this? From the moment, at 8.20 p.m. on the evening of the murder, when the police revealed that Jill Dando died from a single bullet to the head, the words 'professional hit-man' were everywhere. This was not, as had earlier been reported, a 'frenzied knife attack'; in fact it was not frenzied at all, and the temptation to see it as the work of someone acting completely without emotion was too strong for many to resist. The idea of the professional killer, the solitary mercenary who kills repeatedly and scientific-ally and has no feelings towards his victims, holds a powerful allure for the public. What could be more theatrical or more chilling than a 'jackal', slipping away from the crime unrecog-nized by anyone to collect his substantial payment and begin preparing for his next assignment? Every paper aired the possibil-ity. In truth such specialist assassins probably do not exist in Britain – as one senior police officer put it, there just aren't enough murders – but there are and have always been more workaday people ready to kill for money. The evidence of the courts shows that they vary widely in quality, from amateurs and fools to experienced criminals and terrorists for whom the occasional murder may be just one aspect of a violent underworld life. Either category would be better described as hired killers than professional hit-men – these are not specialists. They are available if you can find them, though that in itself would usually be difficult and risky if you are not already in the criminal milieu. And what they charge must be anyone's guess; the idea of a 'going rate' is surely another popular mirage since this is not a market where clients shop around.

If Jill Dando had been the victim of a reasonably competent hired killer you would expect to find that the murder was committed efficiently and briskly, with no wasted gestures and with the minimum risk of capture, identification or detection for the killer himself. In some ways that was how it was, and in others not. The shooting was certainly brisk and with the possible exception of the closed gate there were no wasted gestures at all. But the killer also ran risks he need not have. For one, he showed his face, which was not necessary. He might, for example, have posed as a motorcycle courier and kept his helmet on throughout, a tried and tested approach that has the advantage that the motorcycle itself is a perfect getaway vehicle. He gave his victim the time to scream and was fortunate that this did not attract more attention from the neighbours than it did. He killed her outside the house instead of waiting another few seconds until the door was open and following or forcing her through it. This would have allowed him to use his gun without the risk of being seen, and if he had pulled the door closed as he left it might have been hours rather than minutes before the body was found. He used a semi-automatic pistol, which as we have seen ejects its spent cartridge cases, rather than a revolver, which does not. That meant he left twice as much evidence at the scene – both bullet and case – as he needed to. And he did not use a silencer, meaning that he ran some risk of stirring half the street to attention. In short, this did not appear to be the work of some idealized professional hit-man and it seemed a risky crime even for a more run-of-the-mill hired killer – surely anyone committing murder for money would take more care with his own safety? And yet, as the police so often say, you could not rule it out. The fact was that this man did get away, and what seemed like luck might conceivably have been a display of confidence and fine judgement.

An explanation that might have accounted for some of these perplexing factors was that the gunman was recruited to do the job, and was an amateur with no clear idea of how to carry it out. He might have been someone so desperate for money he was prepared to do something far outside the realm of his experience, or he might even have been a friend or associate of the person who wanted Jill Dando dead, doing the job as a favour. Such a person would not necessarily have been a criminal and might have had no relevant expertise beyond a reasonably cool head and perhaps a familiarity with firearms. He would have been able to carry out the killing without showing emotion because he would have felt little or none, and he might have been prepared to take risks because he simply saw his opportunity and snatched it. Such a man, too, might have broken into a run as he left the scene and then slowed down when he realized that someone (Upfill-Brown) was watching him – actions which do not suggest someone acting to a well-laid plan.

Finally, there was the killer doing his own work. The only reason for thinking of a hired gunman was that the murder seemed to have been carried out efficiently, but as we have seen it was not necessarily efficient at all. And in any case such signs of despatch as there were did not rule out a killer motivated by personal rage, envy, greed or deranged love, for such people do not always act in what the press calls a 'frenzy'. They too can be efficient, particularly if they are eager to get away. Certainly there were no grounds for assuming, as some reports suggested, that because only one shot was fired this was not a crime of passion; there were plenty of precedents for people killing for love without emptying their guns, just as there were precedents for contract killings in which a number of shots were fired.

The crime scene raised one further question, in many ways the most challenging of all: the matter of opportunity. It was very difficult to see how the killer and his victim came to encounter each other at that time and in that place. Jill Dando did not visit the Gowan Avenue house often or with any regularity. For one thing she spent a great deal of time out of London in the preceding weeks, either abroad for *Holiday* or around Britain and Ireland for *Antiques Inspectors*. For another thing, since the turn of the year she had lived mainly in Chiswick with Alan Farthing and in the month before the killing they had spent only two nights in the Fulham house. Yes, she still conducted her business from there but her visits tended to be short and could occur at any time of day and on any day of the week. Even she could often not have predicted more than twenty-four hours ahead when they would happen. So how did the killer know he would find her there, on that morning, at that time?

There were three possibilities. The first was that she told someone, either the killer himself or a third party from whom, somehow, the killer got the information. The second was that she was followed, either all the way from Chiswick or from some point along her route. And the third was that the killer took a gamble. Taking these in order, the police never disclosed the outcome of their investigation into who knew about Dando's movements that morning but it is safe to assume that it was a short list comprising at the very most a handful of people who were personally or professionally very close to her. Detectives had to consider the possibility that either deliberately or accidentally the information was passed from one of these to the killer. We will return to this. As to other parties, Dando herself had made no appointments to meet estate agents or tradespeople in

Gowan Avenue, no deliveries were due and if she had arranged to meet anyone else there nothing in her telephone bills, correspondence or any other records available to the police indicated who it might have been.

So far as could be established with any confidence, she was not followed that morning. The various closed circuit television cameras that caught her visiting the petrol station, shopping in Hammersmith and at various points on the road were scrutinized exhaustively and showed no sign of anyone trailing her either in a car or on foot. It was possible none the less that there was a car, keeping its distance or adopting slight variants on her route to avoid detection, but this would have been very difficult. And what would have been the role of this car? The driver was either the killer himself or an accomplice. If the former, after trailing her to Fulham he had to find time to park and then to get to her doorstep before she entered the house. If it was the latter, and this was an accomplice, he might have phoned ahead to let the killer know she was about to arrive. Neither of these could be ruled out, but on the whole detectives were impressed by the evidence suggesting she had not been followed.

The simple gamble, too, seemed a long shot given the irregularity of her visits to Gowan Avenue, but an informed gamble was a different matter. That she lived there was no secret: besides the fact that her name still appeared on the electoral register, any number of taxi and minicab drivers, local tradespeople and residents and even visitors to the area knew her address. Her engagement to Alan Farthing was public knowledge, and on that basis someone might have guessed that she was spending much of her time away from the house. It might even have been possible to deduce that she would still have kept clothes and work things there. On that basis, if she did visit her own house, when was the most likely time? First thing on Monday morning, at the start of the working week, would be as good a guess as any. If this was the killer's approach, however, there should have been evidence that he had hung around Gowan Avenue in vain on previous Monday mornings, and in the early stages of the investigation there was none. Of course, the more he knew the easier it would have been for him to pick the right day. If he had access to Dando's work schedule, for example, he might have been aware that she had finished filming for *Holiday* and *Antiques Inspectors* and that on Monday 26 April she was in town. And if in addition to that he knew that she had no appointments at BBC Television Centre that day, then he might have felt justified in waiting for her in Fulham. The more such knowledge we assume, however, the more the killer belongs in the first category – those who had been told of her movements.

The crime scene as a whole, then, was tantalizingly equivocal. Although it supplied a great deal of information, there was hardly a single detail which allowed the investigator to say to himself: 'Well, at least we now know *this* for certain,' or 'We can rule that out now for good.' Instead there was a chain of ambiguities and uncertainties. While some of the evidence pointed to a hired killer, it was doubtful whether such a person would have taken such risks. The sightings of waiting men and running men suggested a team, but it remained possible – more likely, even – that there was just one man. The gun and cartridge case might have been altered specifically for this killing, but equally it was possible that the killer merely bought them as they were. In the same way, it was hard to believe that a gunman who acted with apparent despatch did not know in advance that Dando would be in that place at that time, but there was still a chance that this was nothing more than guesswork.

Hamish Campbell called Operation Oxborough 'a 360-degree investigation', by which he meant that at the outset nothing was ruled out and everything was possible. It was to be a characteristic of the Dando case that reducing the number of degrees to be scanned would be extraordinarily difficult. According to Sherlock Holmes's maxim the detective should first eliminate the impossible and then whatever was left, no matter how improbable, must be the truth. This particular murder defeated such logic: there was so little that was categorically impossible that even when those things had been checked and eliminated Campbell and his team were left with a superabundance of possibilities.

# 11. Motive

*'If it was a stalker we would like to think there was evidence
Jill Dando was stalked. There is none.'*

There remained the matter of motive. From the outset this was
the most astonishing aspect of the crime, why it took the public's
breath away and why so many of those close to Jill Dando
struggled to accept what had happened. She was a popular, kind
and harmless woman; who could possibly have wanted her dead?
What could have prompted anyone to shoot her in the head?

One of the first suggestions raised was Serb revenge, but as we
have seen the police always showed scepticism about this: the
notion, they said from the earliest days, was 'far-fetched'. Why
they were so sure of this, in an inquiry where there was so little
that they could be sure about, was initially unclear, but later they
were to explain that there was no intelligence information to
support the theory. Their assumption appears to have been that
if Serbia sent a team of killers to London this would have been
noticed by some branch of the British or allied intelligence
services. If such a team had already been in place in Britain or if
it had been improvised from among Serbs living here, then MI5
would have known about it. And if the team had left the country
afterwards they would have been detected doing so. It may be
that the quality of intelligence about Serbia and Serbs during this
period was so good it justified this confidence, but at the same
time there was more than one precedent to encourage doubt.
For years British intelligence about the IRA, for example, was
patchy enough to make slip-ups commonplace, while the out-
break of the war against Saddam Hussein in 1990 found MI5 so

poorly informed about Iraqis in Britain that many perfectly innocent people were rounded up as undesirables. On its own the absence of intelligence information about Serb killers was probably not enough to eliminate this theory.

There were, however, plenty of other reasons to be sceptical. If the Belgrade government or some extremist group loyal to Serbia had wanted to strike a symbolic blow against Britain they would have been very unlikely to pick Jill Dando as their target. Even allowing for her appearance on the Kosovo appeal there must have been hundreds of high-profile targets more closely associated with the war, most of them politicians and military people, few with any sort of security protection. Their addresses would have been as easy to find as Dando's and their movements were if anything more predictable. If the object of the assassination was to show Serbia's reach or to undermine the British will to fight, how much more appropriate to kill someone like this? And whoever was the target the attack had no symbolic value if it was not claimed. This, indeed, was the principal objection: no plausible claim was ever received to link the murder with Serbia. Even after the passage of weeks, by which time the killers could have been safely in Belgrade, no one had confirmed Serb involvement. As a propaganda act, therefore, it generated no propaganda at all. That, and the absence of any other supporting evidence for a Serb link, rendered the idea at least far-fetched, if not quite impossible.

The possibility of a link to *Crimewatch* was also quickly taken up. It was very difficult to believe, first because, as Nick Ross pointed out, there was no precedent for such an attack and no logic. Why should someone pick on a television personality who was, after all, merely the mouthpiece for a police appeal? And why would a criminal who had been caught once take the extraordinary risk of committing or commissioning a murder purely for revenge? If the theory was correct, moreover, this criminal would have to be drawn from a small pool of candidates. Since 1995 Dando had presented fewer than fifty episodes of

*Crimewatch* so the number of cases with which she had personally been involved was modest, in the region of 100. Where the crimes had been solved the culprits were obviously known to the police and a list of those with the capacity to commit murder could have been very quickly compiled. Those few not still in prison were easily traceable, so they could all be interviewed in short order. This was done by the Oxborough team, once, swiftly, in the days after the murder and again, much more laboriously, over the months that followed. It produced no leads. Other possible links to *Crimewatch* were suggested but they all suffered from the same flaw: no rational criminal would carry out such a crime. That left the possibility of an irrational criminal, a madman or an obsessive, and such people fell into a different category.

The word 'stalker', like the phrase 'professional hit-man', causes a frisson. The notion of an obsessed stranger following, harassing and even attacking the object of his obsession is every bit as theatrical as the cold-blooded assassin. It is frightening and inexplicable, capable of reducing anyone, however innocent, to the status of prey. In the headlines it was associated first with celebrities: film stars, pop singers, television actors and politicians would occasionally appear in court hoping to rid themselves of stalkers and telling stories of relentless abuse and harassment. But once the phenomenon had acquired its name it came gradually to be recognized as something common, afflicting people in all walks of life; here was a whole new class of criminals who had previously been lost among the nuisances, the writers of obscene or threatening letters, the causers of criminal damage, the rapists and the assaulters. Scarcely a day passed without some new tale of madness and misery appearing in the papers. Stalking became the most talked-of crime of the late nineties and it is little wonder that the first thought to come to many minds when the news of Jill Dando's murder broke was that she was the latest victim.

She had been stalked before. John Hole was in his late fifties when he first began to admire Jill Dando. A civil servant at the end of his career, he was single and unlucky with women and lived alone in a village near Ashford in Kent. Watching *Holiday* and *Crimewatch*, he thought Dando was 'so sweet', 'lovely' and 'like the typical girl next door'. After a while he tried to make contact with her; it was Valentine's Day in 1995 or 1996 and he sent her a card. Even though he received no answer he found he liked the feeling of writing to her, so he did it again. Addressing his letters to her at BBC Television Centre, he wrote about her screen appearances, what she said, how she looked and what she wore, and he told her about himself. She did not write back. Then he wrote asking her to meet him, but still got no reply. Frustrated, he eventually decided to act. He travelled up to London to find out – 'by perfectly legal means', as he stressed later – where she lived. The district was no secret, since at least one magazine had informed its readers she lived in 'upmarket Fulham', so all he had to do was go to a local library and comb through the electoral register street by street and house by house until her name came up. It might have taken a couple of hours. When Dando finally wrote him a letter asking to be left alone he was undeterred, as he thought he could 'win her round'. So he plucked up his courage and visited the house in the hope of talking to her. In fact he went three times, but she was never in. Then he began waiting for her outside Television Centre, again without success. He was still sending the letters and cards and now he also tried to reach her by phoning the BBC when he thought she would be there, but the switchboard would never put him through. Dando wrote to him again, politely explaining how unwelcome all this was, and it was when he ignored this second letter that she finally asked her employers to deal with the matter. The BBC sent a hand-delivered letter to him warning that he risked prosecution for harassment, and shortly afterwards the story of 'lovesick loner John Hole' and his pursuit of Jill Dando appeared in the *Sunday Mirror*. Interviewed, he admitted he was a 'sad old man' and told the paper: 'I just wanted to get to know her and I would have liked to have gone out with her.'

By then, fearing legal action, he had stopped trying to contact her.

Hole insisted that all he ever wanted to do was meet Dando, that he had never been rude to her in any way and that he never contemplated violence of any kind. It was easy to believe he was harmless: he cut a pathetic figure, appearing physically feeble, shabby and older than his years and admitting that he had only ever experienced rejection from women. But Dando could not have known that while he was pursuing her. She was accustomed to over-the-top fan mail, including proposals of marriage, requests that she wear particular items of clothing and detailed commentaries on her performances. But Hole had crossed the line between tiresomeness and menace. He was astonishingly persistent – the campaign lasted two or three years – but what made him frightening was his attempts to meet her, and particularly his visits to her home in Fulham. Foolish as he was, he was a genuine stalker. 'I am her number one fan,' he told the *Sunday Mirror*. 'Sometimes when you are attracted to certain people you like to think you are chasing after someone. Unfortunately for Jill she fell in my sights.' Interviewed after her murder, he insisted that his feelings had changed after the BBC letter and particularly after he learned of her involvement with Alan Farthing. He had finally lost interest.

If it had happened once it could happen again. Another fan could just as easily have crossed the line, found her address and lain in wait for her. She was certainly vulnerable and, as the press pointed out, there were a number of reasons – the engagement, the *Radio Times* cover – why a deranged fan might have decided to attack her in the spring of 1999. But there was a simple problem with the stalker hypothesis in the early days, which the police put in plain terms: 'If it was a stalker we would like to think there was evidence Jill Dando was stalked. There is none.' In other words she was not receiving unwanted mail – or at least no more than usual, and none from any particular suspect individual – she was not being followed or telephoned by a persistent fan, indeed she was not being harassed in any way. Everyone who knew her testified that she was perfectly happy and relaxed in the days and weeks before her death and had expressed no concern about being pursued. So if the killer was a stalker he had apparently not stalked her in the familiar fashion. Nor for that matter did he attempt to explain himself or talk to her on the doorstep before he shot her, as you might expect from an admirer, however unhinged. And, importantly, after killing her he escaped.

The best-known instance of a stalker killing a celebrity is the murder of John Lennon by Mark Chapman in New York in 1980. Chapman, aged twenty-five and originally from Atlanta, Georgia, was a lifelong Beatles fan who, during a depressive period brought on by losing his girlfriend and a job he loved, became fixated with Lennon. After working for a spell as a security guard in Hawaii he resigned one day – signing himself off as 'John Lennon' – bought a gun and took a plane to New York. He said later that he followed Lennon for several days and waited around outside his home in the Dakota building in Manhattan. In the course of 8 December he spoke to the singer, asking him to autograph his copy of J. D. Salinger's *Catcher in the Rye*. Then at 11 p.m., seeing Lennon once again outside the Dakota building, he produced his gun and fired five shots at him, four of which hit their target. Lennon died on the way to hospital. Chapman remained where he was and meekly surrendered to police when they reached the scene. His motives and thoughts remain obscure, but one thing he said afterwards was that he had wanted to 'save' Lennon, perhaps as the catcher in the rye of Salinger's book wanted to save children from falling over a cliff.

The United States also offered the best-known example of a woman celebrity murdered by an obsessive fan. This was the case of Rebecca Schaeffer, a television soap opera actress aged twenty-one, who was shot on her doorstep in 1989 by a nineteen-year-old fan, Robert Bardo. Bardo had paid a private detective to find Schaeffer's address and he also showed her photograph to people in the streets of Los Angeles, asking if they knew where she lived. One morning he rang her doorbell and she told him to go away. An hour later he rang again, and again she appeared and told him to go away. Enraged, he pulled a gun from a bag and shot her twice. Bardo ran from the scene but the following day was arrested in an Arizona town for deliberately obstructing traffic. Once in custody he immediately confessed to the killing.

The murder of Jill Dando was different from these two in obvious ways. Chapman, if he did not actually announce his intention of killing John Lennon, left many clues and hinted about it on a number of occasions. He followed Lennon, hung around his home without concealing himself and, when he had done the deed, made no attempt at escape. Bardo, too, made no secret of his determination to meet his idol. When he finally found her he seems not to have intended murder from the outset, but tried twice to talk to her. When he was rejected he shot her, and though he fled he effectively gave himself up within twenty-four hours. The Dando killing – ten seconds and one shot, with no known prior contact and a swift, complete getaway – seemed to have nothing at all in common with these.

But Chapman and Bardo are only the most famous of their kind. Academic work on stalking is still in its early stages but it is already clear that stalkers come in many forms and behave in a large variety of different ways. One sub-class that has been identified and was potentially relevant to the Dando case was given the name 'predatory stalker'. These men fantasize about assaulting – usually raping – their chosen victims but in the first instance they gain gratification, not by terrorizing their victims, but by gathering information about them, by covert observation and by planning an attack. They avoid alerting their victims, partly because they derive a sense of power from these preparations – they know something the victim does not; they believe they hold the victim's fate in their hands. They are a small minority among stalkers but apparently an unusually dangerous one: an Australian study found that of a group of 145 stalkers just six conformed to this pattern, but it also found that they were the most likely to pursue their fantasies to the point where they actually carried out an attack. One case study in the literature involved a lonely man in his mid-twenties who followed a woman for a year and hung around her home at dead of night fantasizing about a sexual assault. He believed he had avoided notice until one day the woman confronted him in a railway station, telling him to stop following her. Humiliated, he decided that the only way forward was to put his fantasy into action so he began to plan in detail an abduction and rape that would end in the woman's death. At the last moment his nerve broke and he sought medical help.

There are examples of similar behaviour involving celebrity victims. In 1998 Jonathan Norman was jailed for twenty-five years after being captured by private security guards outside the Hollywood home of Steven Spielberg. Norman had kept scrapbooks and diaries about Spielberg and his family and fantasized about raping him. He had found the director's address in a tourist map of the homes of stars and watched the house for a month, making more than one attempt to break in. When he was arrested he recounted to police the detailed scenario he had imagined for the assault on Spielberg and he was carrying razor blades, adhesive tape and handcuffs which he had intended to use.

Again, however, in important respects the Dando killing did not fit the predatory pattern – there was, for example, no rape or attempted rape, and the murderer completed his task and escaped. Where the predatory stalker model might have been relevant was in the way that the perpetrator could stalk his prey invisibly, without advertising his intentions to her or anyone else. If Dando was not stalked in the conventional and frightening sense, then perhaps she was stalked in this more remote fashion. It could not be ruled out. All the more so because one piece of information that came into the Oxborough incident room in the first days of the investigation pointed to someone who might have been doing just that. An Internet site called 192.com offers a service combining – perfectly legally – telephone directories, electoral rolls and street maps, so that users who enter a name can almost instantly find the telephone number, address and map location to go with it. In late April 1999, after the managers of 192.com heard about the Dando killing, they ran a check to see whether her name had ever been entered in their system and they found that it had. On Sunday 22 November 1998 a user somewhere had keyed in the words 'Jill Dando'. Her phone number was ex-directory so it was not displayed, but the screen offered a map; it was called up and Gowan Avenue was shown, with a highlight around number 29. Finding this in their records, the 192.com managers immediately contacted the police and a hunt began for this person who had traced Dando's home address five months before she died.

While the Serb and *Crimewatch* theories had a low priority for investigators and the 'loner/obsessive' theory (they avoided using the word 'stalker' in this case) had a much higher one, the potential motive that received most urgent and intensive attention in the first months after the killing was the personal one. The overwhelming majority of murder victims are killed by someone they know and if only for that simple statistical reason detectives had to view this as the likeliest explanation for Jill Dando's death. Perhaps there was a resentful former boyfriend or a jealous colleague, a friend or relative with a grudge. Or perhaps it was something she knew about or was involved in – a 'secret compartment' in her life that contained a criminal, financial or sexual connection capable of providing a murder motive. If this was the explanation, if the killer or the person who hired him was indeed someone she knew, that would resolve one of the principal mysteries of the case: how she came to die while on an apparently random visit to Gowan Avenue. It might have been somebody with a legitimate reason to know about her movements.

This was without doubt the most sensitive area of the investigation. In all murder cases the bereaved find it hard to accept that the victim's life must be scrutinized and this often creates difficulties for the police. It is also a commonplace that such people insist that the victim 'couldn't possibly have been mixed up in anything nasty'. 'We would have known,' they say. Sometimes they can be unpleasantly surprised and the police are used to this. In this case, moreover, detectives looking into Dando's life were dealing not just with a loyal family but with most of the press and most of the country. This woman had been – or so it seemed – everybody's friend. The idea that she might have had contact with criminals, for example, was impossible to square with her wholesome image, just as that image left little room for promiscuity or even for short-term relationships with men. As the detectives dug, therefore, they were aware of the possibility that they might come across something that would shatter the whole basis of Dando's popularity.

## 12. Needles in Haystacks

*'It's a hell of a piece of work, but it's do-able.'*

As the months passed the flow of police disclosures and public events in the Dando investigation slackened. The media interest, however, did not, and ever-stranger stories appeared in print. In June the *News of the World* reported: 'MI5 called in to catch Jill's killer'. Following a direct intervention by the prime minister, the paper said, the security service was helping the Met. The *Mirror*, meanwhile, announced that a palm print had been found on the front gate taken from Dando's house. 'If we can pinpoint a firm suspect we can match the print against him,' a detective on the case was reported to have said. The *Mail on Sunday* demanded to know in July why police had not interviewed a convicted rapist who worked for a security firm used by the BBC. This failure, the paper claimed, had so outraged one retired detective that he was undertaking his own investigation of the case. In August the *People* led its front page with the story: 'Spurned Mafia boss killed Dando'. MI6, tipped off once again by Israeli intelligence, had concluded that the killing was ordered by a senior figure in the Russian Mafia who became enraged after Dando rejected his advances when they met in Cyprus during one of her last filming assignments. The *Sunday Mirror* reported a 'major breakthrough' under the headline: 'Jill's killer bought gun in pub'. Three men were said to be suspected of involvement in the transaction, which took place in the Midlands, and police were on their trail. And another *News of the World* story announced: 'I know who killed Dando', quoting an 'underworld supergrass' who was in touch with Scotland Yard but bargaining for money and an amnesty for his own crimes. All of these stories were denied or dismissed by the police and it is tempting to conclude that they were merely further evidence of how the press abhors a news vacuum.

Despite the lower profile, the police investigation was grinding on. Everything was now down to the slow work and a senior detective summed up the prospects in June 1999: 'It's probably not going to happen overnight but we have every confidence in our ability to attack it thoroughly enough to uncover the answer. We've been there. We've done it, and it's feasible. It's a hell of a piece of work but it's do-able.' It would be wrong, however, to infer from this a mood of blithe confidence, for the crime reporters were not the only ones anxious about progress: so were some of the most senior figures in the Metropolitan Police. As we have seen, for reasons of morale and public confidence they desperately wanted this crime solved, but their thoughts and expectations had run beyond that. If there was any risk that the killer might *not* be found they were determined that there should be no doubts or questions about the quality of the investigation. No hint of negligence should attach itself to this one; it must not be another Stephen Lawrence case.

One practical legacy of the Lawrence affair was the introduction of a new 'murder book' to guide senior detectives. As the mistakes in that 1993 case were exposed, police forces across the country recognized a need to reassess the way in which murders were investigated and this led to the creation of a new manual for detectives. Contained in a black, ring-backed folder, it was similar in many ways to the process paths used in modern business, indeed its opening page was a flow diagram of boxes and arrows of a kind familiar to managers the world over. The manual broke down the business of murder investigation into a series of discrete steps and choices, each carefully defined and given its proper place in the order of events. A detective following its guidance would always know where he stood, what he needed to do next and how to be sure a task was complete. Predictably some officers moaned about 'idiot guides', but the idea was surely a sound one. Not only did the murder book encourage the use of best practice, but it also increased accountability, since anyone wishing to check on progress could test the conduct of the case against the instructions in the book. This was standard modern project management with all its virtues – everyone knows what they should be doing – and some of its vices – if the book itself is flawed you're in trouble.

The Dando case was among the first to be done by the new book. And as the process demanded, the investigation was periodically reviewed by officers from outside the Oxborough team. This was another Lawrence legacy: the Met now had squads of officers whose sole job was to scrutinize long-term investigations to determine whether they were up to standard, an exhaustive process involving examination of the computer database, interviews with officers and scrutiny of everything from overtime allocation to media policy. At the end of a couple of months the review team would produce a report giving a stream of separate verdicts and offering detailed suggestions for changes or actions that might bring results. However useful this was it could also be an ordeal for those under the microscope and within a year of Dando's death the Operation Oxborough team had endured it twice; the second review report, submitted in the spring of 2000, ran to nearly 250 pages.

DCI Campbell himself must have felt the pressure. At the time of the murder he had held the status of Senior Investigating Officer in murder inquiries for just a few months, indeed it was only recently that officers of his rank had been allowed to run such cases – before that it had been a job reserved for higher ranks. So it was probably to be expected that the Met leadership felt some anxiety at seeing this all-important case in the hands of a relatively junior detective. That, presumably, was why a more senior officer, Detective Chief Superintendent Brian Edwards, was given an oversight role with Operation Oxborough two weeks after the killing, with a brief to handle strategic matters while Campbell remained responsible for day-to-day management.

They were not short of manpower. Campbell had a full-time team of around forty-five, comprising one detective inspector, seven detective sergeants, about thirty detective constables and six civilians. This unit was not created specially to deal with the Dando murder; it already existed on 26 April, with half a dozen other cases on its plate, a couple of them difficult ones. It was allocated the Dando case simply because on the day it happened that Campbell was the SIO on call, the next cab in the rank, and in the months that followed he continued to have responsibility for those other cases alongside the Dando work. Where Operation Oxborough was different from other investigations, however, where it received preferential treatment in terms of resources, was in what happened once it was under way: the team was ring-fenced. Campbell did not go back on call and the team was not required to take on new cases, even after a year. The bulk of the team was therefore available to work on the Dando murder for the bulk of the time, and increasingly so as the other cases were solved or wound down – a big commitment that was approved at the highest level. The Metropolitan Police, therefore, were giving the Oxborough team the clearest run possible. What were the detectives actually doing?

'We are all suspects,' said Jon Roseman a few weeks after the murder, and to those who knew Jill Dando best it must have seemed that way. Of all the possible lines of inquiry none had a higher priority for the police than the search for a motive in her personal and professional life, and that meant investigating the members of what Campbell came to know as the 'inner core': Roseman, Alan Farthing, Bob Wheaton, Jenny Higham, Allasonne Lewis, Nigel Dando, Nick Ross, Simon Bassil and a dozen more. How do you look for a killer in such a group? By simple, logical steps. First came the question of whether any of these people actually pulled the trigger. The evidence of Hughes and

Upfill-Brown made it clear that the shot was not fired by a woman, so that ruled out half the group. With the men there was the straightforward matter of opportunity – though there were many mysteries about this case the time and location of the killing were not among them, so everyone was interviewed in detail about their movements on the day of the murder, what they were doing at 11.30 a.m., who could vouch for them and whether there was time or opportunity for a dash to Fulham and back. Alibis were checked and double-checked until detectives were satisfied that none of these people had fired the fatal shot.

Of course the gunman and the person with the motive were not necessarily one and the same – in fact at this stage detectives tended to believe that more than one person was involved – so the people of the inner core had to be investigated much further. Did they have a motive? And did they have associates, possibly criminal ones, who might have committed the murder or put them in touch with hired killers? This was a far more complex business involving many weeks of work and overlapping several other parts of the investigation. These people were asked about their relations with the victim and what they knew of her relationships with others, and their stories were cross-checked one against another. In many instances private papers were taken away for examination in case they contained evidence either of some suspect dealings with Dando or of unexplained payments that might have been to a killer. Large quantities of documents were also removed from Dando's homes and from the BBC and the Roseman Organization, to be sifted for anything helpful, anything unusual, anything suspect. The slightest hint of any contact with firearms or with the military or criminal worlds was probed to the limit. One person, for example, had a son who had been in the Royal Marines; the son was closely questioned and required to provide supporting evidence for his movements.

Detectives, meanwhile, were studying Dando herself. All her phone records – from her mobile and the land lines at Gowan Avenue and Chiswick, her office phone and e-mail at the BBC and the room lines in hotels she had visited on her recent travels at home and abroad – every one was analysed. Anyone she called who seemed of interest was questioned, and *their* phone records were often examined as well. From this and other work emerged what came to be known as the 'middle group', composed of people well known to Dando but not intimate with her, and as the investigation of those in the inner core approached its natural limit so attention turned outward to this larger, more disparate and more distant collection of people. All 486 names listed in her Filofax address book were contacted, for example, as well as many of her BBC colleagues in London and the West Country and all of her ex-boyfriends back to Weston days. By now the questionnaire was a polished product. What was your relationship with her? When did you last see her? Where were you on the day of the murder? What kind of car do you drive? Have you ever held a gun licence? And so on, at considerable length.

They constructed a biography of Dando from childhood to death, using it to identify further individuals they needed to interview or events or periods that might yield a motive. In particular detectives set themselves the task of reconstructing in intimate detail the last twelve months of her life. They wanted to know about every telephone call, every meeting, every credit card transaction, cheque payment and cash withdrawal, every journey short or long, every hairdressing and leg-waxing appointment, every taxi ride, every filming assignment, every formal function, every breakfast, lunch and dinner, every casual encounter and as far as possible every conversation she had, even every word that she spoke. This was a tall order, especially as she had not kept a detailed diary in that period, but it was seen as a vital one and for very simple reasons. It seemed inconceivable that anyone who bore her a grudge sufficient to justify murder would not have expressed those feelings to her in some way at some stage in the twelve months beforehand. Or, on the other hand, if there *was* a secret compartment in her life that contained something capable of causing her death, it was hard to believe

that at some time in that year she would not have opened it. In
either case some trace would surely remain.

The premise of all this work, which entailed such a vast amount
of research and interviewing, was belief that the killer or the
person behind the killing was probably somebody known to
Dando, but while this was the dominant strain of the investigation
in the early months it was by no means the only one; separate
teams of detectives were busy on other matters. Considerable
effort, for example, was poured into the matter of mobile phones.
The witness evidence included many sightings of people using
mobile phones in and around Gowan Avenue on the morning
of 26 April and the question was raised whether it was possible
to trace them. The short answer was, maybe. Mobile phones
(provided they are switched on) constantly exchange signals with
the network masts, or base stations, so in principle it should be
possible to locate any phone at any time and a few prosecutions
have come to court in Britain involving evidence derived from
such tracing. But they were very different cases from this one.
Where the number is known, tracing can often be done with
reasonable accuracy through the network companies, but in this
case what the police were looking for was not numbers but calls
made to and from a specific area. That is a very different matter.

Britain has four mobile telephone networks and it was easy to
identify which base station for each network was nearest to the
murder site. That meant four stations. But each base station
covered a fairly large area and to ensure continuous coverage its
maximum range needed to overlap with the maximum ranges of
several other base stations on the same network. This meant that
mobile phones around Gowan Avenue could be in touch with
eight, ten or even a dozen different base stations. And the compli-
cations did not end there, for when a particular base station was
busy it had the ability to bounce a call on to another, less busy,
station. This added once again to the number of stations that may
have been involved, bringing the total as high, potentially, as
twenty – covering much of west London. The total number of

calls handled by those twenty base stations inside two hours on a given Monday morning would be enormous. It seemed an Everest of a job, but it was attempted. The Dando team commissioned the telephone industry (and, by some accounts, government security specialists at GCHQ, the electronic eavesdropping agency) to sift out from the data held by the four companies those calls which could have been made to or from the relevant Fulham area at the relevant time. After some months they were presented with a file of 80,000 items.

What should they look for? For a start, calls made to and from numbers relating to people who knew Dando, and if any part of this can be called easy, that was it, since by now those numbers were all on file. Beyond that detectives were looking for suspicious calls, which could mean any number of things. It might, for example, mean instances where the caller and receiver were both on mobile phones, or cases where one user made several calls between 10 a.m. and noon. Each of these might yield a list in the hundreds from which callers would be identified, listed and, if they were of any interest, traced and interviewed. But here lay another large obstacle, for about one third of mobile phones in Britain in 1999 were unregistered, that is to say they had been bought off the shelf with ready-made numbers and no one necessarily knew who the user was. Professional criminals use these phones and if they're clever they take the additional precaution of throwing them away after each job. So even if all the necessary data survived and it was possible to identify suspect calls, a proportion of the users making those calls – perhaps one third – could still not be identified from their numbers. Jill Dando's killer could easily have fallen into that group. Of course these unregistered phones might be traced through the numbers they called, or else they might be tied to the phone manufacturers and from there to individual retailers and purchasers – but that was a whole new field of investigation.

Another high-technology inquiry involved the 192.com contact and the search for the person who called up Dando's address on the Internet. It was evident from the start that the user had come to 192.com through AOL – this was his or her service provider – but AOL were unable to help since they routinely deleted such records within fourteen days. 192.com, however, still had some details of the contact. To access such a site a user's computer must provide a certain amount of information about itself, indicating, for example, what sort of software it employs so that the site can respond in the appropriate way. This is done in a matter of moments on first contact, without the user being conscious of it, and this was the sort of data that 192.com retained, deep in its databases. It required very lengthy analysis, without any certainty of success, and then extensive detective work to follow up such leads as could be found.

More traditional but if anything even more labour-intensive was the business of hunting down witnesses from the streets of Fulham and analysing their evidence. Again and again officers revisited Gowan Avenue and the surrounding roads, knocking on doors and stopping passers-by to ask them if they had been in the area and seen anything. Campbell had appealed for such witnesses to come forward on the afternoon of the killing; he had done so again on *Crimewatch* and he never failed to do so every time he spoke to the media. Did you see a man waiting? Did you see a blue Range Rover? Did you see a man running? Did you see anything at all that was suspicious, either on that day or in the weeks beforehand? Over time the file built up until it comprised eighty-nine sightings in the whole of the morning of 26 April. And while they constantly added to the list, detectives were working equally hard to whittle it down by tracing the men who were seen. Three particularly important people were traced and eliminated: one was a builder who was working on a building at the Munster Road end of Gowan Avenue that morning and spent some of the time out on the street. Another was a man working for a gas company, visiting properties in the area that morning – he was the fair-haired man seen by the window cleaner. The third was a man picking up his daughter and grandchildren from a Gowan Avenue house to take them on a birthday treat. One way or another by Christmas of 1999 fifty-nine of the eighty-nine sightings were accounted for – an impressive total but one which still left thirty to be explained.

Of those thirty, eleven were regarded as particularly suspicious because of the clothing or behaviour of the men described. These included, of course, some of the familiar waiting and running men, but also the drivers of dark blue Range Rovers, and this was a substantial line of inquiry in its own right. One of the earliest pieces of information to come in on this subject had been an anonymous call made to the *Daily Mirror*, which the paper reported to the Dando team. The caller claimed that a man had been seen in a street near Bishop's Park just after the murder getting into a C registration blue Range Rover. This at first aroused considerable interest but lengthy investigation revealed that the call was part of a private vendetta against a man who had no connection with the crime. In the same way a sighting in Fulham Palace Road proved to be of a Cherokee Jeep rather than a Range Rover, and was once again eliminated, while the Range Rover captured on Putney Bridge by the traffic camera was eventually tracked down and found to be unconnected. Another approach adopted was to trace all blue Range Rovers registered to owners living in the Fulham area – there were twenty-five – and then assess each in turn, interviewing the more promising drivers about their doings on the day. Nothing was found. A list was acquired of every dark blue Range Rover in the country, together with its present and past owners, and any promising leads were followed up, while stolen Range Rovers were investigated and lists were compiled of Range Rovers leaving and entering the country. On top of this, Campbell was constantly appealing to the driver or drivers who were seen that morning to come forward and he found it baffling that none did.

When it came to the search for people who might be obsessed with Jill Dando detectives soon found themselves mining a rich seam. They looked at her mailbag, at general mail to the BBC

which mentioned her and at the log of calls to the corporation's
duty office. They looked, too, at the tributes sent by letter or
e-mail on her death (in all, the Oxborough team was to examine
more than 13,000 e-mails). And they were left in no doubt that,
like many women appearing on television, Dando had plenty of
persistent admirers, some of whom might be capable of behaving
in peculiar ways. So far as possible they were identified, listed in
order of priority and, where significant, investigated. Top of this
list, of course, was John Hole, her one known stalker, who was
the subject of intensive scrutiny over several weeks. Another
figure who attracted special attention was a businessman living
in Fulham who was found to have a strong fascination for Dando.
Though subsequent press reports that he kept a 'shrine' to her
and that he had fled to Australia once the police became interested
in him were exaggerated, he was regarded for some time as an
important suspect. The Internet was another source of leads.
There had been a dedicated Jill Dando fan site, which was closed
down on the day of the murder, while pictures of her also
appeared on dozens of other celebrity sites. And there had been
some Jill Dando pornography, part of that Internet subculture in
which the faces of celebrity women are attached to the naked
bodies of models. People were traced who had downloaded
hundreds of pictures of her and stored them in their personal
computers. These too were added to the list and any who seemed
significant were questioned. Over the course of the investigation,
in fact, by one means or another detectives identified no fewer
than 140 men whom they regarded as having, or suspected of
having, an 'unhealthy interest' in Dando.

  Combing through the friends and associates, studying Dando's
life, sifting the mobile phone calls, tracing the 192.com user,
seeking out new witnesses, eliminating men seen in Gowan
Avenue and identifying men with an unhealthy interest – these
were just some of the 'high-volume' inquiries under way during
the summer, autumn and winter of 1999. Others included sifting
the thousand or more names supplied by members of the public

either as possible killers or as resembling the face in the E-fit, and tracing any that were of interest. Officers were tracing and interviewing criminal armourers, gun dealers and potential sources of Remington ammunition, as well as legitimate holders of de-activated 9mm 'short' automatics. They were revisiting and re-interviewing criminals caught as a result of *Crimewatch* appeals. They were seeking parallels with other murders or serious crimes involving a similar weapon or similar modus operandi, from political assassinations to armed robberies. And much more.

Every line of inquiry, moreover, yielded a database of its own containing dozens or perhaps hundreds of names, addresses, telephone numbers, car ownership details, personal descriptions, criminal records and so forth. This, after the inner core and the middle group, was the basis of the third, outer pool of potential suspects, that amorphous collection of names and sometimes mere descriptions choking up the Oxborough computer system. As far as possible interesting connections were followed up – a Range Rover driver with criminal associations, a Dando fan who worked near Fulham, a man resembling the E-fit who was a past member of a gun club. Day in, day out such people were visited and questioned, while a few of them merited more long-term attention. One was a former funeral director who was arrested in May after telling police that he was one of the running men seen in Fulham Palace Road. He claimed he had been in the area for work purposes and was running to escape a man who wanted to have sex with him. This man, it transpired, was well known in west London as an eccentric and had a record as a hoaxer, but he was none the less the object of close scrutiny. He was arrested and questioned and his house was searched before he was ruled out, even though one simple fact appeared to exclude him from the start: at 6ft 4in tall he was far taller than the man seen by Hughes and Upfill-Brown, and than any of the running men. Another, more serious line of inquiry involved a mechanic from the East End of London who aroused sufficient suspicion to be the target of a surveillance operation in the autumn of 1999. Though officers soon found that he was a professional car thief specializing in Mercedes models, he did not prove a valid suspect for the murder. He was subsequently jailed for conspiracy to steal cars on evidence gathered by the Oxborough team.

It was, as the officer said, a hell of a piece of work. Eliminating just one man could take an officer five working days. Picking the name off a list, he could find details of address and current employment fairly easily through national computer records. Then he would have to research the man's background, looking for criminal or firearms connections, ownership of a Range Rover and the like. Once he was ready to approach the man and question him there might be difficulties catching him at home; he might have changed jobs or address, or simply gone on holiday. And when they finally spoke he might, for example, have no memory of where he was on 26 April, and nothing on paper besides a till receipt. The officer would then have to go to the source of the receipt and question staff or view security videos before finally deciding that the suspect was telling the truth, after which he would return to his desk and start with the next name on the list. Of course not every inquiry would be so complicated but many were and very few could be dealt with in a couple of phone calls. In the first twelve months hundreds of names were fully investigated and eliminated in this way.

Laborious and unspectacular as they were, these methods had worked before. Senior officers could point to terrorist cases which were investigated in this fashion for years before the breakthrough came. For Brian Edwards and Hamish Campbell the challenge was to manage it all and to keep the balance right. They might have a relatively large team but their resources were not infinite and every hare could not be chased. Priorities had to be set and frequently reviewed, with effort always set against potential results. One line of inquiry might be pursued a certain distance, until a particular result was achieved, and then frozen while manpower was switched to another promising area. Then after a certain time the first line might resurface and, if it was thought worthwhile, be tackled again. And while it might seem that the flow of information into the incident room was potentially endless, the senior officers were convinced this was not the case. The murder had been planned; it occurred on a particular date in a particular place; at least two witnesses saw the killer, who used a particular type of gun and distinctive ammunition. Above all, detectives were sure, there was a motive, a reason for wanting Jill Dando dead. All of these factors defined the crime and gave it limits, provided the investigators did not lose sight of their priorities and avoided distractions. Huge and fluid though it appeared, this was, as the detectives put it, a 'finite network'.

Once every six weeks or so Hamish Campbell would give a press conference or an interview. He was unfailingly upbeat and determined – 'Believe, and the answer comes,' he once said – and he almost always revealed some new nugget of information. In July 1999, for example, he described the strange markings on the cartridge case. In December 1999 he revealed that the gun was smooth-bored. In January 2000 he told the story of the 192.com caller. In each case the revelation made headlines and prompted excited speculation in the press (for example, many papers presented the crimp marks as the killer's 'signature'), but these titbits were new only in the sense that they were new to the public; in each case Campbell had been aware of them for months. That he should have revealed them in his own time might seem like window-dressing, as though he was attempting to reassure press and public that his investigation was making steady progress, and no doubt such thoughts played their part. But it is also true that by spacing them out he gained impact. Police experience in such matters showed that too much information at one time could blunt their message and that a single, simple fact placed before the public at the right moment was most likely to produce a useful response. Campbell, in pulling the rabbits out of his hat one by one, was trying to focus public attention on this most high-profile of cases in a manageable way. Could someone account for the markings on the cartridge case? Had anybody seen or handled the gun? If the person who contacted 192.com did so for innocent reasons, could he come forward? Each appeal produced leads, although never a breakthrough. In other ways, however, things were moving forward.

The search for someone with a personal or professional motive to kill Dando continued through the summer and autumn of 1999, but despite a huge commitment of man-hours almost nothing turned up, certainly nothing pointing towards the killer. Dando's legacy gave no lead for she died intestate and the £600,000 residue of her estate after tax went to her father, Jack. Very few of her associates in the inner core and middle group had the opportunity to commit the murder and those without alibis seemed to disqualify themselves from suspicion on other grounds. Nor, anywhere in the paperwork or in the associations, histories, statements and interviews of the two groups, was there any strong indication that any of them had the motive or capacity to recruit someone else to do the job. Throwing the net wider produced a similar lack of results. Examination of the period in 1997 when she spoke of herself as single and dining out with three men in a week yielded no substantial leads; study of her turbulent period of contention for the *Six O'Clock News* in 1998 likewise. Despite all the digging there was still no trace whatever of the secret compartment. Slowly, very slowly, detectives began to form the view that the reason they could not find it was that it probably wasn't there, either in Dando's life or in those of her friends and close colleagues. Reporters who asked whether she was really the uncomplicated woman she seemed were told: 'That's what we find at the moment.' Had she been secretly promiscuous? 'From what we know, Jill Dando was a perfectly normal woman, no more and no less.' Were all the ex-lovers in the clear? 'There is nothing that has led us to believe that any past boyfriend or friend has had a motive or opportunity to kill her.' Eventually Campbell himself would tell an interviewer:

'I've read her diaries and her letters, seen her mementoes. I know what she did in minute detail. People say there must be something in her life that explains it but there's nothing which suggests a catalyst for her killing.'

Other lines of inquiry, meanwhile, were proving slightly more fruitful. Among the high-volume tasks carried out by the Oxborough team was contacting every person called Dando in the country to find out if they had anything to say. One of these was a woman who was listed in her local telephone directory – outside London – as J. Dando, and she told officers about an unusual call she had received in December 1998. The caller was polite, but also inquisitive. He asked the woman about Jill Dando, whether she was related to Jill, whether she knew her and whether she knew where Jill lived. He kept the woman on the line for some time, possibly as long as ten minutes, chatting amiably but always with an inquisitive edge and never giving any information about himself or explaining the reason for his interest. The woman had received a number of calls over the years from people who hoped she might be the television celebrity and she was not particularly surprised by this one, but she remembered it because of how long it lasted and because the caller was so polite. She had no memory of an accent or of any other distinguishing characteristics to his voice, beyond saying that he 'sounded white'.

Here then was a fresh instance of someone apparently crossing the line that divides normal fan behaviour from unhealthy interest, and it came three weeks after the 192.com inquiry and four months before her death. And there was more. On 1 February 1999, it was discovered, three extraordinary calls were made to utility companies in London in relation to Jill Dando's accounts. The first came at 6.31 p.m. when a man called her gas supplier and, introducing himself as James Dando, said he was her brother and he wanted the account switched to his name, but at the same address. Explaining that he lived at the house and that Dando was not often there, he also asked to change the method of payment to a monthly direct debit. He was told that none of this could be done over the phone but that a new payment form would be sent to the house. The call ended. Fifteen minutes later, at 6.46 p.m., Thames Water received a call from a man who said he was living at the Gowan Avenue address and asked for details of the state of the account. These were declined. And three or four minutes after that a man phoned the electricity supplier, gave Jill Dando's fourteen-digit account number, said he was her brother James and tried, in vain, to have the billing switched to his name, once again at the same address.

These calls made little or no sense. Three times in twenty minutes a man presenting himself as Jill Dando's brother asked to take over payment of her utility bills, but *at the same address*. Unless he had access to the house he would never receive these bills, so he would not have the opportunity to pay them. Even if the utility companies had agreed to the changes over the phone, the only consequence would have been that the name on the bill became 'James' or 'Mr J.' instead of 'Jill' or 'J.' The futility of it all was demonstrated to the full when the letter from the gas company duly arrived at 29 Gowan Avenue. Though it was addressed to 'Mr J. Dando' Jill Dando did not notice; she sat down, filled in the direct debit form and sent it back, completely unaware that anyone else had been involved. However baffling they were, these phone calls showed at the very least that there was a man somewhere who knew Jill Dando's address, had an unusual and apparently quite irrational interest in her affairs and was in possession of her electricity account number. More than that, the date may have been significant. The calls were made on 1 February. On the previous evening, 31 January, Jill Dando and Alan Farthing had announced their engagement to friends at their party in Chiswick. That news reached the press the following day and was in print in that afternoon's London *Evening Standard*. In other words, someone could easily have read the story on the journey from work that evening and started making the calls as soon as they arrived home.

Three months later, and just six days before Dando died, it happened again when a man phoned British Telecom and asked to have her account switched to his name. This time he did not pretend to be her brother but said he lived at the Gowan Avenue house and was able to supply Jill Dando's telephone number, which was ex-directory. Once again his request was refused. Although the police could not prove that this was the same man who made the earlier calls it is almost inconceivable that it was not. Was the date of the BT call significant? It was 20 April, the day the photographs featuring Dando in leather appeared in the press.

So there were now four signs: the 192.com inquiry; the call to the woman named J. Dando; the December calls to the utility companies and the April call to BT. It was tempting to link them all together and draw the conclusion that, in a peculiar way, Jill Dando was being stalked after all. Calmly, it seemed, a man somewhere might be assembling information about her: he had her home address, her ex-directory telephone number and her electricity account number. He was trying to learn more and in tentative ways he was trying to interfere in her life, to make little changes. Was this someone behaving towards Dando as a predatory stalker might, exerting a form of control and showing himself that by indirect routes he was able to get close to her without her knowing? Perhaps, but on the other hand it might all have been much less sinister than it seemed. The 192.com inquiry might have been nothing more than somebody fooling around on the Internet. The call to Ms J. Dando could have been just another fan call that happened to be a long one. The utility calls could have been made by a third man, or even two different men, and as detectives pointed out it was just about possible that they were part of some half-baked attempt at credit fraud in which the bills would ultimately be used as proof of identity. Such doubts were strengthened when, early in 2000, thanks to a herculean effort of detection over nine months, the 192.com man was finally traced. They had started with a list of 1,600 people, narrowed it down to 100 and then to just one. It was a man; he lived in Wales and he had no particular interest in Jill Dando. Apparently he was experimenting with the website and the name popped into his head simply because he had been watching television. Though once again he was investigated closely police were soon satisfied that he had nothing to do with the murder or the utility calls.

There was something else to add to the file, however, another line of inquiry which had borne fruit in a way not made public. Shortly after the killing detectives had said there was no evidence that Dando was stalked in the conventional sense – in other words they had nothing to show she had been harassed or followed in the period before her death. This was true at the time but by the summer a witness had emerged whose testimony suggested something different. He was a plasterer employed during the spring of 1999 at a property on Wardo Avenue, the street that runs parallel to Gowan Avenue immediately to the north. He recalled that at 11 a.m. on Monday 12 April, two weeks before the killing, he was walking down Munster Road towards a café when he saw a man standing outside the primary school opposite the corner of Gowan Avenue, a little more than 100 yards from Dando's house. And between thirty-five and forty minutes later, when he was walking back, the plasterer noticed the same man in the same place. Then the man must have moved, because when the plasterer reached the house where he was working in Wardo Avenue he looked up and caught sight of the man at the corner of the street. He was wearing a baggy suit, possibly double-breasted, and on his head was a hat – a trilby or pork-pie hat with a fairly narrow brim, made of patterned material, possibly tartan.

A week later, on Monday 19 April, the same plasterer was walking along Wardo Avenue towards a bookmaker's on Fulham Palace Road in the early afternoon when he spotted the same suspicious man again. This time the man was standing on the corner of Wardo Avenue and Sidbury Street, which leads to

Gowan Avenue. He was about 180 yards from Dando's house, though not in sight of it. Again he was wearing a suit, but this time no hat. And that was not all. Two days later, on Wednesday 21 April, the plasterer spotted the man again in Sidbury Street. On this occasion he was in shirtsleeves and using a mobile phone; as the plasterer passed he became agitated and tried to hide his face by looking down at the ground.

Here were three sightings of a man behaving oddly in the vicinity of Dando's home, two of them on the Mondays immediately preceding the murder (which also took place on a Monday) and the third on a Wednesday. Perhaps this was the answer to the all-important question: how did the killer know his victim would be there on 26 April? Perhaps he did not know after all but simply employed trial and error, hanging around near her home again and again until finally she turned up. There were still a number of unexplained sightings of men in the hours before the murder and two of them could be linked to the plasterer's information because of the hat. The first took place at 8.50 a.m. A woman aged forty-two was driving her ten-year-old son to school along Gowan Avenue when the boy's eye was caught by a man behaving strangely at the roadside, on the opposite side of the road to the Dando house and some distance from it. The man seemed to be pacing up and down very quickly. The boy told his mother to be careful in case the man walked in front of the car. Both of them looked at this figure as they passed him and saw that he was dressed oddly as well. His suit seemed old-fashioned and far too big for him and he was wearing a hat. As described by the woman it had a wider brim than the hat seen by the plasterer, but it was in roughly the same style. The second sighting was in the evidence of the woman driver who reported the Range Rover following her along the road after 10 a.m. Just before that happened she had been sitting in her car waiting to cross Munster Road and enter Gowan Avenue when she saw a man who she said 'looked out of context' and acted strangely. At first he was standing by the glazier's and then he crossed the road, looking up and down, she said, as if he was checking the name of the street. What made this sighting especially interesting now was her description of him: he was wearing clothes that did not fit and as she watched he took off a hat he was wearing and stuffed it in his pocket.

Men in hats are a sufficiently rare sight in the streets of modern London to suggest a link between these three sightings, but they also matched in other ways. In each case the hat was of roughly the same design; in each case the man was in his thirties or forties, tall, wearing a dark, ill-fitting suit; and in each case he was behaving in a manner that was strange enough to attract attention. There seemed, therefore, to be some grounds to suspect that this could be one man who loitered in or near Gowan Avenue on three successive Mondays, and also on the Wednesday before the murder. Was this the gunman?

By the end of 1999, then, things were changing in important ways inside Operation Oxborough. As we have seen, the search for a killer with a personal or professional motive appeared to have drawn a blank. In similar fashion the chances of a criminal connection were dwindling too. Metropolitan Police officers run thousands of paid informers across London and they provide tip-offs on all categories of crime, yet despite constant urgings not one of them ever reported so much as a whisper of reliable information about the murder of Jill Dando. Moreover the reward now stood at £250,000, making it the largest in British criminal history, and still no one had come forward from the criminal community to claim it. Again there were grounds for suspecting that this was for the obvious reason – that no one in that community knew anything about the crime. That in turn suggested something about the murder weapon. The strange crimp marks on the cartridge case had always appeared crude, and the smooth bore indicated a gun that had been tampered with. The stubborn silence from the world of criminal armourers now lent weight to the idea that both might be the work of the same amateur hand, the hand that fired the fatal shot.

Campbell's public utterances offered some clues to the change. In press conferences and interviews he was always asked about the various possible motives and over the months his answers changed subtly. At first he tended to rank the 'personal or professional' motive and the 'loner/obsessive' motive equally, but with a bias towards the former. As 1999 turned into 2000, however, the emphasis shifted and the idea that Dando might have been murdered by a loner/obsessive gained precedence in his comments. It would be wrong to construe this as simply a logical progression, for the force of circumstance was playing its part. Instinct, habit and experience had driven the inquiry first and foremost towards the personal or professional motive: this was the cause of most murders and it was surely the most likely cause of this one. Other possibilities had been explored from the start but in the scale of priorities this one had come top. 'Clear the ground around your feet', was a constant refrain from Edwards, meaning that detectives should do the obvious things first. This, so far as they were concerned, was the obvious thing. By the end of a year of searching and sifting, however, it was looking like a dead end – 'We came to realize the crime was not making sense,' Campbell would say later, and the Oxborough team as a whole was beginning to accept that priorities must change. It was a matter of percentages. As ever, very little could be ruled out completely, but surely it was possible to say now that the chance of the killer being someone from Dando's circle of acquaintance and the chance of professional criminal involvement were both far lower than at the outset. On the other hand, the chance that it was a stranger acting alone and for a motive other than a conventional criminal one had grown proportionately.

## 13. The Man with Many Names

*'Now I know where you live.'*

Munster Road, reached by turning right from Jill Dando's front door, is a popular rat run for drivers in a hurry to get through Fulham. Walk down it past the school and you soon reach the lights at Fulham Road, where a left turn takes you abruptly into latte and Chardonnay country – Starbucks, Café Flo and the rest of them, cheek by jowl along the street. Cope's fish shop, where Dando bought those Dover soles, is squeezed in here and just across the way is Dancer Road, where she tried to park her BMW. Cross over there and carry on past the end of Dancer Road along the south side of the street and soon you are at the mouth of Crookham Road, where the first house on your right, a redbrick Edwardian structure, is number 2. A steep flight of steps leads up to the front door and there the array of buttons tells you that the building is divided into flats. Flat B is at this level, to the right of the front door and overlooking the street. In 1999 and 2000 this was the home of Barry Michael George, an unemployed man well known in the area. The distance between his door and 29 Gowan Avenue is about 750 yards and if you walk briskly and are not held up crossing the roads you can cover it in six minutes.

Barry George, who was roughly the same age as Dando, had lived in west London all his life. His father, Alfred, came from an army background and over the years worked in a variety of jobs, including bus conductor and prison officer, while also serving for a time as a special constable in the Metropolitan Police. In 1954 he married an Irish girl, Margaret Bourke, in a church in Hammersmith and they had two daughters, Michelle and Susan, before Barry arrived on the scene on 15 April 1960. The marriage, troubled for some years, ended when the boy was seven, with Alfred moving away – he eventually settled in Australia – and leaving the children in their mother's care. By that time it was evident that Barry was a difficult child. He was epileptic, although the condition was not diagnosed until he was in his teens, and it seems that he had serious behaviour problems. From the age of five or six he attended a special school locally in Hammersmith and when he was old enough he was sent away to Heathermount, a boarding establishment near Ascot for what were then called 'maladjusted' boys. Barry probably attended until his mid-teens, at which point he returned to London to live with his mother and prepare to enter the adult world.

Within a month of his sixteenth birthday he was working as a messenger at BBC Television Centre in Wood Lane, west London, near his mother's home. It was just a short-term contract, probably a holiday relief post, but he would come to regard it as one of the highlights of his life. From May to September of 1976 he wheeled his trolley around the circular corridors of what has been called the 'concrete doughnut', delivering and gathering letters and parcels. He was a slim, eager young man, obviously not bright but obliging enough. His epilepsy, now recognized and treated, was mild and need not have affected his work. In fact as far as we know nothing much marked him out as strange at this time apart from his name, which was a false one. In the offices he visited, in the post-room where he was based and in the personnel department where he was registered as an employee, he was known not as Barry George but as Paul Francis Gadd, which was the real name of Gary Glitter.

He had been an admirer since schooldays – when Glitter reached the peak of his pop success in 1973–5 George was in the age-group to which the gang anthems most appealed – but it is one thing to be a fan and quite another to adopt a version of your hero's name. Evidently Barry George did not want to be

Barry George any more; there may have been some resentment towards his absent father here, or perhaps he wanted to put his troubled childhood behind him. At the same time he positively wanted to be, not 'Gary Glitter', which would have been obviously eccentric, but the next best thing. It was a conversation point, something to make him interesting, and on the basis of his behaviour later in life it is easy to imagine him making use of it as he travelled around Television Centre. His dealings were not with celebrities, although no doubt he spotted some along the way, but with junior staff in the offices, many of them young women secretaries. He was called Paul Gadd, he would say. Yes, just like Gary Glitter – in fact Gary was his cousin . . .

After his spell at the BBC we do not know what work he found, or whether he found work at all. To judge once again by the pattern of his later life he was probably unemployed for most of his late teens and early twenties, not an unusual fate in those years and one that doesn't seem to have troubled him; increasingly he was content to live on benefits. To the outsider, looking back, it seems that his was now a life with little or no structure, with no long-term friendships and very few elements of continuity except that he remained in west London, in easy reach of his mother's home. What survives from this period, and what the police and the press found when they came to investigate his background, is a series of recorded episodes, of glimpses.

The first of these occurred one evening early in 1980 when 'Paul Gadd' was arrested in Kingston, southwest London, by police following up a complaint about a man pretending to be a detective. The man had aroused suspicion when he visited a private house in the area, showed what appeared to be a false identification card and asked to see a woman called Caroline, who lived there. On his arrest, Gadd was found to be in possession of just such a false card, a mock-up as feeble and unimpressive as the story he went on to tell. He said he had encountered the woman the previous night after seeing her being pursued by her husband and had tried to reassure her by saying he was a police

officer and showing the card. The following evening he returned
to her home merely to see if she was all right, he said. Police
soon found that Gadd had used the same card on at least five
previous occasions, including attempts to persuade drivers to give
him lifts, so he was charged with impersonating a police officer
and tried. Pleading guilty, he was eventually given a £5 fine.
The affair does not seem to have embarrassed him in the least,
for outside the court he posed for a photograph and spoke freely
and boastfully to a reporter, claiming that he was twenty-three
years old (he was twenty), a musician who played the synthesizer
and the former boss of a company that ran three pop groups.
More than that, he was a cousin, not of Gary Glitter, who by
now was slipping out of fashion, but of Jeff Lynne, the lead singer
of the Electric Light Orchestra.

This incident is eloquent in several respects. Although four
years have passed and he is no longer a teenager, he is still using
the name Gadd and far from outgrowing his pop fantasy he has
simply updated and embellished it. Moreover he wants to show
it off, seizing the opportunity of a local newspaper reporter's
interest to parade his false connections and accomplishments,
making himself as newsworthy as he can manage. Even stranger,
however, is what we learn from the detail of the case: George
had recently applied to be a policeman, for the fake warrant card
was made up using a Metropolitan Police insignia clipped from
a letter he had received turning him down for a job. That the
pop star's cousin wanted to become a police officer and thus an
authority figure – like his special constable father – is striking in
itself, but that when rejected he should have refused to accept
the decision is doubly so. He chopped up the letter, made himself
a warrant card and went out on to the streets of London saying
he *was* a detective. And what did he do next? He followed a
woman who was a stranger to him all the way to her front door.

The story of his Kingston court appearance featured in a west
London local paper in May 1980. Three months later Paul Gadd
was in the news again, this time as a karate champion. He walked

into the offices of the *West London Observer* with a large trophy in his arms and announced that he had won it at the British karate championships for breaking forty-seven tiles with his feet. He was photographed and the story was reported in good faith, with the additional detail that when he was not training at karate Gadd was a session musician and a singer with a band called Xanadu. Again this was a fiction. The paper soon received complaints and investigated, and a few weeks later it announced that Gadd had lied and that his trophy was a fake. It was another telling affair: when Barry George wanted people to believe he was a martial arts champion he simply bought a trophy and declared he had won it. And it wasn't enough to tell the people that he met: he had to go to a newspaper so that his claim would be published.

The karate story opens up another side to George's character: his interest in, and admiration for, physical prowess. For a time at least this ran concurrently with his fascination for pop glamour, as the Xanadu tale shows, but it soon became dominant and with it came a new name: Steve Majors. This was in honour of Lee Majors, star of *The Six Million Dollar Man*, the children's television hit of the later 1970s. Majors played the handsome test pilot Steve Austin, whose 'bionic' limbs made him a superhero. Barry George borrowed the actor's surname and his character's first name and for the next few years this was how he introduced himself to most people. It may be relevant, too, that by the early 1980s the actor Lee Majors had moved on from playing the bionic man to another series called *The Fall Guy*, in which he was a movie stunt man. Another of George's claims, which became a long-lasting one, was that he was a professional stunt man. There was at least some truth in this, for he was a proficient roller-skater and by some accounts landed small parts in skating displays for a time. Certainly he was sufficiently competent and plausible to persuade someone to stage a stunt event early in 1981 at which he was to jump on skates over four double-decker buses. A television camera crew turned out to film, and a reported crowd of 5,000 was there to watch, as he climbed a scaffolding tower on a wet

and windy evening and then careered down a ramp. He clipped
the last of the buses and tipped forward on to his stomach as he
landed, but otherwise completed the stunt in one piece and was
quickly on his feet to acknowledge the applause. It was a moment,
perhaps, when reality matched his aspirations.

In December of 1981 George enlisted with the Territorial
Army in White City – again very close to his mother's home –
and not just with any old unit but with the Parachute Regiment.
Over the following eleven months he attended twenty-nine
voluntary training days under the name of S. F. Majors. These
were heady times in which to be associated with the armed
forces, and particularly the Paras, since mid-1982 saw the victory
in the Falklands War. No doubt some of the excitement, and the
glory of the two Victoria Crosses won by men of the Parachute
Regiment, found its way down to George as he attended his
physical training and his firearms instruction. It was the beginning
of a sustained interest in militaria and in guns. He was still a TA
member when, in August 1982, he applied to join the Kensington
and Chelsea Pistol Club in the Cromwell Road, west London,
once again giving the name of Steve Majors. While his application
was considered he was allowed to use the firing range as a
probationer and in the next six weeks he attended eight times,
trying his hand at pistol shooting. Then in mid-September the
application was turned down and the visits ended. Two months
after that he parted company with the TA after failing a proficiency test.

Although George was now an adult, pretence still played a
large part in his life. Later events and later diagnoses suggest that
he was fully aware they were pretences and that his various names
and roles – as pop manager, karate champion, soldier, stunt man
and cousin of the stars – were part of a conscious effort to give
himself status and importance. He wanted to impress people,
and particularly women. It is no surprise that this was largely
unsuccessful and that he had little romantic or sex life and in
consequence he felt, as his counsel would soon say in court,

rejected and lonely. It is clear that he was also somewhat desperate. The Kingston episode had shown that he was capable of following a woman, which was an alarming sign in itself. One night that same summer of 1980, just a few weeks after his first conviction, he went further. He followed a woman who worked at his benefit office in Kensington, struck up a conversation and eventually asked her out, and when she brushed him off he tried to kiss her and put his hand on her breasts. Hitting him with her bag, she got into her car and drove off. Later the same night he followed a second woman, this time in Hammersmith, again asking if he could take her for a drink. By her subsequent account he got into a lift with her at her block of flats and tried to put his hand up her skirt.

He was arrested and charged under the name Paul Gadd and pleaded not guilty when the case came to court early in 1981. In evidence he admitted meeting both women separately on the same night and inviting each of them for a drink but after that, he said, his memory was a blank until several hours later. He observed that he saw 'no harm in being friendly'. Significantly, the defence also relied on medical and psychological evidence: the court was told that he was epileptic and registered disabled, and a neurologist testified that George showed signs of a 'considerable personality disorder' which manifested itself in 'inappropriate behaviour'. Convicted of the assault on the benefit office worker but cleared of the other charge, he was given a three-month suspended sentence.

Early the following year he again attacked a woman and this time it was a far graver matter. It happened one night near Turnham Green Underground station in west London. A twenty-one-year-old woman was walking towards her home in Acton after seeing her boyfriend off at the station when a young man fell in step with her and struck up a conversation. Though she was uncomfortable about talking to him she was unable or afraid to shake him off, and so found herself responding to his questions. Was she going home? Yes. In that case he would see her to her door. Was she a student? Yes, she was. What did she study? French and German, she replied. At this the man announced that he too knew some German and proudly spoke a few words. The exchanges continued in similar vein for a few moments longer and then, in a stairwell near her home, the man grabbed her, twisted her arm behind her back and put his hand over her mouth. Now in control, he pushed her to the ground, pulled down her jeans and pants and tried to rape her. Then he ran off. For several months the police were unable to track down the attacker and it may well have been the next episode in George's life that led to his arrest.

One night in January 1983 George was arrested outside Kensington Palace, then the residence of the Prince and Princess of Wales. The details remain vague, but it appears that he was found in bushes somewhere near the palace perimeter wearing combat gear and carrying a rope and a knife. At least one police officer took the view that he was hoping or intending to break in and he was taken to a police station for questioning. No charges were laid, however, and the official record includes the words: 'Released after everything is considered. It appears he is a fanatic when it comes to military things.' It is in some ways a baffling outcome since if only the few details above are correct he might have been charged with a variety of offences, but it leaves the strong impression that Barry George was not regarded as a serious threat to royal security. Why was he there? If he really was intending to break into the palace, then perhaps he was hoping to copy Michael Fagan, the drifter who had caused a national sensation the previous year by breaking into Buckingham Palace and sitting down on the Queen's bed for a chat.

Very soon after this incident he was arrested and charged with the rape, and it may be that the two were linked – for example that fingerprints taken after he was detained near the palace were linked to the earlier offence. Certainly the story told in local press reports seems unlikely. This was that the turning point in the rape investigation came when a detective visited George at home and tricked him into saying a phrase in German that he had also used in his conversation with the rape victim. Then, the reports said, once he realized that he had given himself away, he confessed. The fingerprint connection seems more plausible, but perhaps some combination of the two occurred. Whatever the truth was, in March 1983 at the Old Bailey in London Barry George, now under the name of Steven Majors, was convicted of attempted rape and sentenced to thirty months in jail. As his previous suspended sentence of three months was still 'live', that period was added to the total.

This spell in prison – he served about eighteen months – seems in some respects to have broken the pattern that had been forming in Barry George's life. In 1980–83 he had been running out of control, doomed sooner or later to land himself in serious trouble. After his release his behaviour appears to have been more subdued. Certainly the sequence of lurid episodes is broken and there are no more newspaper stories or court appearances to shed their occasional light on his life. The pretences continued but they were in a lower key, and though his relations with women remained very troubled he seems to have been able to keep on the right side of the law. His criminal record is a crude indicator: between 1980 and 1983 he acquired three convictions while between 1985 and 2000 there were none.

His first home after his release was a hostel in Stanhope Gardens, near the Natural History Museum, and there he presented himself to management and residents under another false identity: Thomas Palmer. Palmer had been a real person, a corporal in the SAS who took part in the ending of the Iranian embassy siege in London in 1980 and in the Falklands War before being killed in a road accident while on undercover operations in Northern Ireland in 1983. After this early death his exploits – he won the Military Medal – had become widely known through newspapers and books and clearly Barry George was one of those impressed by them. Paul Gadd and Steve Majors were not completely discarded but for the next few years he was usually 'Thomas' or

'Tom' to those he met. To some of them at least he claimed to have been a member of the SAS himself and, as we shall see, his interest in firearms and militaria remained strong. After a short while in Stanhope Gardens he was assigned the Crookham Road flat and from then on the cosy little district around the bottom of the Fulham Road was his patch. Over the next fifteen years he rarely worked for any sustained period, if indeed he ever did. The only job he could recall when questioned later by the police was a spell as a bicycle messenger in the late 1980s, but no details of that were traced. As before, he was happier living on benefits, no doubt in part because he was able to live very modestly. Like many epileptics he did not drink alcohol nor did he smoke. He rarely left London and when he travelled within the city, which he liked to do, he was able to do this free of charge because of his disability. His mother appears to have done most of his laundry for him.

How did he pass the time? To the outsider it seems like a great chasm of years and months and weeks with little or nothing to fill it, but the whole notion of time, as would become clear, had a limited meaning to George. This was a man generally content to drift along. On the evidence of his later years, his principal activity was probably going out and wandering around, trying to make contact with people. Certainly by the mid- to late 1990s he was well known in the area around his home, among both local people and shopkeepers. Staff and customers at Jazzy G hairdressers, for example, were accustomed to him dropping in for a chat. Nicholas Baker, who ran the reference section of Fulham public library, knew George well. So did Mary Quinn, the manager of Go-Gay dry cleaners, and so did the owner of the paint shop, staff in the banks and cafés and many others. Neighbours in Crookham Road grew accustomed to this stocky, dark character who appeared in a variety of garbs, sometimes a sober suit, sometimes combat gear and sometimes jeans and leather jacket. He often seemed preoccupied but at the same time was always keen to chat in his peculiar way, earnest and self-important yet at the same time transparently childlike. He was, many concluded, a fairly articulate simpleton.

Another way he filled his time – an unconscious strategy, perhaps – was by becoming a complainer, a person with grievances. At the council housing office he was a frequent visitor, calling in with a complaint once a week or once a fortnight. His rent was often in arrears but he was reluctant to take responsibility for that and interested instead in grumbling about neighbours or about repairs that were needed. At times he became angry and had to be ejected. His health, too, was often on his mind, for he came to believe very strongly that he suffered from a number of complaints which were either not being diagnosed or not being taken sufficiently seriously. Chief among these was scoliosis, a spinal condition, but there were others. He consulted medical reference works in the library and argued with successive local doctors about his symptoms, until by the late 1990s most of the practices in Fulham refused to have him on their books. In several west London hospitals, too, he was a well-known but less than welcome visitor. A third area of grievance was the police, who he felt at times victimized him. He himself was occasionally the subject of complaints and he believed the police did not give him a fair hearing, perhaps because he had a criminal record. In the early 1990s he was questioned in connection with the Rachel Nickell murder in Wimbledon – he was never a serious suspect and was soon ruled out – and no doubt this stoked his sense of injustice. It amounts to a pattern: whether it was welfare, health or the police, Barry George usually had some problem that preoccupied him, that required him to conduct research in the library and latterly on the Internet, and to consult experts – doctors, solicitors and so forth – seeking their opinions and giving them the benefit of his. It also gave him something he could talk about to other people he met.

Some of his problems were connected with the flat and the state he kept it in. A barrister acting for George would later say that he was 'a collector *par excellence*', but this was somewhat misleading. The truth was that he was chronically untidy and had no housekeeping instinct whatever. Almost everything that came into his flat, provided that it did not actually stink as it decayed, simply remained there. There were two rooms, a hall, a bathroom and a kitchen, and it seems that he himself never tidied or cleaned them but filled them progressively with rubbish, some of it in bags or boxes and some loose on the floor. One man who visited the flat in the late eighties would say that even then, when George had been living there for only two or three years, all but one room appeared derelict. Inevitably, even though the worst of the domestic rubbish tended to go in the bins, the flat became smelly and unsanitary, and just as inevitably the neighbours complained and the council became involved. There were also complaints that George played his television or stereo too loud and at odd times of the day and night, and these too brought in the council and the police. Each incident in turn, no doubt, was added to George's catalogue of injustice.

His continuing taste for fantasy – if that is the right word – also helped the time to pass. In 1986, once again under the name Paul Gadd, he got himself listed in a music industry directory as managing director of a technical company called Xanadu, giving his mother's address in Acton and naming Jeff Lynne as another executive. At other times he said he had been a roadie with rock bands, or a musician and singer. In fact he could not play a note and a neighbour who once offered to teach him the piano soon gave up in exasperation. George talked, however, of being a music student and on his visits to Fulham library he would often look up courses in that or some other subject and send away for application forms. These, when they arrived, would be brandished for a time as though they were degree certificates, on at least one occasion to practical effect – both Barclays Bank and Barclaycard issued him with free mobile telephones as part of their student package, apparently on the strength of application papers alone. In another mode he was still Thomas Palmer, the SAS man, and he continued to read books and magazines about the special forces and about guns and weaponry. Periodically, he would buy pieces of military gear: camouflage clothes, epaulettes and so forth. At one time he considered applying again to join the army, although nothing came of it. The year 1991, however, brought a big development in his life, for that November Freddie Mercury died of Aids-related illness. Now George was Barry Bulsara, a cousin of Mercury, whose real name had been Bulsara. Whether he adopted this personality before or after the death is not clear, but if it was before it was not long before; certainly there is evidence he was using the name just weeks after the death. Why Bulsara? Like Gary Glitter, Freddie Mercury was a rock and roll showman, and no doubt George liked the music and enjoyed the act. As before, he adopted the real name rather than the stage name, which gave him something to explain or elaborate upon when he introduced himself to people. And this identity could be complex and interesting to others, for unlike Glitter, who had sunk into booze and bankruptcy in the eighties, Mercury was dead, a martyr to a dreadful disease while at the height of his fame and success. In fact death and the sympathy that accompanied it had given the Queen singer a respect and even a respectability that he had not enjoyed before, and as a 'cousin' George could hope that a little of this might rub off on him.

As the nineties passed Barry Bulsara became his preferred identity. At the first anniversary of Mercury's death George was among those who gathered outside the singer's London home for a memorial event and there he boasted of his family connection to other people in the little crowd. In later years he repeated this and those close to Mercury eventually felt the need to deny it all, perhaps at the point when they began receiving mail addressed to Barry Bulsara. He had a digital mock-up photograph made of himself with his arm around Mercury's shoulders and had at least one business card printed in this name – one subsequently emerged that read: 'Bulsara Productions Inc.' and then beneath: 'Barry Bulsara. Fredderick Bulsara Mercury. Company directors', with his Fulham address. When the Princess of Wales died he was among the many thousands who brought flowers and his bouquet was marked as coming from Barry Bulsara, Freddie Mercury's cousin. At the funeral he wandered among the crowd near Westminster Abbey mentioning the connection to whoever would listen. Yet even though he worked very hard at being Barry Bulsara, his other identities never quite disappeared. Some people in Fulham knew him by several names and linked these names to his dress: sometimes he would be out and about dressed like Freddie Mercury, and sometimes as Thomas Palmer. They would even joke with him about it all.

The main use to which he put the name, however, was in making contact with women. Two stories later unearthed by the police illustrate how he went about this. The first was told by Sophia Wellington, a young woman who in 1991 worked for the BBC in White City. Leaving her office after 10 p.m. one winter evening she walked to a bus stop half a mile or so away and was waiting there when a man came up and introduced himself as 'the late Freddie Mercury's cousin'. Did she work for the BBC, he asked. Yes. He then told her that he was not happy with the corporation because of the way it had treated Freddie and the family during his final illness. He talked some more and she said little in reply, feeling uncomfortable in his company. Then her bus came and as they parted he gave her a business card which identified him as 'Barry Bulsara – singer, pianist, entertainer'. The other story was told by Alison Hoad, who in 1997 visited Fulham to deliver her six-year-old son to an audition. Emerging from Parsons Green Underground station, she produced a map and was trying to find her bearings when a well-dressed man came up and asked if she was lost. She gave the address of their destination and the man said he was going that way and would accompany them. It was more than a ten-minute walk, along to Munster Road and then up to a street beyond Gowan Avenue, and on the way the man exchanged greetings with a number of shopkeepers on Fulham Road. As they walked he told Hoad and her son that he was Freddie Mercury's cousin and he had been to court that day on a matter related to the singer's will. In fact, he said, he was the manager of Mercury's fan club and he invited the two of them to visit the club offices, which were nearby – at this point he gestured in the general direction of Crookham Road. Hoad, by now uneasy, declined and they continued together right up to the door of the house where the audition was to take place. There George said he would wait so that he could guide them back to the station, but Hoad told him that was not necessary and to her relief when she emerged later with her son he was gone.

The pattern is there. George wanted to have something to say to these women, and more, to seem interesting and important to them, and being Barry Bulsara was the best he could do. In itself the pretence is relatively innocent; it is the underlying need to connect with women on the street that is not. For Barry George, twice convicted in his earlier years of desperate sexual acts against women he did not know, still could not find a satisfactory, stable relationship. True, in 1989 he got married. The marriage certificate issued on 2 May of that year at Fulham Register Office shows that Barry Michael George, a stunt man of 2B Crookham Road, took as his bride Itsuko Toide, a Japanese student living at the same address. He was twenty-nine and she thirty-four and her father's profession was given as tax accountant. The couple had met while he did some voluntary work at a Japanese community centre in west London and she was studying English, but the marriage lasted only a few months and there are grounds for suspecting that it was never a normal relationship. Neighbours in Crookham Road said they were surprised when a Japanese woman moved into the flat and George announced that she was his wife, and before anyone had the chance to get to know her Toide had packed her bags and left. There were rumours at the time of domestic violence and they seem to have been accurate – on one occasion she told the police he had raped her, but she did not press charges. The marriage may have left one significant legacy for George, for we know that a few months before it began he visited a branch of Cecil Gee and spent no less than £1,200 on clothes, including a suit and a dark blue cashmere overcoat – just the sort of outfit a man might wear to his wedding and bought, perhaps, with his fiancée's assistance. These remained in his possession long afterwards.

Besides his short marriage, George's dealings with women in these years were overwhelmingly those that took place on the street. At bus stops, in tube stations, in queues and waiting rooms, in parks, on trains, at tourist sites – in short wherever he could count on an opportunity to strike up a conversation, he spoke to women whom he did not know and some at least of those women found him threatening. He was too eager, too persistent. And it did not stop with conversation. Look again at the Wellington story: how did he know that that particular young woman at a bus stop in Shepherd's Bush worked at the BBC? Perhaps, she thought later, she had been carrying a BBC bag, but then again perhaps not, perhaps he had followed her all the way from her office, a location which he knew well. There was a precedent: that is what he did back in 1980 with the woman benefits officer. In fact we know that in the eighties and nineties George made a habit of following women and sometimes pestering them, a habit that his own counsel would later admit in court amounted to 'totally unacceptable behaviour'. Police would trace a number of women who could testify to this. One, for example, said he left a note on her car saying that he had been watching her. Another said he walked up to her as she let herself in at her front door and said: 'Now I know where you live.' A third said that she was approached by a man answering George's description who spoke to her about the SAS and tried to kiss her. As none of these stories has been tested in court they must be treated with caution, but the picture they paint can be confirmed at least to a degree. When police eventually searched the flat at 2B Crookham Road they found, among many other things, a map showing the location of a woman's house with her name, and when they traced her and asked her about it she was completely unaware of George's interest. Most extraordinary of all, however, was his hoard of photographs, the great majority undeveloped, for they show that he often took a camera with him when he went out to follow women. In all there were 2,597 pictures, taken mostly in the early 1990s, and they featured 419 different women, the majority of whom, once again, had no idea they were being watched.

Totally unacceptable as it was, this behaviour may have been under some sort of control, at least in the sense that he acquired no further convictions. It was probably fortunate that there seemed to be so little focus to his following activities and that George switched his attention from woman to woman by the day, the hour or even the minute. That is presumably one reason why so few of the films were ever developed; he had lost interest and moved on to something or someone new. On a handful of occasions, however, he was the subject of complaints and he was questioned in connection with two or three serious sex offences, although none of these made it as far as a courtroom. Whether he was lucky and got away with crimes or whether his habit of following women and his record were simply drawing suspicion towards him, we can only guess. Looking back, there are some grounds for believing that time was calming him, for as the years passed he had progressively fewer formal contacts with the police: between 1997 and 2000, the record shows, he was stopped by officers three times in the street, and that was all.

This, then, was the tenant of 2B Crookham Road. He was single, unemployed and in April 2000 he was just turning forty. Although he had a criminal record including sex crimes nothing had been added to it for seventeen years and the convictions were long since, in the legal sense, 'spent'. He had a long-term interest in militaria and pop music, while his proudest moment was probably his spell of employment twenty-four years earlier at the BBC, whose offices he still visited occasionally to pick up free publications. His flat looked as though someone had tipped a skip of rubbish into it from a great height. He filled his time with roaming London, with imaginings and pretences, with grievances and complaints, with a search for human contact and for a sense of importance – and with the furtive following of women. He had been diagnosed at least once as having a personality disorder. His Fulham neighbours either indulged or endured him; some found him funny while others pitied him and a few, most of them women, thought he was creepy. As for his family, he had long since lost touch with his father, while his sister Michelle had married and moved to Ireland and the other sister Susan had died during an epileptic seizure in 1986. Only his mother remained and she ranked as his closest friend. By most definitions Barry Michael George, known generally by now as Barry Bulsara, was a loner. Whether he was also an obsessive was a matter which would be much debated but either way it should be no surprise that early in the year 2000 detectives on the Jill Dando murder investigation began to take an interest in him. In fact, if there is anything surprising here it is that they did not do so much earlier.

# 14. A Particle

*'Link guns, link loner, link obsession with Jill or odd behaviour with women'*

The name Bulsara first entered the Operation Oxborough data-base in the first weeks of the investigation as a result of a series of calls to the incident room by staff at Hammersmith And Fulham Action for Disability, or Hafad, an advice centre in Greswell Street, half a mile from the murder scene on the other side of Fulham Palace Road. They wanted to report the following strange sequence of events. On the day of the murder a local man known to them visited the centre and spoke to various people about his health problems. He had a carrier bag full of papers and it was clear he had a long story to tell, but since Hafad dealt with people only by appointment he was asked to return at noon the next day. In due course he left, but he did not return to keep his appointment, turning up instead on the Wednesday, two days later, and this time in an agitated state. His concerns were now different: he was no longer asking about health matters but wanted the Hafad people to tell him the time of his Monday visit and to describe for him the clothes he had been wearing. The reason, he explained, was that he was afraid the police would suspect him of the Dando murder – he had had trouble with the police before – and he wanted the information so that he could pass it on to his solicitor. Again he spoke to several staff members, making a considerable fuss, before leaving.

The people at Hafad understandably thought this suspicious and the centre's director, Lesley Symes, rang the police that afternoon (28 April) to tell the story. Although she declined to give his name over the phone, she explained that the man had mental health problems and she said that his visit on the Monday took place at 11 a.m. The time was obviously important: 11 a.m. was half an hour before the murder and the Hafad building is just six or seven minutes' walk from Dando's house. Although Symes's information was logged in the Oxborough computer system, however, no officer was despatched to Hafad to follow it up, and after two weeks the staff there grew impatient. So on 12 May a second call was made to the incident room and it was in the course of this call – sixteen days after the murder – that the name Barry Bulsara was first mentioned. The caller was Elaine Hutton, the finance officer of Hafad, and she wanted to give the police more information about the suspicious man, presumably in the hope of galvanizing them into action. She gave the name by which he was known at Hafad and his correct address and she said that several of her colleagues believed Bulsara resembled the man in the E-fit picture that had recently been released. Finally, she gave a different time for that Monday visit: Bulsara had called in at Hafad at 11.50 a.m., she said, or about twenty minutes *after* the murder.

These two calls were made, of course, at the busiest and most difficult time of the investigation, when the running and sweating men dominated inquiries and when the flood of information coming in was, to use Campbell's later phrase, 'approaching unmanageable proportions'. But the two Hafad calls did not go completely unnoticed, for three days after Hutton phoned an instruction was entered into the police computer system to 'T.I.E.' – trace, interview and eliminate – the Barry Bulsara who was said to live in Crookham Road. This requires a little explanation, for such instructions are part of a police process that is almost mechanical. Certain officers in every inquiry have the responsibility to review all the information that is coming in and look out for specific items, no matter how minor, that need to be followed up. Each of these is or should be marked and numbered, with a note attached in the computer system spelling out exactly what step must be taken. These notes are called 'actions', and the action relating to Barry Bulsara was number 1637 in the Oxborough file. But just because an action has been 'raised', as the police put it, does not mean that it will be dealt with immediately, for there are usually so many they have to be ranked according to priority. A low-priority action, therefore, goes into a queue where it may wait some time before being 'allocated' to a named officer to be dealt with. Action 1637 was just such a low-priority action and it remained in the queue, unallocated, for nine months.

Campbell would later acknowledge that this amounted to a failure in his investigation but looking back we can see at least some reasons for it and among them, probably, are two further calls that came in from Hafad *after* the action had been raised. The first was made by Susan Bicknell, the organization's welfare officer, who had the longest conversation with Bulsara during his visit on the day of the murder. She rang in a week after Hutton to say that Bulsara had appeared to be 'very flustered' when she saw him and that she thought he might have witnessed something to do with Dando's death. In her opinion, she added, he did not look like the E-fit at all. And so far as the time of his visit was concerned she endorsed Hutton's version, saying that her meeting with Bulsara took place at about midday. (In fact Bicknell had a note of the encounter written a week afterwards which put the time at 11.50 a.m.) The last of the four calls from Hafad came from Elaine Hutton, who rang once again on 14 June to express concern that more than six weeks after the murder nobody from the police had yet visited Greswell Street to follow up their information. Again she identified Bulsara by name and this time she added his date of birth. She also said that when he called on the day of the murder he was wearing a casual jacket and a yellow shirt and was carrying a plastic bag. It may well be that these two later calls had the opposite effect to what was intended, for taken together they were likely to make Hafad rather less interesting to the police. The Hafad man now appeared to be dressed in the wrong way – nothing like the eyewitness descriptions of the gunman – and by Bicknell's account he did not resemble the E-fit and was merely a potential witness rather than a suspect. In the early stages of the investigation the job of tracing such a man could well have been regarded as of marginal importance, although the delay that followed was surely excessive.

Through the summer and autumn of 1999, as we have seen, other matters absorbed the attention of Operation Oxborough and it was only as priorities began to change, as the chances of the murderer being either an associate of Dando or a criminal were perceived to be diminishing, that the step was taken which would ultimately bring action 1637 to the surface. This came when Hamish Campbell ordered a re-examination of the entire suspect list. Despite all the work that had been done there were still hundreds of names on the list and inevitably the majority were those which had initially been allocated a low priority. Campbell now wanted them sifted and rated again, and a questionnaire and points system were created so that every suspect would be scored and ranked in the revised list. For example, did the name come from more than one source? If it was only one source, was it known or anonymous? Was this merely an E-fit likeness or something more? Was the suspect named, or identified merely by address or description? Had the informant given information before? And so on.

Even when this process was complete Bulsara did not jump to the head of the queue and another two or three months passed before action 1637 was finally allocated. (One of the tasks completed in the interim, incidentally, was the solution to the mystery of the utility caller, who after long investigation proved to be a journalist. He was not publicly identified and what he was hoping to achieve by meddling with Dando's bills was not disclosed, but he was not a suspect for the murder.) It was not until 24 February 2000, therefore, that the job of finding Barry Bulsara was given to Detective Constable John Gallagher, a tall, dark, heavily-built officer who had been on the team since the day after the murder. Gallagher, who had no fewer than twenty-five other actions on his plate at the time, visited Hafad in early March and interviewed the four staff members who had been involved in the events of the previous April. In broad terms they confirmed the essentials of the story — Bulsara's details, his two visits, the clothing he wore — but something new emerged about timing which was to cast the matter in a different light. Looking back, at least two of them believed that on the day of the murder Bulsara arrived at the centre somewhat later than the messages to the police had previously suggested. One of them, the receptionist Rosario Torres, believed it was around 12.30 p.m., while Lesley Symes, the director, thought it was actually after lunch. Hutton, for her part, gave a time around midday, while Bicknell said 11.50 a.m.

Gallagher tried to speak directly to Bulsara but it was surprisingly difficult to make contact. Three times in March the detective called at the flat but no one was at home and though he pushed a card through the letter-box Bulsara did not call him. Why this was we do not know, but it may have been connected with a cycling accident, for the tenant of number 2B had recently been knocked off his bicycle in the King's Road, suffering leg injuries, and it is possible he was receiving treatment somewhere. Meanwhile Gallagher pursued his researches by other means, notably by reviewing police records both at Scotland Yard and in local stations. From these he learned a little of the story of the man born Barry Michael George: he had committed two crimes against women, although that was a long time ago and since then he had no convictions; he had been a suspect in two or three investigations, and he used a variety of names. More information about his behaviour came from local people around Crookham Road, while from Department of Social Security files Gallagher learned that George was unemployed and registered disabled.

In early April, after two further visits to the flat and one to the home of George's mother had still drawn a blank, Gallagher submitted his first report and it was seen by Hamish Campbell. Though George was still not regarded as a strong suspect the detective was urged to carry on at least until he had spoken to him, so after one last unsuccessful visit to the flat Gallagher resorted to a method often used when tracking down elusive people: he established where and when George collected his benefit and waited there with a colleague. Sure enough George turned up, wearing a camouflage jacket and still limping from his injury. Asked why he had not called the station in response to the card Gallagher left at his home, George said he had assumed the inquiry was about the bicycle accident and had sent the card to his solicitor. He was driven first to Hammersmith police station and then to his mother's home where, as she looked on, he made a statement.

On the day of the murder, he told Gallagher, he spent the whole morning at home in his flat. At about 12.30 or 12.45 – he could only guess at the time because he didn't have a watch or a clock – he left to go to Hafad because he wanted help with some problems he had. He was on foot and his route took him to the bottom of Fulham Road, then into Bishop's Park and along Stevenage Road to Greswell Street. He estimated that this journey took him between ten and fifteen minutes. He didn't spend long at Hafad and when he left he walked straight to Fulham Palace Road and to the offices of London Traffic Cars, a minicab company, where he intended to ask for directions to Rickett Street, two or three miles away in Earl's Court. His plan was to visit the offices there of the charity Colon Cancer Concern because he wanted to pick up some information about bowel illnesses. To his surprise he was offered a free lift in a cab and he took it. Afterwards he walked home and spent some time in the flat and he did not learn about the murder until told by a neighbour in the course of the evening. He had not known before then where Jill Dando lived. Asked about his appearance that day he said he was wearing either a dark suit and coat with a white shirt and red tie or a T-shirt, jeans and trainers. He thought he probably had a couple of days' growth of stubble. And as for knowledge of firearms, he said he had once been a member of the Territorials and had received some training with rifles.

After taking the statement Gallagher drove George home. The detective now had several new leads to follow up and in one case the answers were right under his nose, for George's visit to the minicab office had been reported on the very day of the murder and details of it had lain in the Oxborough computer system ever since. The manager of Traffic Cars, Ramesh Paul, had called the police early that evening to say that 'around the time of the incident' one of his drivers carried a fare from the firm's office on Fulham Palace Road to an address in Earl's Court. The Traffic Cars office is only 150 yards north of the end of Gowan Avenue so Paul thought this information might be significant. Two days later, the police computer record showed, Paul rang in again to report something else which he thought 'very odd': the same man who had taken the taxi on Monday had returned to the cab office on that day, the Wednesday, asking for confirmation of the time of the trip and what he had been wearing. Unlike the Hafad calls, the Traffic Cars information was investigated in the spring of 1999 and statements were taken from Paul and from the driver in question, but the inquiries led nowhere because the man could not be identified, and in fact the description given was wildly off the mark – Paul thought the man he had dealt with had spiky blond hair and an east European accent. Until Barry George pointed it out, the similarity between the events at Traffic Cars and the sequence at Hafad had not been noticed.

Looking at the Traffic Cars information in April 2000, Gallagher and his superiors could see that it not only confirmed part of George's story but also provided important evidence about timings, for the taxi to Rickett Street was logged as having left at 1.15 p.m. Where the Hafad witnesses were at odds about time, here was something concrete and contemporaneous which provided a firm anchor for George's story that he left home some time after midday, walked through the park, paid a brief visit to Hafad and then went straight to the minicab office. And this in turn left him with no alibi for the murder. If, as he suggested himself, he reached Hafad later than 12.30 p.m., he would have had plenty of time to commit the murder, go home to Crookham Road to change his clothes and then walk to Hafad.

The lack of an alibi on its own, however, is not enough to make someone a suspect, so what grounds, if any, did the police have at this stage for regarding George as a possible killer? He was the right age, height and build; his hair was the right colour and he had volunteered that he might have been wearing roughly the right sort of clothes on the day; he lived locally and had a history of offences against women; he had been in the Territorials and thus knew something about guns, and neighbours in Crookham Road reported that he was still keen on things military. Above all, he had behaved suspiciously. Some of the Hafad witnesses said he was agitated when he arrived on the day of the murder, while his return visits to both Traffic Cars and Hafad in pursuit of details about timing and clothing were very strange indeed. And when DC Gallagher had finally tried to make contact with him a year later he had been unusually hard to find. It all added up to something well worth pursuing, so by the middle of April 2000 the name of Barry George was at the top of the suspect list.

The obvious next step was to search his flat. Just before 8 a.m. on 17 April, therefore, Gallagher led a specialist police search team to 2B Crookham Road where, as there was no answer to their knock, the door was forced. Inside they found a chaotic jumble of bags, boxes, old furniture, bare boards, litter and filth, and slowly and methodically they set about their task. The search took two days – it had to be extended because of the state of the flat – and produced a large haul of material. No guns or ammunition were found, although there was a part of a holster and an SAS-style knife, both of which were seized. Various items of clothing were taken away, including the three-quarter-length

Cecil Gee coat George had bought in 1988, a few months before his wedding. And there were documents, notably a large amount of material about guns and military matters and a smattering of items relating to Jill Dando. The former included a copy of *Guns and Weapons* magazine, a catalogue from a firm which sold militaria, a book called *Ambush and Counter-Ambush*, two photocopied pages from *Exchange & Mart* relating to firearms, a guide to joining the Territorials with some completed application forms and also various handwritten items relating to makes of guns. As for the Dando documents, they were a mixture. Among the heaps of newspapers in the flat were a number dating from April and May 1999 which were dominated by news of the murder. There were also four copies of the 27 April 1999 edition of *Ariel*, the BBC's internal newspaper, which dealt at some length with the same story. Then there was an envelope containing messages of condolence at Dando's death which had clearly been written by staff in shops along Fulham Road. And most intriguing of all, the searchers found two handwritten notes evidently written by George, both containing the same passage: 'Although I did not know Jill Dando personally, my cousin Freddie Mercury was interviewed by her back in 1986. I was present with him, so for this reason I feel it poignant to bring together the situation of Jill's death and my coming to Christ . . .'

Besides all this the searchers made one further important discovery. This was the undeveloped photographic film, dozens and dozens of rolls scattered around the place, all now gathered up, taken away and sent to be developed. Very soon these would establish Barry George as the strongest suspect to be pursued by the Oxborough team.

As the search concluded on 18 April 2000, the first anniversary of the murder was just a week away, and this was an occasion that would be widely noted. The curiosity of the media about the state of the investigation had been mounting for weeks, with editors eager to have something special for their readers. Hamish

Campbell was once again much in demand, as were Alan Farthing and others who had been close to Dando, while *Crimewatch UK* was to present a fresh appeal. The public appetite had been whetted in March when a fund was launched to raise money for an academic chair of crime prevention in Jill Dando's memory. Farthing, Nick Ross, Sophie Rhys-Jones (by now the Countess of Wessex) and Sir Cliff Richard all attended the publicity event, held at Claridge's. The slogan was 'Not for Nothing'.

Campbell gave interviews to *The Times*, the *Guardian*, the *Observer*, the London *Evening Standard* and several other papers, and though he never mentioned the names Bulsara or George the articles that resulted are none the less interesting in retrospect. On the one hand they dwelt to a striking degree on the detective himself. Readers were informed, for example, that despite his 24-carat Scottish name Hamish Campbell was English, brought up in a middle-class family and sent – an unusual background for a policeman – to public school. Despite having the brains for university he chose instead to join the Metropolitan Police, where he was soon a detective working in criminal intelligence and later the anti-terrorist squad. Over the years he acquired three commendations, as well as a wife and children. Though a 'devoted family man' he was also a hard worker, at his desk every day by 8 a.m. and frequently still there at 9 p.m.; only his equable temperament and his ability to maintain a distance from problems prevented him qualifying as a workaholic. And if he ever felt the pressure he had the perfect outlet for stress: twice a week he attended a judo class. In press terms this was all standard personal background – you would not have been surprised to read where he lived, what his wife was called or what make of car he drove – except that such attention is not often given to a policeman, and even more rarely to a mere chief inspector. Hamish Campbell was becoming a celebrity. It was as though, in the absence of a known killer, the mantle of Jill Dando's fame had descended on his shoulders.

So far as the investigation itself was concerned Campbell

confirmed in these interviews the trend of his thoughts over recent months. The probabilities, he believed, had narrowed considerably and it was now his 'gut feeling' that the killer was a loner. Nothing had been ruled out – 'no one is ever going to be ruled out until someone is charged' – but in some areas the absence of evidence, like the dog that didn't bark, had become evidence in its own right. There was no sign of a motive in her private life and no information from the criminal underworld, and after such a long time you had to wonder whether this was because neither was relevant to the murder. On the other hand the loner theory seemed stronger and stronger. 'When you look at the sort of people who have been obsessed with her, they worry me,' he said. 'They are people who have been trying to talk to her, write letters to her, who have wanted to meet her, and you just need one to take the murderous extra step . . .'

In the *Crimewatch* programme, broadcast on Wednesday 19 April, Campbell took these suspicions further as he made a completely fresh appeal for the public's help. Referring to the many theories that had circulated about the case, he said: 'What I want to do is to put all that to one side and look at one very strong possibility: that Jill was killed by a person working on his own.' As he had a year before, he worked through a sequence of dramatized sightings in and around Gowan Avenue but this time the focus was on men seen *before* the killing, and not just that morning but also on the man seen by the plasterer in the preceding weeks. Conceding that there were differences in the various descriptions given, Campbell pointed out that there were also similarities. 'We have a dozen witnesses describing a man in his thirties or forties, tall, wearing a dark suit and agitated. Three of them said his suit was too big; another three saw him in a Trilby hat; several mentioned the mobile phone. He's the main person that we wish to speak to.'

*He's the main person.* Campbell was now stating a belief that this was indeed one man who had been seen waiting for his chance to kill Jill Dando. And he went on to paint a portrait in words. This man, he said, 'clearly has an interest in guns and firearms' and was 'very likely' to have relevant specialist magazines. He was 'very likely to be alone, perhaps a loner, someone who is emotionally isolated' and he was also 'very likely to have had an interest in Jill Dando, or if not Jill, an unhealthy attraction, infatuation or obsession with women'. Campbell said he wanted the viewers to think about anybody they might know with some or all of these characteristics. 'People need to look back in time, link guns, link loner, link obsession with Jill or odd behaviour with women,' he urged. More than that, he addressed himself directly to the killer. 'I feel sure he's watching now,' said the detective. 'And what I also know is that nothing has been resolved by this killing and it won't be resolved. But there's one opportunity and he can ring us now here on *Crimewatch* or he can ring the inquiry team and speak to somebody . . . I feel sure that will resolve it.'

This was sensational television – the notion that the killer was in the audience was guaranteed to send a shiver of excitement through every watching home – but it was also an important moment in the investigation. Although Campbell spoke of it as a 'very strong possibility' he was more or less committing himself to an entire scenario: his killer was a man who had planned the attack and waited around wearing odd clothes as he sought his opportunity; his killer had known what he was doing as he handled the strange bullet and the strange gun; his killer was an obsessive, although he was not necessarily obsessed with Dando. Gone, at least for the moment, were the caveats about alternative, innocent explanations for some of these things. Gone were the requests for people to come forward and eliminate themselves. Gone too were the old uncertainties about the origins of gun and bullet. And then there were the remarks about the killer's likely character: 'There is something odd about him; he might be alone but isolated . . . not married, having difficulty with previous relationships with girlfriends . . . separate, away from society and groups of people.'

All of this plainly owed a good deal to the criminal psychologists Campbell had consulted in the course of the inquiry, as
did his final words promising the killer some kind of emotional
closure if he confessed. These people had been involved from
the start and the leading Home Office 'profiler', Adrian West,
had argued in favour of the loner theory within weeks of the
killing, but at the time the investigating team had been sceptical.
What prompted the change of heart, the apparently wholehearted
conversion to the loner theory? In part at least the answer was
simple – Campbell himself remarked around this time: 'We've
got to start making choices here.' As we have seen he also felt
that the other main lines of inquiry were all but exhausted, to
the point where the returns scarcely justified the effort. And then
there was Barry George. That Campbell's team had a man in
their sights at exactly this time who appeared to meet a number
of the new criteria for suspicion – 'link guns, link loner, link . . .
odd behaviour with women' – certainly adds an intriguing extra
element to the equation. Campbell had been told about George
on 5 April, had read the statement he made on 11 April and had
authorized the search that began two days before the *Crimewatch*
broadcast. He was live in the studio on the evening of 19 April
when he described the 'emotionally isolated' character he wanted
the public to look out for and to call in about. The coincidence
is striking.

Once they were developed, the hundreds and hundreds of photographs of women in the street added up at the very least to
strong evidence that George had what Campbell was calling
'an unhealthy attraction, infatuation or obsession with women'.
Even if he never went near any of these women he had clearly
followed them, and this was surely a form of stalking. What
was more, detectives were also picking up from other sources
evidence of George's habit of striking up conversations in the
street with women he did not know. Taken together with his
criminal record from the early 1980s this provided further

grounds for suspicion. And then there were the photographs involving guns. There were two: one taken indoors and the other outdoors. The former showed a man wearing a gas mask and military clothing, posing with a pistol in his hand, while in the latter a man was standing by a wall in the street, somewhat further away, again wearing fatigues and this time holding a submachine gun. Detectives were sure that in both cases the man was Barry George, while police firearms experts stated firmly that the pistol in the indoor photograph was a blank firer, and not only that but one that showed signs of having been tampered with. It was a Bruni 8mm model, made in Italy, and some of the metal close to the muzzle had apparently been cut away, revealing a spring.

A fortnight passed before the clothes removed from the flat were sent for scientific examination. Detectives held out little hope that, after a year, they would carry any traces of the murder, but the effort had to be made and on Tuesday 2 May the various sealed paper packages were delivered to the forensic science laboratory in Lambeth, south London. The Cecil Gee coat was the first to be scrutinized, senior scientist Robin Keeley removing it from the bag, placing it on his table and, by dabbing various parts of it with pieces of sticky tape, lifting off samples to be examined. Over the next couple of days he examined these various specks under a powerful microscope and most were everyday components of household dust, but one of them proved to be something quite unexpected. From the piece of tape marked as having been used to dab the inner left pocket of the coat had come a single, spherical, metallic particle which Keeley recognized instantly as firearms discharge residue.

Firearms discharge residue, on which Keeley is an authority, is what is left over after the 'live' parts of a round of ammunition are ignited. When the trigger is pulled the firing pin strikes and sets off a primer cap containing a volatile mixture of chemicals and that in its turn detonates the propellant, which by exploding sends the bullet on its way. In this process very high temperatures are reached inside the cartridge case and the chemicals in the primer tend to fuse into thousands of metallic particles. Many of these are expelled from the gun through the barrel, while some remain in the weapon and on the cartridge and others are scattered from the sides of the gun. By this last route some at least will normally land on the firer. As to their composition, these particles can have various chemical make-ups, depending on the contents of the primer cap before firing. All standard primers contain three basic ingredients: lead, barium and antimony. Some have only these, while others have one or more additional ingredients drawn from a short list: silicon, calcium, tin and aluminium. Residue particles from any normal gunshot will contain some of these elements, so for example a single particle may be made of lead and barium, or of silicon and antimony, or of calcium, lead, barium and antimony. Of course the 'additional' ingredients from the second group will only be present if they were in the primer cap of the ammunition to begin with – in other words, silicon can only appear in the residue from primers that include silicon when they are manufactured.

Back in June 1999, when Robin Keeley examined residue particles he lifted from hair that had been close to the wound in Jill Dando's head, and others that came from the upper parts of the coat she was wearing when the shot was fired, he found a variety of chemical compositions. Two combined just the basic ingredients of lead, antimony and barium; one was aluminium and barium; another, from the right shoulder of the coat, was aluminium, lead and barium. This was enough for Keeley to conclude that the primer cap of the round that killed Dando was made up of four elements: the three basics, plus aluminium. Now, nearly a year later, he was looking at a residue particle from Barry George's coat and it clearly contained three elements: lead, barium and aluminium. In short, it was consistent with the shot that killed Dando. On 5 May Keeley phoned Hamish Campbell to give him the news.

As evidence, how strong was this? The particle was minute –

just over one hundredth of a millimetre in diameter and quite invisible to the naked eye – and it was solitary, for although Keeley looked for others on the clothes that had been seized he found none. It was also most unexpected, since firearms discharge residue tends to be rapidly lost from clothing and other moving surfaces. And the particle itself was not unique and could have come from any gunshot in which the primer contained aluminium, which was by no means a rarity. But this was a negative view. As Campbell and his team looked at it, the significance of the particle was quite different. Here was a suspect who fulfilled a number of the criteria for suspicion – a follower of women, a gun enthusiast, a loner – and now, in a coat removed from his flat, a particle of firearms discharge residue had been found. That alone suggested that he didn't just know about guns but had fired one. Furthermore he had probably done so in the not-too-distant past, since cleaning, and particularly dry cleaning, would be likely to remove the particle. And to cap that, the composition of the particle matched. It could have been one of the majority of types which were definitely not used in the Dando killing, but it was not. It was the same type. To the detectives, a case for prosecution was taking shape.

On the same day that Keeley first looked at the coat a surveillance operation had begun in Crookham Road. From a window in one of the buildings opposite a fixed camera watched the front of number 2 all day and every day, generating videotapes in copious quantities. George was also followed and a male undercover officer was assigned to approach him and try to win his confidence. The tapes showed George coming and going from his home, occasionally in an eccentric manner: he would skip and jump up and down the steps and sometimes enter and leave the flat directly by jumping through a window rather than using the outer and inner doors. Tailing him proved at times a surreal experience, as officers toured London – Kensington, the West End, Victoria, Wimbledon, Chiswick, Putney, Tooting – following George's meanderings. Sometimes he talked to tourists, sometimes he appeared to follow women and sometimes he visited Internet cafés. On 22 May he went to two BBC buildings in White City. None of this was evidence. As for the undercover officer, he learned very little.

While this was going on – and incidentally it later emerged that George was aware he was being followed – Campbell authorized another search. The first search, even though it had been extended, had only scratched the surface of what was in the flat and detectives were eager to see more. So once again Gallagher led a team to Crookham Road, arriving this time before 7 a.m. and finding the tenant at home. George wanted to refuse the searchers entry but Gallagher, according to the later police account, placed both hands on George's chest and pushed him out of the way. The search team spent seven hours in the flat and although they seized some more newspapers with stories about Jill Dando and some more handwritten documents referring to guns, there were no dramatic discoveries. Among the firearms documents, however, one would turn out to be of special interest: a notebook with the name 'Steve Majors' on the cover. Inside it were handwritten details of three guns, a Heckler & Koch submachine gun, an 8mm blank firing 'government automatic' and a Browning pistol. The first two were familiar to detectives, since they were the makes of gun that featured in the two photographs already taken from the flat. The man in the outdoor photograph was holding what appeared to be a Heckler & Koch, while the gun in the indoor photograph matched the second gun on the list – the 8mm Bruni blank firer is a copy of a Colt weapon known as a 'government automatic' or 'government pistol'. Perhaps this list was a confirmation that George had owned these two guns, and if so it suggested that he might also have owned a third. (Although the Browning on the list was a 9mm pistol, it should be noted that it was not a 'short' model of the kind used to kill Dando.)

By the middle of May plans were being laid for the next move, which was to make an arrest. This would be a dramatic step. In the thirteen months since the investigation had begun only one man had been formally arrested and that was the funeral director, who was never half as strong a candidate. An arrest now, coming just a month after the *Crimewatch* programme had caused a surge of public optimism about the case, would inevitably be greeted as a breakthrough, so the police had to be all the more confident that they were not making a mistake. The arrest, of course, was not an end in itself and Campbell prepared a three-pronged drive to ensure that the event produced the maximum in terms of results. First, there would be a new search of the flat, of a character and on a scale quite different from the two that had gone before – no matter how much effort it took, if there was so much as a crumb of evidence in 2B Crookham Road it was to be found. Second, George was to be placed on an identification parade once he was in custody and as many as possible of the significant witnesses should have the chance to pick him out. And third, he was to be questioned in depth by officers trained in interview techniques. With luck decisive evidence would quickly turn up, but even without it there was a chance that, when confronted with what was already in hand, George might either confess or incriminate himself under questioning.

The arrest was made at 6.30 a.m. on Thursday 25 May 2000. Barry George was handcuffed and taken to Hammersmith police station where his clothes were removed for scientific examination and he was issued with a white paper 'babygro' suit. Meanwhile in Crookham Road the search began. After an initial tour of inspection by forensic scientists, searchers in paper oversuits and plastic overshoes moved in to begin the business of logging and boxing up every movable item in the flat short of the bigger pieces of furniture. One by one the boxes were filled, taken out and loaded into a lorry, to be transported to a police depository in south London for subsequent examination. The process of emptying the flat alone took until Friday lunchtime, by which time the total of packing boxes had reached 104. After this came a 'deep search', which involved lifting floorboards, removing

fixtures and fittings and inserting cameras in wall cavities. A
sniffer dog was also brought in.

The search had scarcely begun on the Thursday before the
first journalists and cameramen turned up in Crookham Road –
police activity on such a scale and so near to Dando's home could
not be kept secret – and the Scotland Yard press office soon issued
a statement. 'Officers investigating the murder of Jill Dando have
this morning arrested a man on suspicion of murder,' it said,
adding that the man was in custody at a London police station.
The media were formally asked not to print any photographs,
likenesses or physical descriptions of the man because identification was an important element in the case. Off the record, 'police
sources' shed a little more light: the development was 'highly
significant', they said, which seemed to mean that detectives
were confident this was their man, and it was not the result of
information received in response to the *Crimewatch* programme,
a conclusion to which many had already jumped.

The *Evening Standard* used its biggest type to announce: 'Jill
Dando – Man Held'. Television coverage during the afternoon
relied heavily on footage of the comings and goings in Crookham
Road, coupled with copious background on the crime, but as
the hours passed details and stories about the suspect trickled out.
He was an unemployed musician; he had once been married to
a Japanese woman; he was a fan of Freddie Mercury; he lived
alone and suffered from ill-health; he claimed he had been in the
Territorials or the SAS. The evening bulletins were straightforward but the following morning's papers went to town. 'Jill
Cops Question Freddie Mercury Oddball', said the *Sun*, with
the additional headline: 'Loner held in dawn raid'. Across pages
two and three ran the banner: 'He lives five minutes away', and
below that: 'Suspect known as the local weirdo'. The same story
was told elsewhere, if not with quite the same gusto. Papers
spoke of a 'breakthrough' in the thirteen-month investigation
and described a mood of confidence among the police. Bulsara,
they explained, was a loner living on benefit who passed himself

off untruthfully as a relative of the Queen singer – in fact, though no one said as much, he was just the sort of person Hamish Campbell had described on *Crimewatch*. Overwhelmingly, but again not quite overtly, this was presented as the end of the police hunt.

Inside Hammersmith police station things got off to a slow start. Medical and psychological assessments were required before officers could begin questioning George, and he also needed time to talk to his solicitor, Marilyn Etienne. In fact it was almost 5.30 p.m. before Detective Constable Michael Snowden, the principal interviewing officer, was able to ask his first real question: 'Can you tell me what you did on the 26th of April 1999?' So began almost eight hours of interrogations spread out over four days, a stop–start marathon that must have been as frustrating for Snowden, Campbell and the Dando inquiry team as it was exhausting for George. Not that he was obstructive, or at least not overtly so; on the contrary, he was polite to the point of deference – constantly calling Snowden 'Sir' – and never showing a hint of temper or irritation. In the early sessions at least he seemed at pains to be helpful, speaking with a strange, stilted formality as if reading from a police officer's notebook. 'I couldn't be definitive and precise about that.' 'They had at some point engaged with me in dialogue.' 'I could have ascertained, having spoken to my solicitor . . .' 'Like I formerly expressed to you . . .' Nor did he show any obvious signs of mental disturbance. He had no difficulty, for example, in dealing with his false identities, reeling off the list of names quite comfortably and acknowledging that they were indeed false. So was it correct that Freddie Mercury was his cousin? 'Not in any sense of the word or meaning,' he said, 'I have absolutely no connection whatsoever.' Did he make a habit of telling lies? 'No. Exaggeration maybe, but not a lie, sir.' As the hours and days passed, however, his physical health became more and more of an issue and he was seen by a police doctor a dozen times. Though the doctor proclaimed him fit to continue he himself complained that he was in pain and throughout the later interviews he clutched his side with one hand. At the same time his answers came more slowly and tended to be more vague and confused than at the outset.

Two issues dominated the questioning: George's movements on the day of the murder and his involvement with guns. On the former, despite sustained pressure on several occasions, he stuck firmly to the account he had given in his statement to Gallagher – he spent the morning at home, walked to Hafad and then to Traffic Cars and after that received a lift to the cancer charity offices. He was asked again about the time he left Crookham Road:

SNOWDEN: If I was to split the day up into morning and afternoon, would you be able to identify what part of the day it was when you went? If you can't give me a time, was it in the period before midday or in the period after midday?
GEORGE: It was getting on to after midday.

In fact he could never be precise about times and still less about dates. It was as though all the years of his adult life were the same to him. He could not remember the year of his own marriage, nor the years of his membership of the Territorials, nor the year when he first moved into Crookham Road. Pathetically, only one date stood out in the whole of his past: when asked about his spell of employment at the BBC he was able to say without hesitation that it ran from May to September 1976. As for the reason for his return visits to Hafad and Traffic Cars, he stated that he feared being accused of the Dando murder and wanted information in case that happened.

GEORGE: I went back there basically to account for my movements so if a situation did come up, I could address it to my solicitor.
SNOWDEN: The reason you went back to Hafad and to Traffic

Cars two days after the murder of Jill Dando was to try and verify
through those two places where you had been on the day that
Jill Dando was murdered. Is that correct?
GEORGE: That and the time. The timing was obviously important if, and only if, something ever came up or came of it, and
obviously it has become apparent now but that was only *if* . . .

On guns, however, he was far less consistent. He began by
categorically denying that he had ever owned any of the guns
listed in the 'Steve Majors' notebook and when he was shown
the two photographs – one with the Heckler & Koch and the
other with the Bruni – he claimed at first that they were not of
him. Only gradually and under pressure did he give ground. Yes,
that was him in the photographs. Yes, he had bought both of the
weapons that could be seen, although he stressed that neither was
a real gun – the submachine gun was a plastic replica and the
Bruni fired only blanks. Pressed about whether he still owned
them he said no and suggested that somebody called David
Dobbins would know their whereabouts. Hearing this, detectives
leapt into action and even as George was still being questioned
Dobbins was traced and interviewed. He told a simple and
surprising story: as a teenager in the mid-1980s he had known
Barry George and seen his two guns; in fact he had handled them
when George was showing them off once, at a time when they
were both living in the hostel in Stanhope Gardens. Then a
couple of years later, after George moved to Fulham, Dobbins
and some friends broke into the Crookham Road flat and stole
both guns. Soon afterwards the Bruni broke and was given away,
while the Heckler & Koch ended up in a children's toybox.
George, in other words, had not seen either weapon since about
1987.

By now it was Saturday and everybody involved was aware that
what is known as the 'custody clock' was ticking. Already on the
Friday evening the police had had to go to a magistrate for

permission to hold their suspect a further thirty-six hours, and
that extension would run out on Sunday morning. They could
seek a further twenty-four-hour permit, but after that they would
have to charge their suspect or release him. A side-effect of this
long wait was that the press had an unusual opportunity to
investigate and write about the suspect. Friday's splash of coverage was followed by a second wave of front-page headlines on
Saturday morning and a third in the Sunday papers, by which
time some juicy details had emerged. 'Jill Man Is PC's Son'
declared one paper, and 'Dando Suspect Idolized Diana' said
another, as more and more details of George's 'weirdo' lifestyle
turned up. His mother and father were tracked down and interviewed, both insisting that they did not believe him capable of
the crime, while one by one the residents of Crookham Road
and the shopkeepers of Fulham appeared in print giving their
recollections and their views. One unnamed neighbour described
George directing traffic in the street with a walkie-talkie to his
ear, another said he was addicted to Diet Coke and a third
that he was hooked on Internet pornography. While reporters
avoided direct speculation about George's guilt and never mentioned his criminal record, the message to a public that had
already been informed through *Crimewatch* that Dando's killer
was a loner was clear: the police had got their man. By contrast,
it should be said that for some readers and viewers following the
events the long delay produced a contrary effect, on the one
hand by sowing doubt about how much evidence the police had
against this man – If they know it's him why don't they charge
him? – and on the other because the more the press dwelt on
how pathetic a figure George was, the less it seemed that he was
capable of such a grotesque crime.

By Saturday afternoon, as it happened, the case against George
was if anything weaker than when he had been picked up. The
search had failed to turn up anything of immediate interest –
certainly no gun or ammunition, nor any sign that George had
either been stalking Dando or tinkering with firearms. The

identity parade, held on the Friday, ended without result. Five witnesses attended, among them Richard Hughes, and no one picked out George. As for the interviews, the suspect had certainly produced some odd answers and had been distinctly slippery on the subject of guns, but on balance their effect had been neutral. And Dobbins, to put it bluntly, had left George gunless after 1987. The detectives had one further card to play, their trump, for in the questioning so far no mention had been made of the firearms residue particle. It had been held back for a final challenge, and on the Saturday evening the trump card was played.

Snowden built up with more questions about guns and about the Bruni in the photograph, and very painstakingly he elicited from George the statement that the last time he had fired a gun it had been the Bruni, at least ten years previously. Then the interrogator raised the tempo.

SNOWDEN: So since that time, when you used that firearm to shoot your blank weapon, have you ever bought or possessed any other firearm ammunition?
GEORGE: No, sir.
SNOWDEN: Did you kill Jill Dando?
GEORGE: No, sir.
SNOWDEN: She was killed by somebody who was in Fulham on 26 April 1999. She was killed by someone who had possession of a smooth-barrelled semi-automatic pistol similar to the type of gun that you've bought in the past. The cartridge left at the scene of the murder of Jill Dando has been examined and it has firearms residue left behind in it, in the cartridge. Do you understand what I'm saying to you, Mr George?
GEORGE: I hear what you're saying, sir.
SNOWDEN: Do you understand it?
GEORGE: I understand and hear what you're saying insofar as you're telling me, sir.
SNOWDEN: The person who killed Miss Dando was seen leaving

the area. He was wearing a dark, three-quarter-length coat. You have stated in interview that on that day you may have been wearing a three-quarter-length coat. Was that you leaving the scene of the crime, Mr George?

GEORGE: No, sir.

SNOWDEN: The police took your three-quarter-length coat from your flat at the time of the search. A firearms expert has examined that coat. Did you kill Jill Dando, Mr George?

GEORGE: No, sir.

SNOWDEN: The inside pocket of your coat has been found to have a trace of percussion primer discharge residue. Did you kill Jill Dando, Mr George?

GEORGE: No, sir.

SNOWDEN: How do you explain the firearms residue in your coat pocket, Mr George?

GEORGE: I can't explain it. I have no knowledge about it being there.

SNOWDEN: Of course you haven't. But how did it get there, Mr George?

GEORGE: I have no idea, sir.

SNOWDEN: Isn't it possible that it got there because you were at the scene of the crime and you were the person that shot Miss Dando, wouldn't that explain how it got there? It's consistent with the firearms residue found in the cartridge at the scene of the crime, could you explain that to me?

GEORGE: I cannot explain that, sir.

At this point the solicitor, Etienne, demanded to consult with her client about this new evidence, of which she had had no warning from the police. The interview was halted and did not resume for more than three hours. As soon as the tape was running again, just before midnight, Etienne declared: 'I have made representations to the custody sergeant that there was significant, sufficient evidence to proceed to charge. My representations have been noted on the custody record . . . In the circumstances, my client has decided to exercise the right to silence.'

After securing a final extension of custody from a magistrate, allowing the police to hold George until Monday morning, Campbell personally made two attempts to question him further. George gave no answers. Time was now running out. In what must have been an anxious series of meetings on Sunday the police reviewed the evidence and its implications with the Crown Prosecution Service – discussions which were certainly followed closely at the highest level of both organizations – before the decision was made. At 8.30 p.m. on Sunday 28 May, eighty-four hours after his arrest, Barry Michael George was charged with the murder of Jill Dando.

# 15. *Regina* v. *George*

*'I have always been quite clear I have never been sure of the exact time.'*

Almost a year passed before the trial began. The police used the time in intensive investigation of Barry George and his background, aiming to extend and strengthen the evidence against him. The defence, meanwhile, recruited Michael Mansfield QC to conduct their case. Known for his work in overturning miscarriages of justice, Mansfield had also acted for the Lawrence family at the public inquiry into the Stephen Lawrence affair. Subtle and dogged, he was well equipped to unpick a weak case and was likely to tackle the job in a manner that would make headlines. For the Metropolitan Police, and for the Crown Prosecution Service which was now in charge of the case against George, the stakes were correspondingly raised. George himself remained in custody at Belmarsh prison in southeast London.

In November the legal wheels began to turn in earnest as the defendant was brought to Bow Street magistrates' court for a two-day committal hearing at which the Crown presented its case in summary and Mansfield argued that it should be thrown out forthwith. His plea was rejected and in due course the trial was listed to open at the Central Criminal Court – the Old Bailey – in February 2001. Behind the scenes the pace quickened further and in this phase two developments occurred that were to have an important influence upon the trial, the first involving the Cecil Gee coat on which firearms residue had been found. As we have seen, this was removed from the Crookham Road flat in the first search on 17 April 2000 and delivered to the forensic science laboratory for examination on 2 May. As the trial approached it emerged that something very surprising had happened between those two dates. On 28 April 2000 the coat and some of George's other clothes were taken from the exhibits room at Hammersmith police station to a police photographic studio at Amelia Street in south London, where they were removed from their sealed packaging and placed on a tailor's dummy to be photographed. They were then returned to the bags, which were re-sealed and taken back to the police station. As the defence was quick to point out, this meant that the coat might have been exposed to contamination – that residue particle, in other words, might have been picked up in the studio.

The other unexpected development, which came at about the same time, was that the defence declared it would be claiming that Barry George had an alibi for the murder. This was entirely new. In his original statement to D C Gallagher George had said he remained at home all morning before leaving for Hafad between 12.30 and 12.45 p.m., while in the course of his interviews before arrest he had said, when asked what time he left home, that it was 'getting on to after midday'. These accounts clearly left open the possibility he had committed the murder, although he had noted on both occasions that he could not be sure of times because he did not wear a watch. Now, in the early weeks of 2001, the defence issued an alibi notice – a kind of statement – which said that George left home much earlier, between 10.30 and 10.45 a.m., that he walked from his home through the park to Hafad and that he remained at the advice centre until about 1 p.m., when he went directly to the Traffic Cars office. By this account he was in the Hafad office at the time that Jill Dando was killed, and the defence did not need to point out that this was roughly consistent with the evidence of some of the Hafad witnesses.

On 26 February the parties in the case of *Regina* v. *George* – prosecution, defence, judge and defendant – all presented themselves at the Old Bailey for what was to have been the opening of the trial. It proved only a short staging post in that direction, for after four days of legal arguments the judge, Mr Justice Gage, was obliged to adjourn the proceedings for seven weeks. He left little doubt that in his view, as in the view of the defence, much of the responsibility for this unwanted interruption lay with the press.

The legal restrictions on reporting criminal cases in Britain are such that between the charging of a suspect and his trial hardly a word appears in newspapers or is spoken on radio or television. The effect of this in the Dando case was startling: for more than a year after the murder it had figured in the headlines at least on a weekly basis and often as a dramatic daily lead story, but once George was charged it suddenly vanished and from the end of May 2000 to the end of February 2001 – nine months – there was virtual silence on the subject. Press interest, however, remained very strong and the approach of the trial brought intensive preparations for the fullest possible coverage. It would be a release of pent-up journalistic energy. Seats in the press gallery were at a premium and there were even suggestions that this might be a 'British OJ' trial, so sensational that its every detail would grip the country. In particular, as the first session began many papers were looking forward to their first opportunity to print photographs of Barry George, since it was assumed the judge would lift a ban long in force. To general surprise, however, instead of lifting it he extended it, and so on day two a barrister appeared in court to challenge this on behalf of the publishers of the *Daily Mail* and the London *Evening Standard*. The challenge was successful and within a couple of hours the *Standard* was on sale across the city with the headline: 'First Picture: Man Police Say Shot Jill Dando'. Beside this was a striking close-up of George's face with moustache, a couple of days' black stubble and a crew cut. His eyes were large, dark and empty and at his neck a tie was tightly drawn around a white shirt collar that was a size too small. He looked like a thug. Inside was another photograph, this time of George in custody, wearing handcuffs.

The next morning the same two pictures were everywhere, while a number of newspapers, notably the *Mail* and the *Sun*, went much further, printing galleries of photographs of George over the years, with captions and accompanying copy. He was in a combat jacket, in karate gear, on roller blades and in Kensington Gardens after Diana's death; he was clean-shaven in one, wore a moustache in another and had a full-grown beard in a third. Although no one used the words 'weirdo' or 'oddball' this time, that sentiment was undoubtedly there between the lines. Mansfield was outraged and as soon as the court was in session rose to denounce what he called a display of 'rampant sensationalism' in which his client had been portrayed as a Walter Mitty figure who constantly changed his appearance, who looked threatening and who had to be kept in handcuffs. It had had 'a devastating effect' on George, who felt 'personally destroyed', but perhaps more importantly potential jury members could not fail to be prejudiced by reading such material. 'This case has had stamped on it an aura of guilt,' declared Mansfield, and for the moment at least a fair trial was impossible. The judge, clearly surprised and shocked by the coverage, condemned what he called 'lurid press reporting' and ordered that in future only one approved picture of George, without handcuffs, could be used, but he ruled that the trial should go on. The following day, however, it was adjourned for seven weeks after a medical and psychological assessment indicated that George was not fit to continue.

When the trial resumed on 23 April it was to begin a further week of legal arguments, but now everything was overshadowed by the question of George's mental and physical health. The whole of the first day's session was lost; on the second the court sat for just an hour; on the third it was four hours, on the fourth two hours and on the fifth a mere thirty minutes. The reason for the lost time was that George was either unwell or undergoing further tests. When he was in court he often seemed poorly, his face pale and his head hanging low, and on two occasions he had to leave the dock suddenly after appearing to suffer attacks of some sort. His behaviour, though, had an unusual dimension, for it was theatrical; as he came and went George did the sort of grimacing and blinking, the unsteady walking and heavy sighing that one might expect from a ten-year-old boy hoping to ham his way out of a day at school. Even the judge was later to remark that it was impossible to watch these performances without feeling scepticism, and to some it seemed that George was actually trying to manipulate the court and interrupt its proceedings at moments of his choice. The judge, however, put little or no pressure on the defence – on the contrary, he bowed to Mansfield's request for five-minute breaks every hour so that George could be put through a routine of exercises to ease his tension, and he also gave permission for someone to sit with the defendant in the dock and keep an eye on his condition.

The reason for this tolerance was that a series of specialists had by now produced reports on George which showed that, no matter how false his symptoms appeared, he was a sick man. Though his epilepsy was of the _petit mal_ variety, which meant that he suffered 'absences' rather than more violent seizures, it was unusually persistent and general. He was subject to frequent absences, perhaps several in one day, and though these were not usually obvious and could pass unnoticed even by him, over the years since childhood they had had a grave impact on his mental development. Between them the psychologists identified half a dozen separate conditions that he suffered from or had suffered from, including attention deficit hyperactivity disorder, somatization, factitious disorder and histrionic/narcissistic personality disorder. The consequences were dismal: his IQ of seventy-six (the average is 100) placed him, in the words of one report, 'on the borderline of intellectual functioning'; his memory was very poor, as were his concentration and his ability to plan and execute complex actions; he was emotionally volatile and inclined to become rigid and stubborn in the face of difficulties, and he was also prone to exaggerating and even making up physical symptoms. This last, like most of the others a long-standing complaint, presumably lay behind some of what the court had seen, but the judge, having read the opinions of no fewer than five experts, accepted that even a false seizure was likely to be an expression of underlying illness. Since the experts were agreed that despite all of this George was fit to stand trial, the judge concentrated on ensuring that the proceedings went ahead as smoothly as could be managed. In fact after a couple of weeks things improved.

Among the legal matters resolved in this unsettled period one stood out as significant and it was an argument that the prosecution lost. Not unnaturally they wanted to include in their case the evidence the police had assembled about George's habit of following women. It was now a big file, including the testimony of half a dozen women who had experienced his attentions as well as some of the photographs that had been found in the flat. These, the prosecution believed, would contribute strongly to the overall picture of George as a man who posed a danger to women and therefore potentially to Dando, but Mansfield objected in forthright terms. While it had been wrong of the defendant to behave in this way, he said, it had nothing to do with the Dando case. For a start there was no similarity – nobody was suggesting that Barry George followed Dando or took photographs of her and at the same time it was plain that he did not shoot or attack these other women – so this evidence could shed no light on the practical, central question of whether he was the killer. What it *would* do, he argued, was create prejudice. A jury hearing this would be likely to form such a low opinion of the defendant that they might not give proper consideration to the evidence that was actually relevant; they might even convict him out of sheer distaste. The judge, for his part, was never in doubt about this so-called 'stalking' evidence. As he told the court, it appeared to him to suggest propensity – 'He's the sort of person who would do this' – which is forbidden in law, and he also agreed with Mansfield that its capacity to cause prejudice far outweighed its ability to help prove that George did the deed. On these grounds, he declared, it was inadmissible. For the same reasons he forbade the prosecution from portraying the defendant as obsessive or referring to 'odd behaviour' and the like. Barry George, he was saying in effect, should be tried for the crime with which he was charged and the prosecution should be required to prove beyond reasonable doubt that he actually did it. And with that the stage was finally set.

Court number one at the Old Bailey is a great Edwardian cavern of a room with creaking oak below and pristine white plasterwork above. The judge's bench runs almost across its width on one side, looking down on the barristers to his left and the jury box to his right. In the well before him sit the usher and clerk while perched high to his left, above the clock and behind the lawyers, is a public gallery with seats for about thirty. Finally, directly opposite the bench across the well stands a dock large enough to accommodate a dozen defendants. Surrounded on three sides by glass, it contains a few large leather seats and behind them is the narrow, white-tiled staircase from the cells below. Among the defendants who have come up those steps are Crippen, Christie, the Krays, Ruth Ellis, Peter Sutcliffe and Dennis Nielsen, not to mention those others less well known who have been acquitted and allowed to make their exit by the little side door of the dock. Though its acoustics are poor and its layout is ill-suited to modern needs, court number one is without doubt an imposing arena of justice and here, on the morning of Wednesday 2 May, a jury of seven women and five men was sworn to try Barry Michael George for the murder of Jill Dando. To outward appearances at least they were a fair cross-section of the population and in the weeks that followed they would show every sign of concentrating on the job in hand. The judge warned them that while they must all have read something about the case in the press, the coverage had been speculative and sensational at times and they must put it from their minds. '*Your* views are the important ones,' he stressed. He also informed them that Barry George suffered from *petit mal* epilepsy and a psychological condition and that he might from time to time have to leave the dock.

The judge himself was businesslike and un-pompous. Sir William Gage is a High Court or 'red robe' judge and so rather more senior than the usual run of Old Bailey judges, and he had a recent record of dealing with difficult or sensitive cases – it was he who tried Sion Jenkins, the Hastings teacher convicted of killing his foster daughter, and he who handled the trial of the killers of Michael Menson, the black musician burned to death in a racist attack on a north London street. In the Dando case he was to prove fair and courteous, if occasionally sharp with the prosecution, whom he tended to hurry along. The Crown case was presented by Orlando Pownall, the senior Treasury counsel, or in other words the Crown Prosecution Service's leading barrister. Handsome, tall, broad-shouldered and pinstriped beneath his gown, Pownall so closely resembles a leading man from a black-and-white movie that the words 'matinée idol' have fixed on him like a brand. He is a low-key advocate, slow, deliberate and quiet, and he questions witnesses with something of a bedside manner: coaxing and reassuring rather than challenging and provoking. He would need all his reserves of stoicism in the weeks ahead. The role of challenger and provoker in this case fell to Mansfield, a far more theatrical figure, whose rolling eyes and waving hands are often called in support of argument. He can be outraged and incredulous, but contempt is probably his strongest suit, while patience and thoroughness are also in his repertoire. There can be few barristers with a greater talent for mastering complex documents and exploiting them on the hoof during the cross-examination of a witness.

On Friday 4 May the trial itself finally began, Pownall presenting before the jury a summary of the prosecution case. This had developed considerably since George's arrest and it was now as follows. Several witnesses in Gowan Avenue in the hours

before the murder saw a smartly dressed man whose general
appearance matched Barry George's. One of these had subsequently picked George out of a video identification parade
even though more than a year had passed and the defendant had
grown a beard in the interval, while at least two others had
indicated that they suspected it was him but could not be quite
certain. Taken together with other witness evidence, said Pownall, these showed that contrary to his own account George was
in the street that morning and although no one saw him do the
deed it was one of several elements in the case which pointed to
his guilt. After the murder he must have returned to his flat and
changed, and then set out by a roundabout route for Hafad,
where, it was suggested, he deliberately drew attention to himself
in the hope of creating a false alibi. Once again contrary to
George's own, amended account – as given in January 2001 –
there was strong evidence to suggest that he arrived at the
disability centre no earlier than 12.45 p.m. From there he went
to the Traffic Cars office, which he left at 1.15 p.m. That he
should have returned to Hafad and to Traffic Cars two days later
to inquire about the time of his visits and the clothes he was
wearing again pointed to an attempt to contrive an alibi.

After the murder his behaviour was strange in other respects.
He appeared to show no further interest in the welfare matters,
apparently so urgent at the time, which had taken him to Hafad
on the Monday. Instead he became absorbed by the Dando
killing. He bought flowers which he said he had delivered to
Gowan Avenue as a gesture from his church; he collected condolence notes from local businesses (although these remained in his
flat); he called at a council office to propose a memorial; he told
a woman on a bus that he was going to speak at Dando's memorial
service – indeed what appeared to be an extract from such a
speech had been found in the flat. To another woman he said
that he was hoping to help the police solve the crime, even
adding: 'I was there you know.'

George was a man, Pownall explained, with a long-term

interest in firearms. Besides the mass of gun literature found in the flat, some of it technical in character, there was proof that in the mid-1980s he had owned a Bruni blank firer and a replica submachine gun. He had showed them off and on at least one occasion had fired the Bruni, in strange circumstances: David Dobbins would testify that, apparently as a prank, George once burst into the Dobbins home at night wearing camouflage gear and fired a blank round, terrifying those present. Though it was known that the Bruni and the replica submachine gun were later stolen from George, various handwritten lists including the one in the 'Steve Majors' book indicated that he had also owned another, possibly a Browning or a second Bruni. Moreover a witness had been found, Susan Coombe, who said that in 1985 she saw a third gun in a box in George's room and that it had a silver barrel and black handle. This gun had never been accounted for.

Although there was no direct evidence to show that before the killing George had a specific interest in, or dislike for, Jill Dando, there were none the less events in his past which pointed in that direction. When, for example, he had accompanied Alison Hoad and her son along Munster Road towards the boy's audition, she recalled him making a strange remark. As they drew level with either Vera Road or Gowan Avenue he pointed down the street and said: 'A very special lady lives down there.' Hoad inferred that this woman was well known, and it had been established that no other celebrities lived in those streets besides Dando. Certainly George was fascinated by the BBC, visiting the offices frequently and collecting copies of the *Radio Times* and *Ariel*. Papers found at his home showed he phoned the BBC on numerous occasions and had various phone numbers and names relating to the corporation, while among his photographs were a few taken of the television screen showing women presenters, albeit not Dando herself. Among the thousands of scraps of paper were two which might also be relevant: one with the handwritten word 'Dando' and the other with the word

'Roseman' – the name of her agent – and a number, although on testing the number proved to have no connection with Jon Roseman. George's 1991 conversation with Sophia Wellington, in which he complained of the BBC's coverage of Freddie Mercury's illness, was also significant.

Pownall said that when it came to his interviews – several hours from the videotapes would be played before the jury – George was devious or dishonest about many of these matters. He claimed that before her death he would not have known Jill Dando if he had met her in the street, even though it was clear he knew a good deal about the BBC. He said he had no particular familiarity with Gowan Avenue, even though he had been registered with a doctor there for a time in 1996. He said he had never owned a gun and that he was not the man with guns in the photographs, until it was proven otherwise.

Finally there was the scientific evidence. The firearms residue particle strongly pointed to a link between George and the murder scene. He had insisted in interview that he had not fired a shot of any kind for years, and yet here was residue in a coat which happened to be one of the garments he said he might have worn on the day of the murder. It was in a pocket, which was one of the few places where such a particle might linger for so long, and evidence from the flat and from the local dry cleaners suggested that the coat had not been cleaned in the interim. Moreover it was chemically a match for the gunshot that killed Dando, perhaps not exclusively so but a match none the less. And there was a further connection through a cloth fibre: scientists had found that the material in a pair of trousers owned by George contained fibres of a kind found on Dando's coat after the murder, although again this was not an exclusive link.

On their own it might have seemed that none of the parts of this case was sufficient to prove George's guilt, but Pownall indicated that it was their cumulative effect that was compelling. This was the police logic from May 2000. George was in the street on the morning; he had no true alibi for the murder;

he behaved oddly on the day and lied about his movements afterwards; he had a fascination for guns and may well have owned one; he had an abiding interest in the BBC and his conduct in the days after the murder was suspicious to say the least. All of these were things that would almost certainly be true of the man who killed Jill Dando. Then, on top of all that, he had in his clothing both a firearms residue particle and fibres which were consistent with what was found on Dando's body and clothes. Was it conceivable, was it possible that there were two men of whom all this was true, and that George happened to be the innocent one? No, Pownall told the jury. 'You can be sure that the components I have described are collectively unique and that, although he may have had no rational motive, this defendant shot Jill Dando.'

That this was a circumstantial case was of no particular significance: it is by no means rare in murders for there to be no direct evidence such as the testimony of an eyewitness to the deed, and many killers have been convicted on the basis of indirect or circumstantial proof. Nor is it unusual for a prosecution to pin its hopes on cumulative effect – that is to say the combination of many small items of evidence rather than one or two large items. This case passed the critical tests, with both the committing magistrate and the judge agreeing that it was strong enough to go before a jury, but that said it remained, in the understated words of one senior police officer, 'not the strongest' that the Crown Prosecution Service had ever presented. If it was to succeed, it would surely need clever advocacy and impressive witnesses to carry it. Over the next five weeks no fewer than seventy-three witnesses would testify for the prosecution.

Susan Mayes was a professional woman in her thirties or forties who lived on Gowan Avenue, towards the Fulham Palace Road end. On the morning of the murder she left home at three minutes to seven, as was her habit, and walked east along the south side of the road, heading for Parsons Green tube station. It was drizzling and she had her umbrella up, she told the court. 'Did you see anybody?' Pownall asked her. 'I saw the defendant,' she replied bluntly. The man she saw was standing on the far side of a burgundy-coloured car parked in the middle of the road outside number 28, the house opposite Dando's. The man looked first at the houses on the even-number side and then across the road at the odd numbers, but when he saw Mayes approaching he turned his gaze towards the ground and as she walked by he kept his head down and wiped the passenger side of the windscreen, possibly with his hand, in what she thought was a furtive manner. She assumed at the time that the car was his and that it was a minicab. She described the man as mid to late thirties, 5ft 9in tall, slightly overweight and Mediterranean – that is to say, with dark hair and slightly olive skin. He wore a black suit with a white shirt open at the neck. On 5 October 2000 Mayes attended a video identification parade (as was his right, George declined to attend further line-ups in person after the first one drew a blank), and she picked out number 2 after a very long, hard look. Number 2 was George. She said in court she was 'very sure'.

Stella de Rosnay, though British by background, was a French baroness by marriage and lived in Paris. On the morning of the murder she was coming to the end of a visit to the home of her son and his family in Gowan Avenue, and at 9.30 a.m. she was in an upstairs front room with her daughter-in-law, Charlotte. As they talked Stella remarked on a man who was crossing the road in something of a hurry and they both looked out at him, taking in his appearance. Stella described him in court as stocky, between 5ft 8in and 6ft tall, with brownish hair, a pinky complexion and a dark grey suit. Charlotte remembered him slightly differently, with pale skin, 'Desperate Dan' stubble and a navy blue suit. Memorably, Charlotte remarked that he was smart – 'not City smart, it was more like estate agent smart'. Both women viewed the video identification parade in October 2000, again with subtly different outcomes, as the jury saw when the tapes of the parades were screened. Stella looked very closely indeed through the two showings of the full tape and then said she wanted to see the men at numbers 2 and 8 again. After leaning forward and examining these even more carefully she said: 'I can't give a positive statement. I can't tell you between 2 and 8. My gut feeling is 2. It's frustrating; it's the colour of the skin too.' Charlotte, after the first two viewings, said: 'I'd like to see number 2 again, and there is another halfway through.' This proved also to be 8. But when she was asked whether she could make a positive identification she said: 'I don't think so.'

Terry Normanton was a very small, very nervous lady in her fifties who lived, like Mayes, towards the far end of Gowan Avenue from Dando's home, and on the morning of the murder she set out at 9.50 a.m. to go to an embroidery class in Bishop's Road. As she walked down her street she saw a man in the road who had a mobile phone to his ear and was looking towards number 29. She had a clear view of him for about a minute, she estimated, and she got as close as eight feet from him. He was in his thirties, 5ft 8in tall, medium build, with black hair to collar length. He wore a black suit and no tie and had a bracelet on his wrist that might have been a watch strap. At a video identification parade in August 2000 she watched the full set of nine faces three times and picked out number 2, but declined to make a categorical identification. 'I'm sure but I'm not quite sure,' she said at the time. 'I don't remember a moustache.' In court she said she was now quite sure, and that only the moustache had worried her.

Though the prosecution produced a few other people who saw a man in Gowan Avenue that morning, these four were the ones who either picked George out or, in the Crown's contention, *all but* picked him out in the identification procedure. Pownall argued that, although it might be unusual to rely on some witnesses who had not made positive identifications, in this case it was justified. On the one hand more than a year had passed since the crime, so memories were being stretched, and on the other all the men in the parades had beards while none of the witnesses was saying the man they saw had one. Thus, to use Pownall's word, the witnesses at the parade were asked to 'predict' what the man they saw would look like if he had had a beard – a doubly difficult task. In this context, he said, it was all the more striking and relevant that Normanton had settled on number 2 and that both de Rosnays had come so close to doing so. And the prosecution was further helped when it emerged in evidence in court, first that Stella de Rosnay had claimed after attending the parade that she was 'ninety-five per cent sure' number 2 was her man, and then that Charlotte believed number 2 was the 'predominant contender' in her choice between 2 and 8.

In cross-examination Mansfield chipped away at these witnesses. He suggested to Mayes that she might have picked out George because she recognized him from the streets of Fulham, where he was a well-known figure. 'Can you be sure you haven't seen him before?' he asked. 'I'm not aware of seeing him.' He also pointed to some discrepancies in the descriptions she had given over the previous couple of years, implying that her memory might not be absolutely reliable. But she was a robust if prickly witness and it was only at the very end of her evidence, in fact in response to a further question from Pownall, that she said something helpful to the defence. She had looked at the man in the street three or four times 'over five to six seconds in total', she said. It did not seem very long and the judge, apparently surprised, checked that he had heard her correctly. With Terry Normanton Mansfield was gentle, but his grounds for doubt were clear. Although she had spoken to the police on two or three occasions after the murder it appeared that it was not until the anniversary, a year later, that she came forward with her account of the man with the mobile phone. This, she said, was because of a medical condition which made her hesitant (and hearing her testify in court there was little doubt about that), but the delay left her account of the man in Gowan Avenue looking a little stale. As for the de Rosnays, Mansfield drilled home the message that, however sure they might *now* claim to be that the man at number 2 was the man they saw in Gowan Avenue on the morning of the murder, when they had actually attended the line-up in October 2000 neither woman had felt able to make a positive identification.

For all of Mansfield's sceptical testing, it was when it was set against the testimony of Richard Hughes and Geoffrey Upfill-Brown, the men who saw the killer leaving the scene, that the prosecution's identification evidence met its sternest test. Both of these men failed to pick out Barry George at parades; both said that the man they saw had a thick mop of black hair and both said he was wearing a coat of some kind. Neither Mayes nor Normanton nor the de Rosnays saw a mop of hair or a coat; in fact they all spoke of shortish hair and a suit. In conspicuous respects, therefore, the two sets of descriptions simply did not match. Pownall addressed this problem by suggesting when questioning the two men that perhaps they were not well placed to describe or remember the person who fled the scene, and in one case he got the answer he wanted. Hughes freely admitted that when he looked out through the blinds of his upper window he had only a glance at the gunman and then only from the waist up. Upfill-Brown, however, gave a different account of himself when he was asked about his power to remember details two years on.

POWNALL (hoping for the answer no): Were you expecting to be able to recollect what you saw?
UPFILL-BROWN: Yes, very definitely, yes I was.
POWNALL: Why was that?
UPFILL-BROWN: Because of the manner in which he [the fleeing man] was behaving. He immediately attracted my attention and I watched him very carefully and made every mental note I could about his appearance and his clothing particularly.

Pownall hurried on to other things.

From Gowan Avenue attention turned to Greswell Street and

the offices of Hafad. Here the question to be addressed was whether Barry George arrived at a time which left open the possibility that he was the killer. By a rough measure he would have needed thirty minutes to return home from the murder scene, change his clothes and make his way through the park to the disability centre, so did he arrive there later than noon? The members of the Hafad staff who saw George that morning each gave different accounts. Rosario Torres, the receptionist, said that when she answered the door to him he behaved in an odd, excited manner. 'I need help! I need help!' he said. 'I'm disabled and you have to help me.' She spent some time in loud conversation with him before Elaine Hutton, the finance officer of the centre, came out of her office nearby to take over, upon which Torres left the two together and returned to her desk in another room. The next thing she remembered hearing that day was the voice of Susan Bicknell, Hafad's welfare officer, calling out: 'Sorry, I'm having my lunch.' This, and her own feeling about the time, led her to conclude that the whole incident occurred at about 12.30 p.m.

Hutton's account of events was different in a number of respects. She said that although she saw and heard George in the building that morning she had no dealings with him, and that Torres not only let him in but also fetched Bicknell to talk to him. As for the time, Hutton accepted that at first, back in April 1999, she had thought George arrived at about 11 a.m., but later she realized this was a mistake. She based her calculation, she told the court, on a belief that George turned up about one and a half hours after she started work, and since she normally started between 9.30 and 9.45 a.m. her first assessment had been that he arrived at around 11.a.m. When she subsequently checked her diary, however, she found that she arrived late that day, at 10.25 a.m., so after doing the sum again she revised her estimate to 'approximately 12'. This was now her position. In cross-examination the defence swiftly established that the word 'approximately' embraced the possibility that George had arrived at 11.50 a.m. and then, with reference to the detail of her statements to the police, pushed the arithmetic a little further.

MANSFIELD: When you came up with 11 o'clock originally, it was because you thought it was either about an hour and a quarter or possibly an hour and a half [after you began work] – if you had started at 9.30?

HUTTON: I think in my head it was about an hour and a half.

MANSFIELD: The statement this year is pretty clear. It says: 'I normally begin at 9.45. I said 11 was about the time he came in, as this time-gap would seem about right – an hour and a quarter.' That is how it is in the statement, do you follow?

HUTTON: Yes.

MANSFIELD: If in fact you started at 10.25 and you add an hour and a quarter to that, it is about 11.40 that he comes in, is it not?

HUTTON: Yes, but these were always guesstimates.

MANSFIELD: Looking back on it, it could well have been 11.40 that he came into your centre, could it not?

HUTTON: I cannot be sure of the exact time. I have always been quite clear I have never been sure of the exact time.

After Hutton it was the turn of Susan Bicknell to testify. As it happened 26 April 1999 had been her very first day at work in Hafad and since she did not know anybody at the time she could not recollect whether it was Torres or Hutton who came to fetch her from her office to talk to Barry George. On the matter of the time at which she went to speak to him, however, she was in no doubt at all. 'Before I walked out of the open-plan office I worked in I looked at the clock, and it said 11.50. I cannot speak for the accuracy of the clock but it said 11.50 and in the time that I worked at Hafad it was never more than five minutes out. So I am assuming it was right on the day in question.' Though she proved in many ways a troublesome and over-talkative witness she was never to vary her view on this point, and it was a view that had remained consistent since the time of the events themselves. Furthermore she denied indignantly that she had called out 'Sorry, I'm having my lunch', the remark which Torres had identified as one of her reasons for giving a time of 12.30. The last Hafad witness was Lesley Symes, the director, but she had seen George only briefly on the day and not spoken to him and perhaps in consequence seemed to have no clear idea of when he was at the centre.

In summary, then, Torres said George arrived around 12.30 p.m. while Hutton said it was approximately 12 but possibly 11.50 (with the defence arguing that her evidence pointed to 11.40) and Bicknell was adamant it was 11.50. The majority verdict among the three women, therefore, gave George an alibi for the murder, but the evidence did not end there. At different moments as the trial unfolded the Crown unveiled three further items which, they said with some justification, altered the picture. One of these was supplied by Jonathan Clark, an expert in telecommunications who investigated a telephone call Barry George made on that Monday. No one disputed that at 12.32 p.m. George used one of his mobile phones to check his credit level with his service provider, Cellnet, a call that lasted thirty-five seconds. If the account given in his alibi notice was correct, that call had to have been made from Hafad, where George claimed to have been from a little after 11 a.m. to a little before 1 p.m. Clark had tested that proposition and found it doubtful. The data from the billing records showed that it was what was known in the phone industry as a 'handed off' call, which is to say that it was picked up first by a mast at Parsons Green, to the east of Fulham, and then transferred halfway through to a mast at Putney Bridge, to the south. The mere fact of such a transfer would normally suggest that the caller was in movement, either in a vehicle or on foot, and by conducting tests on the ground Clark had concluded that the most likely location for calls involving a transfer between those particular masts was Bishop's Park or the streets immediately to the north of it, including Doneraile Street. From Hafad, however, the signal was 'extremely poor', he declared, and he rated as 'very unlikely' the proposition that the call was made inside the premises.

At about the time that phone call was made, an American woman called Julia Moorhouse was walking along Doneraile Street when she had an encounter with a man who she thought was 'slightly odd'. Describing this man in court thirteen months later she said he was in his early to mid thirties, heavily built with very dark hair that was well-trimmed. She thought he might be southern European. He wore a bright yellow, hip-length jacket of a type she associated with sailing and he was carrying a mobile phone. Moments after she first spotted him close to the halfway point of the street, her attention was attracted by helicopters circling overhead and she was still looking up at them when the man came up to her and explained knowledgeably that they were police helicopters. After a short exchange with him she set off again in the direction of Stevenage Road, only to find the man falling in step with her, still talking. He mentioned the Territorial Army and she was left with the impression he had supervised training for them in some way. She also thought he had a harelip. They turned the corner into Stevenage Road together and soon she went into a house there, while she believed he continued northward. She estimated that they parted at about 12.35 p.m.

It was very difficult to listen to this account and not link it with Barry George. The hair and build were right; the behaviour was right and the topics of conversation were right. He also has a harelip. In fact almost the only jarring note was the minor one that she said he was wearing a yellow jacket while Hafad witnesses recalled a yellow shirt or T-shirt. As with the phone call it was the timing that was significant, for Moorhouse's evidence was also in conflict with the defence account of George's movements. The prosecution asserted that Moorhouse and Clark provided strong confirmation that Barry George was making his way from his home to Hafad at around 12.30, a time consistent with his being the murderer. The story behind these two items of evidence is revealing and important, for they emerged very late in the day. Although Julia Moorhouse first contacted the police on the day of the murder – in fact she was one of the very first people to provide information to the Dando investigation, phoning in soon after 1 p.m. – she did not make a formal statement to the police until 26 February 2001, the day on which the first phase of the trial began. And it was not until around the same time – more than eight months after the arrest – that Jonathan Clark was commissioned to investigate the mobile telephone call. Why did these elements arrive so late? Because they were prompted by Barry George's alibi notice, served in January. Until then his position had been that it was 'getting on to after midday' when he set out for Hafad, but now that the defence case was that he left before 11 a.m. the prosecution needed to counter-attack. Clark and Moorhouse were their principal weapons, and they had one more, although it was of a lesser calibre. A CCTV camera at the gates of Fulham football ground captured an image of a man heading north along Stevenage Road at 12.43 p.m., and the man appeared to be wearing a yellow shirt. The image, in fact, was so fuzzy and fleeting that the judge indicated he did not believe it helpful, but for what it was worth it was put before the jury as further support for a later arrival time at Hafad.

Where Mansfield had been able to turn the evidence of the Hafad staff to his advantage, he made less headway with these witnesses. On Clark he made no impression beyond confirming that the expert, while confident his findings were right, could not be absolutely certain about them. Moorhouse he made only a small effort to challenge – over the nature of the yellow garment she described and the absence of any carrier bag – before stating bluntly to the judge: 'If there is a suggestion that the person she is talking about is the defendant, it is not accepted.' Instead Mansfield employed a quite different line of argument which he had developed while cross-examining the Hafad witnesses, which was that George had indeed spent the entire period in the advice centre – most of it waiting to be dealt with. The Hafad staff were in general agreement that George's visit had lasted around fifteen minutes, a duration which until January George himself had accepted, but Mansfield had set about stretching this. Torres agreed that she probably spoke to George for around five minutes, and then somebody dug out his file, which might have taken a few more minutes. Bicknell said that she took a few moments to skim the file and pick up her diary before going out to see George, and then she had a conversation with him. By playing on Bicknell's evident tendency to gabble, Mansfield in cross-examination illustrated vividly to the jury that any conversation with her risked being a long one. Then he added the image of Barry George not really listening, and simply talking on and on about his problems, to evoke the picture of an exchange that could easily have lasted quite a long time. Bicknell herself conceded it might have been more than twenty minutes.

Mansfield went on to suggest that George had been left in a waiting area – in effect ignored – in between these encounters with the various members of staff, and furthermore that at the end of the discussion with Bicknell she had suggested that he wait while she went to fetch something and then failed to return. Though they could not disprove all of this, none of the Hafad witnesses was prepared to accept that anyone would be kept waiting in such a way in their offices. Mansfield, meanwhile, got a little help from the Traffic Cars manager, Ramesh Paul, who agreed that George might have been in the minicab office for up to twenty minutes before he took the cab at 1.15 p.m., which meant he might have left Hafad earlier than thought. By the end of all these endeavours, therefore, the defence version of the timings looked like this: George arrived at Hafad at around 11.15 and left at, say, 12.45 for the minicab office; of the intervening ninety minutes he spent around thirty in dealings with the staff and around sixty simply sitting and waiting. The Crown version was that Moorhouse and Clark proved that George reached Hafad much later, around 12.45, and after a brief visit went on to the cab firm.

While the jury followed all this evidence and watched the witnesses come and go from the box, they were also able to form some impressions about Barry George himself. They knew nothing, of course, about his criminal record in the early 1980s or his habit of following women. No doubt, however, most of them had picked up something from the earlier newspaper coverage about his 'weirdo' tendencies and the judge himself had told them he was epileptic and had a psychological condition. Their own eyes and ears now told them a little more. The man in the dock was a heavy figure, thickset though not at all athletic. His shoulders were round, his waist ample and his face pudgy. He had thick black hair which was neatly cut, broad, arched eyebrows and sideburns running down to a tidy beard and moustache. He routinely wore blue shirts and one of two dark blue sweaters, occasionally with sleeves rolled up. Two seats from him in the dock sat the woman social worker who had been assigned the tasks of helping him to follow the proceedings and monitoring his demeanour for signs of *petit mal*, while behind were three uniformed dock officers. George moved and looked about very little except to drink water from a plastic cup that was often refilled, and in general he cut a hunched and passive figure. He appeared to pay attention, however, consulting papers that were referred to, sometimes taking notes and occasionally having messages passed forward to the defence team. Only rarely did he catch the eye of his sister Michelle, who loyally attended every day, sitting near to the dock. And only twice was there a recurrence of the scenes which had been seen during the legal arguments before the jury was sworn, with George seeming unwell and leaving the dock.

To this picture the jury could add other things. A video of the flat at the time of the first search was shown, as were several hours of videos of the interviews before arrest, all pointing to a strange and possibly disturbed man. They heard about his various identities, his enthusiasm for militaria, his concern about his own health and his habit of complaining about wrongs he felt he had suffered. They may have picked up other things, for example that he talked to strangers in the street and that they usually seemed to be women. Alison Hoad stated clearly that she found him threatening, while from the evidence of Sophia Wellington the jury might even have guessed that he was capable of following women. On the other hand, when they were told he had lived continuously for fifteen years in the same council flat a few of them may have deduced that he had not been in prison in that period. In the same vein they were told that between 1997 and April 2000 official records showed he had been spoken to by the police only three times. It probably counted against him in the jury's eyes that he declined to attend identification parades after the first one, and that he had changed his account of his movements on the morning of the murder.

A few witnesses offered personal insights into George the man and one was Sally Mason. A Fulham woman who had known him for fifteen years, she was called by the prosecution because it was to her that he was alleged to have said of the murder: 'I was there you know.' Pownall opened his questioning by asking her to cast her mind back to the days immediately after Dando's death. Did she remember meeting George at that time? Although it was clear that on the basis of her statements Pownall expected her to say yes, she said no. The relevant conversation, she insisted, took place not in April 1999 but in April 2000. Pownall's discomfiture was evident – there was a world of difference between remarks made days after the murder and remarks made a year later – but he settled for what he could get. Mason explained that she had met George in the street at about the time of the anniversary of the murder and the subject had come up: 'I think he said to me that he was being followed by the police, and I said, why? And he said he went to Fulham police station and told them he could help them solve the murder of Jill Dando because he was there.' Exactly what was meant by 'there' was not clear, but Mason offered her own view: 'I thought it was one of his fantasies,' she said. Mansfield, cross-examining, picked up a phrase she had used about 'Barry being Barry' and asked what she meant. 'He's harmless enough,' she replied, 'but reality drifts up on him. I've never known him to be violent or aggressive to anybody.'

A contrary impression might have emerged from the evidence of Susan Coombe, who knew George when he was calling himself Thomas Palmer, way back in 1985 in the Stanhope Gardens hostel. It was Coombe who described seeing a third, silver-coloured gun in George's room, a story which she stuck to firmly in court, but before that she dropped in a revealing remark. Pownall had begun by asking her about the other guns, the replica submachine gun and the blank firer, and she described George showing these off to other residents in the hostel. Then Pownall asked: 'Did you ever see any other weapon?' 'Yes,' came the reply, 'a knife that Tom used to carry and a small silver gun in a box . . .' That Barry George might have been in the habit of carrying a knife in the mid-1980s was no part of the prosecution case, almost certainly because it counted among the elements excluded by the judge's pre-trial rulings. Pownall did not pursue it, but it remained in the air, a fleeting insight but a vivid one.

However scrupulously the court avoided the direct explo-ration of George's character, the impression that the jury formed of it would be as important to the outcome of the trial as any of the other big issues in the case. If the jury was to accept the prosecution argument that George shot Dando without a rational motive after waiting for her in the street, that he then tried to contrive an alibi and that he was now misleading the court, then they also had to believe that he was both irrational and devious. That was what Pownall suggested to them. The defence, by contrast, was happy for George to be seen as a local Fulham character who lived in a world of his own and spent much of his time on the streets talking at people rather than to them. What they challenged was the idea that he was wicked or dangerous. He was a bore, Mansfield implied, but he was a harmless, scatter-brained and innocent one.

★

It was the judge who observed that as far as hard evidence was concerned the case turned on three matters: the Gowan Avenue identifications, the visit to Hafad and the scientific evidence. The last of these took up the greatest share of the court's time, leading into a number of byways and dead ends. Mansfield's defence was that the particle of firearms discharge residue had arrived on Barry George's coat as a result of accidental contamination and thus offered no proof whatever that George fired the shot that killed Dando. As the trial progressed he indicated two principal routes by which it might have travelled and the first was that, having emanated from a gunshot unconnected with the Dando murder, it made its way on to the coat via the clothes of one of the police officers involved in searching the flat. Police witnesses questioned about this pointed out that the coat was found in the first minutes of the first search and immediately sealed in a bag, so that the opportunity for contamination by the police was small. On the other hand, when pressed by the defence they were forced to concede that the precautions taken against such accidental contamination had been lax and incomplete. The searchers wore 'blues' and not special oversuits, and plain boots rather than disposable overshoes; some changed into their blues at home and some outside 2 Crookham Road; they travelled in a van that had not been cleaned or sampled, having passed through police stations where firearms were sometimes handled. It seemed a sorry picture and there were signs that the judge was shocked by the absence of rigour, but was it significant? Mansfield fell a long way short of showing that the searchers were the vehicle for the particle, but then he didn't need to do that; all he had to show was that they might have been.

More exhaustive attention was devoted to the coat's visit to the Amelia Street photographic studio, which Mansfield described with justice as 'an act of crass forensic folly'. Who was responsible for the decision would be disputed, but it was established that DC Gallagher, the same officer who had first questioned George, had been acting under instructions when he took it to the studio and removed it from its bag to be photographed. How likely was it that the particle arrived on the coat there? Much of the argument centred on the other items which had passed through the studio in the months beforehand, and whether they might have been the source. Slowly, over time, the prosecution seemed to show that most of them – they were largely items of clothing from crime scenes – had no known connection with firearms or that where they did the ammunition involved was not of the specific kind to give rise to the relevant particle. The cleaning supervisor from Amelia Street was produced, along with an office manager, to show that the studio was frequently cleaned (there was even a discussion about the size of vacuum cleaner head employed), and evidence was introduced of scientific sampling in the studio in early 2001 which showed no trace of firearms residue. Mansfield conceded nothing in the face of all this, insisting that the door was being shut after the horse had bolted and standing by the general point that the possibility of contamination at Amelia Street simply could not be excluded.

It was in the final stages of the prosecution evidence that Robin Keeley, the scientist who found the firearms residue particle, entered the witness box. A small, serious man with mousey hair and large spectacles, he proved to be the sort of expert witness who constantly qualifies both his own remarks and those of his questioners. Led by Pownall, he explained what primer discharge residues were and how the particle found on the coat, comprising lead, barium and aluminium, was a chemical match for the particles produced when Dando was shot. Asked how strong the link was in scientific terms, he seemed less than enthusiastic. Such particles were never unique to a particular gunshot, he said, in fact the five basic kinds of primer discharge were 'all as common as each other'. He went on: 'The most you could say is that it *could* have come from that ammunition – or any other ammunition which had the same composition.' This was not what the prosecution wanted to hear, so Pownall tried again: how common were particles containing the three elements lead, barium and aluminium? 'Not uncommon,' came the firm answer. 'Ammunition with aluminium primers is not uncommon.' There followed an hour or more of questioning in which nothing much went right for the Crown, and it reached its climax with a strange revelation. Keeley had had a Remington 9mm round taken from the laboratory storeroom and fired, and when he compared the residue from that with the residues found at the Dando murder scene they did not match. Whether this was important – and Keeley insisted that it was not – scarcely mattered; it was utterly baffling. Mansfield by now was laughing openly and it was fortunate for the prosecution that this chaotic exchange took place late on a Friday afternoon, so that when Pownall and Keeley resumed the examination after the weekend break some of the damage could be repaired. Reluctant though he was to endorse the particle as a firm link between George and the murder, the scientist was even more reluctant to accept that it had arrived on the coat, as the defence suggested, by innocent contamination. It was most unlikely, he thought, that it had got on to the coat either during the search or at the Amelia Street studio. His views were endorsed by a second prosecution expert in this field, Graham Renshaw, who suggested at one stage that the chances of such contamination were akin to those of winning the lottery. Although on reflection he shortened those odds somewhat, he remained of the view that the probability was low.

Cross-examining Keeley, Mansfield quickly drew out an acknowledgement that in the scientist's own laboratory, 'even when you take as many precautions as you can, contamination arises'. Then, in a clever passage, he tackled one of the key problems of the case for innocent contamination: was it possible for such a particle to find its way into the *inside pocket* of a coat if it arrived in some casual way? Mansfield had the coat produced and given to the witness and then he asked Keeley to lay it out across the front of the box and show roughly how he had handled it when it arrived in his lab. Keeley laid the coat flat on its back and then its front, explaining that he would have done this first to make himself familiar with the garment. Then he showed how he would dab the coat with pieces of sticky tape to lift off any traces for subsequent examination. At Mansfield's request he showed how he had dealt with the inside pocket, pulling it inside out, laying it flat against the coat lining and dabbing it, then laying it flat the other way and dabbing the other side. Mansfield was triumphant: this, he said, showed that the particle need never have been in the pocket. Having arrived on the outside of the coat through innocent contamination it could have found its way on to the inner lining near the collar when Keeley first turned the coat over. Then it could have slipped down to near the pocket during the examination and finally attached itself to the inverted pocket lining as Keeley laid it this way and then that to do his sampling. This could explain how it ended up on the piece of sticky tape identified as carrying the pocket contents. Keeley admitted this was possible, though unlikely.

As for the fibre evidence, the prosecution had never given it much weight and when the scientist who found it appeared he soon demonstrated why. Geoffrey Rowe of the Forensic Science Service testified that he had found on Dando's coat a single strand of blue-grey polyester half a millimetre in length, and that matching fibres were later found to be present in the fabric of a pair of trousers taken from 2B Crookham Road. Rowe, however, was even more reluctant to ascribe any particular significance to this than Keeley had been with the particle. Blue-grey polyester was 'relatively common', he said, and there was also a risk that such a fibre might be transferred along a chain of people. He seemed almost to remove the matter from discussion when he stated that he had an eight-point scale for rating the value of any fibre as evidence and that this one fell into the second category from the bottom. It was 'weak', he said, and 'weak is as low as I can go without ruling it out'.

The prosecution case took five weeks to present; the defence was finished in less than three days. Mostly this was because

Mansfield had already presented most of his arguments and elicited much of the evidence he needed through the prosecution witnesses, and for the rest it was because Barry George did not testify in his own defence. This is the right of every defendant but on this occasion it was the subject of a lengthy argument over whether the jury was entitled to infer anything from George's silence. It was a legal grey area in cases where mental and physical health were the issue but Mansfield eventually won his point and the judge agreed to direct the jury that the defendant's silence must not be held against him. The jury were thus denied the chance to see him cross-examined by Pownall, and to hear him account in particular for his alibi notice and the evidence of Julia Moorhouse and the mobile phones expert.

Mansfield's opening speech caused a sensation. For the most part the media had found the trial lacking in excitement, with the evidence too technical and the arguments too fine to make good day-to-day copy. After a flurry of early reporting, interest dwindled and there were many days when the number of journalists attending was down to a handful. On Thursday 14 June, however, Mansfield suddenly grabbed the attention of the press with a barnstorming speech claiming that the nature of the murder and the burden of the surrounding evidence pointed, not to his client, but to a Serb plot. It was obviously a professional assassination, he said, and the Serbs had both the means and − after Dando's television appeal and the bombing of the Belgrade television centre − the motive. Anonymous callers had claimed the attack on behalf of Serbia and the strange crimping on the cartridge case was a trademark of east European armourers. There was even a police intelligence document (based on information from an unnamed informant) from the summer of 1999 saying that the hit squad was despatched to London by the Serb warlord Arkan. This squad, Mansfield went on to argue, included the gunman and a driver, and on the morning of 26 April they waited in a blue Range Rover parked at various points in or near Gowan Avenue. As Dando arrived the gunman stepped out and the

Range Rover moved off, waited around the corner, picked him up inconspicuously once the deed was done, and then sped away. What impact this had on the jury is unknown, but it was headline news that night and the next morning. In fact the small print of Mansfield's presentation made clear that while he was convinced the killer was a 'professional', it did not in his view *have to be* Serbs who were behind it. His real purpose was to show that no unanswerable logic of the case pointed to a lone gunman as the killer, let alone to his client.

Perhaps more directly pertinent to the issues of the trial were two other points Mansfield made. The first of these was his attack on the Crown's case relating to guns. 'There is no evidence since the mid-1980s,' he said, 'that this defendant has owned, possessed, carried or bought any weapon or ammunition from anyone . . . The fact that this defendant undoubtedly had an interest in things military including weapons, as manifested in a multitude of lists that he made, is no more indicative of possession of such items than it is of all the other things of which he made lists. For example, no one suggests he owned a rocket-propelled grenade launcher; no one suggests that he served with the SAS in Cambodia, Malaya and Borneo; nor does anyone suggest that he had a sound studio equipped with the sort of hardware supplied by companies listed in great detail on another handwritten list.' Nowhere in his flat or elsewhere, for that matter, had any evidence been found to suggest that George could have altered firearms; he had neither the tools nor, on the evidence, the expertise, and no chemical traces had been found even to show that he might have done such work in the past.

The other all-out assault was directed against the prosecution arguments on motive, which were certainly slender, and here again Mansfield dwelt on what was not there. Barry George, he said, had never met or attempted to meet Jill Dando. 'He did not follow her, nor stalk her. He did not hang around outside her address. Amongst all the photographic materials, there were no photographs of her in the street or off the television screen. There were no signed – fan-style – photographs or posters. Amongst all the lists relating to organizations and individuals found at 2B, there is no mention of Jill Dando. There were no diagrams or maps showing her address. There were no videos of her television appearances. Of the 800 newspapers and magazines accumulated at 2B, only eight predating her death have articles about her, and none of these had been marked up, highlighted, circled, cut out, put to one side or filed. It is of special note that he did not have the current *Radio Times* for the week in which she died, which featured her on the front cover. Over the many years and months before her death, those who had got to know this defendant do not suggest he was wandering around muttering about, or obsessed with, Jill Dando, as someone he knew or wanted to know, or as someone who had done him or Freddie Mercury some disservice.' In sum, Mansfield argued, it was hard to see on what grounds Barry George entered the frame at all, for given the state of his flat the prosecution could not argue that he had carefully sifted through it at any stage to remove incriminating evidence.

The defence evidence began with a chain of minor witnesses from in and around Gowan Avenue on the day, testifying either that they saw nothing suspicious around the time of the murder or that they saw a blue Range Rover. The purpose of both was clear. The other significant defence testimony came from John Lloyd, the expert who had been recruited by the defence to review the evidence relating to the particle. Introduced by Mansfield as a man with exceptional qualifications, long experience and an international reputation in his field, Lloyd proved to be a small, elderly man with wild hair, an avuncular manner and a monocle. A single exchange sums up what he had to say.

MANSFIELD: From a forensic science point of view, what significance do you attach to the finding of one particle in this case?
LLOYD: There could scarcely be less residue at all. The presence of a single particle does raise serious doubts as to where it may

have come from. It might have been something which is just a casual contamination. Some laboratories have in fact not reported findings as significant when so little residue is found. It should be said that in this case, this is the first occasion when it has been suggested that a single particle could be a relic of an event which has occurred a year ago. It is quite a unique suggestion.

These observations were never seriously challenged, let alone disproved, and they gave some explanation for Robin Keeley's earlier discomfort. The prosecution, Lloyd was saying, was taking evidence that some experts would simply discard and construing its meaning and significance in ways that had never previously been attempted. To claim that it helped to prove George might have shot Dando was 'incredible', he insisted, and quite unsupported by scientific experience or knowledge. On balance, in fact, Lloyd believed it was more likely that the particle arrived on the coat by innocent contamination than that it came from the shot that killed Dando and remained on the coat – even in the pocket – for a whole year. The following morning Mansfield declared: 'That is the case for the defence.'

The concluding phase, of closing speeches from Pownall and Mansfield and the summing-up by the judge, took five days and produced few surprises. Pownall dismissed the Serb theory as an absurd distraction and mocked the Range Rover sightings as a hodge-podge – some were new cars, some old, some carried two men, some one, some were blue, one was black and some weren't even Range Rovers. By contrast, he said, there was an 'underlying unity' to the sightings of a man by Mayes, Normanton and the de Rosnays and that unity extended also to the descriptions given by Hughes and Upfill-Brown. Like the others they both said they saw a tallish, thickset man in his thirties who had black hair and dark clothes; if there were differences over clothing and length of hair that could surely be put down to human error. As for the Hafad issue, Pownall was contemptuous of George's alibi notice, which he portrayed as 'the abandonment of his original timings in preference for those he perceives to be more advantageous to him'. Instead of helping the defendant, however, it had backfired, since the evidence of Moorhouse and the mobile phones expert showed him to be a liar. Nor, said Pownall, did the evidence of the Hafad staff themselves give strong support to George's story, for only Susan Bicknell had been confident of a time before noon and for all anybody knew the clock she looked at may have been wrong by an hour. (This was apparently an afterthought by Pownall, since he had never produced any evidence for it.) George's behaviour in the days that followed the murder and a year later when the police began to take an interest in him only confirmed his guilt, while his lies under questioning put it beyond doubt. Was it a coincidence that this man should have had in the pocket of his coat a firearms residue particle perfectly consistent with the shot that killed Dando? Pownall left the answer to the jury.

Mansfield began his response with a spectacular display of courtroom oratory. Raising the issue of Dando's popularity and the strong feelings her murder had evoked (it was he who likened the shock at her death to the Cuban missile crisis and the death of Diana), he told the jury: 'It would do no justice to her memory were you to allow those feelings to mould together a non-existent case because in some unconscious way there is a desire to make somebody pay.' Turning to the evidence he did not immediately repeat the Serb theory – only a few days had passed since he spelled it out in his opening – but instead concentrated his attack on identification and Hafad. Mustering the evidence of witnesses who were in Gowan Avenue in the half-hour before the murder and saw nothing, he asked where the gunman was during this time and pointed out that the prosecution had no answer, just as they could not account for the complete absence of eyewitness evidence showing Barry George running or walking back to Crookham Road after the killing. This, he said, was because George did not do it and was not there. As for the identification witnesses, he poured scorn on a prosecution that relied on people

who had not picked their man out of a line-up and accused the
Crown of wanting to 'drive a coach and horses' through safe-
guards built up over a century to protect the innocent from
mistaken identifications. 'What you are being asked to do is
unprecedented,' he told the jury, 'and we ask you not to do it.'
Only Susan Mayes provided a positive identification, and she
had seen a man beside a car more than four hours before the
killing. Other evidence showed that minutes after she left the
street both the car and the man had disappeared, so wasn't it
likely that the man simply got in the car and drove off? (George,
Mansfield had shown, did not drive and had no car.) As for the
'underlying unity' of descriptions given by the witnesses, he
derided it as 'underlying disunity', pointing in particular to the
coat and mop of hair seen by Hughes and Upfill-Brown but not
the others, and to the contrasting descriptions of the man's
complexion as both olive-skinned and pink.

On Hafad Mansfield reminded the jury of the evidence of
Bicknell and Hutton, who said that George arrived or might
have arrived by 11.50 a.m., a time which ruled him out as the
murderer. The belated suggestion that the clock in Bicknell's
office was wrong by an hour, he asserted, was a measure of the
prosecution's desperation, for had there ever been the slightest
chance of proving such a thing they would have done so through
witnesses. No, George had a solid alibi and the evidence for it
was overwhelming. So far as the firearms residue was concerned
Mansfield not only repeated the evidence of Lloyd that it was
'incredible' to rely on a single particle found after the passage of
a whole year, but attacked the police, and in particular Hamish
Campbell, for the incompetent manner in which they allowed
the coat to be exposed to the risk of contamination. Finally he
urged the jury to remember that there were other possible
explanations for this murder – in his view much more plausible
ones – and that no force of logic made Barry George the obvious
suspect. He urged them to think about the scene of the crime,
about what was really known about the death of Jill Dando, and

to reflect on whether it was not more likely that the killer was somebody engaged in a business he knew well. Perhaps, suggested Mansfield in his closing words, it was somebody who came from a part of the world where it was normal to crimp bullets.

The judge's summing-up was thorough and – in keeping with his handling of the whole trial – even-handed, notable only for a number of directions to the jury which were themselves strictly by the book. He told them to keep cool heads, set aside prejudice and remember that they must be sure of their verdict. The defendant was obliged to prove nothing; lies alone, even if proven, could not be held against him, nor could his failure to testify. The evidence about his interest in celebrities must not be taken as a reflection on his character, for its sole purpose was to prove that he had lied when he said he would not have known Jill Dando, and likewise his interest in militaria was relevant only insofar as it suggested that he owned a gun. There were particular warnings, too, about identification evidence which, the judge said, was problematic and should be treated with caution. As to the leading issues of the case, he gave the jury a formula to help them in their deliberations. It was one that both prosecution and defence knew of and accepted, and it greatly simplified the matter. If the jury members were not *sure*, on the basis of the identification evidence, that the defendant was in Gowan Avenue on the morning of the killing, then they must find him innocent whatever their views on other questions. If they were not *sure* that the defendant arrived at the Hafad office later than 12 noon, rather than before that time, then they must also find him innocent even if they accepted the Gowan Avenue evidence. As for the particle, that had a lower status: they could reject the forensic science evidence and still convict if they were satisfied on the other two.

At 10.40 a.m. on Wednesday 27 June the twelve members of the jury retired to consider their verdict. By that evening they had not reached a decision and they were sent to a hotel for the night. All through Thursday, Friday and Saturday they continued to debate the issues, still without reaching the unanimous agreement required by the judge. Their number, meanwhile, shrank to eleven as one of the women jurors was discharged following a family bereavement. Late on the Saturday afternoon, before sending them back to their hotel for the remainder of the weekend, the judge informed them that, given their evident difficulties, he would now accept a verdict agreed by ten out of the eleven. This brought no swift conclusion to the matter and for more than five hours of the Monday session they remained enclosed in the jury room, still locked in argument. Then at 4.10 p.m. the court was called into session – judge, lawyers, defendant, public gallery and a throng of journalists – and the jury filed in. They had reached a verdict by a majority of ten to one. What was that verdict, asked the clerk, guilty or not guilty? 'Guilty,' said the foreman. After a brief interval in which his criminal record was read to the court, Barry George was sentenced to life imprisonment.

# Afterword

There could be no tidy outcome to this affair. So incongruous, so outlandish and so cruel was the murder of Jill Dando that the explanation for it, if it ever emerged, was always likely to challenge comprehension, to leave people surprised or confused. This outcome went beyond even those expectations, for it was so untidy as to be perverse.

One indication of the unease the conviction aroused, albeit a contrary one, was to be found in the newspaper coverage the next morning, where for the most part caution and judgement were thrown to the winds in the effort to demonize Barry George and show that he *must* have been the man who pulled the trigger. No longer was he an oddball or a weirdo; he was the 'chameleon killer', a 'sex monster', a 'mad assassin' and 'The Beast'. In the avalanche of words and pictures, readers could have been forgiven for forming the impression that George had a string of rapes on his record, an armoury of guns in his home and a shrine to Dando in his bedroom. The case against him was grossly distorted and luridly embellished while his personal history was presented only in travesty. Most strikingly, a new theory of the murder emerged which raised it to a different level of sensation: George had been obsessed with the Princess of Wales and had stalked her, and he had killed Jill Dando as a substitute. There was even less evidence to support such a notion than there was to justify the Serb assassination theory, but that was no constraint: 'He tried to kill Di too', announced the *Sun*.

They were protesting too much, and no amount of bluster could conceal the weakness of the case on which this conviction was secured. There was no confession and there was no motive. There was no gun, no sign that George had ever owned a gun capable of firing bullets and no indication of where he might have procured such a gun. There was no evidence of a prior interest in Dando, let alone an obsession, and no serious possibility that if he had had such an interest he could have concealed it. The only positive identification of George in Gowan Avenue that day was by Susan Mayes, who four and a half hours before the murder saw someone who did not have the hairstyle, the complexion or the coat described by witnesses who actually saw the gunman. The forensic evidence was both tainted by the police themselves and discredited by the defence expert, and the testimony of two prosecution witnesses, Bicknell and Hutton, appeared to give George an alibi. It was hardly surprising that a guilty verdict should have provoked widespread disquiet or that the defence should have immediately announced its intention to appeal.

Amid all the sound and fury, however, something important changed, for though her name and face were once again everywhere for a day or two, Jill Dando was slipping out of the foreground. Alan Farthing, who had been a frequent though discreet visitor to court number one over the preceding months, read a statement in the street outside in which he expressed the hope that the trial would 'act as some kind of milestone' for those who loved her and were still trying to come to terms with their loss. This natural wish is likely to be granted, not least because Farthing did not make it a condition that Barry George, towards whom he showed no bitterness, should remain behind bars. The case will be talked about and written about for many, many years, but the controversy is now about George and it has at last become detached from the person and the personality of Jill Dando. Nothing can change the fact that the name of this talented, charming presenter who commanded so much respect and affection will always be associated with violent death, but for her family and friends, whose thoughts of her are so different and who have had to endure a great deal, there is the prospect of peace.

# Index